'MY BROTHER'S KEEPER?'

'MY BROTHER'S KEEPER?'

Recent Polish Debates on the Holocaust

EDITED BY ANTONY POLONSKY

ROUTLEDGE

in association with

THE INSTITUTE FOR POLISH–JEWISH STUDIES, OXFORD

First published 1990
by Routledge
11 New Fetter Lane, London EC4P 4EE

Simultaneously published in the USA and Canada
by Routledge
a division of Routledge, Chapman and Hall, Inc.
29 West 35th Street, New York, NY 10001

© 1990 Antony Polonsky
© Translation, selection and notes: Institute for Jewish Studies, 1988

Typeset in 10/12 Times by Columns of Reading
Printed in Great Britain by T.J. Press (Padstow) Ltd.,
Padstow, Cornwall.

British Library Cataloguing in Publication Data

'My brother's keeper?': recent Polish
debates on the Holocaust.
1. Poland. Jews. Genocide. *1939–1945*
I. Polonsky, Antony   II. Institute for
Polish–Jewish Studies
940.53′1503924
ISBN 0–415–04232–1

Library of Congress Cataloging in Publication Data

'My brother's keeper?': recent Polish debates on
the Holocaust/edited by Antony Polonsky.
p. cm.
Bibliography: p.
Includes index.
1. Holocaust, Jewish (1939–1945)—Poland—Public
opinion.   2. Public opinion—Poland.
3. Anti-semitism—Poland.   4. Poland—
Ethnic relations.   I. Polonsky, Antony.
II. Institute for Polish–Jewish Studies (Oxford, England)
DS135.P6M9 1989
940.53′18′09438—dc20   89–6208

The publication of this book has been made
possible through the help of Mr Edward
Roche, to commemorate his family,
Rozenholc and Reichstein of Łódź,
who perished in Treblinka.

CONTENTS

Acknowledgements ix

1 INTRODUCTION 1
Antony Polonsky

2 THE POOR POLES LOOK AT THE GHETTO 34
Jan Błoński

3 THE DEEP ROOTS AND LONG LIFE 53
OF STEREOTYPES
Stanisław Salmonowicz

4 A REPLY TO JAN BŁOŃSKI 59
Władysław Siła-Nowicki

5 GUILT BY NEGLECT 69
Ewa Berberyusz

6 THE 'JUST' AND THE 'PASSIVE' 72
Teresa Prekerowa

7 THE MISSION THAT FAILED: A POLISH 81
COURIER WHO TRIED TO HELP THE JEWS
Maciej Kozłowski

8 'THE BLACK HOLE': CONVERSATION WITH 98
STANISŁAW KRAJEWSKI, 'A POLE AND A
JEW IN ONE PERSON'
Ewa Berberyusz

9 DO NOT SPEAK FOR ME, PLEASE 110
Kazimierz Dziewanowski

10 DIFFERING ETHICAL STANDPOINTS 118
Jerzy Jastrzębowski

11 IN A SENSE I AM AN ANTI-SEMITE 123
Janina Walewska

12 POLISH REASONS AND JEWISH REASONS 134
Jerzy Turowicz

13 THE EIGHTY-FIRST BLOW 144
Kazimierz Kąkol

14 PILATE'S GESTURE 150
Ryszard Żelichowski

15 THE DISSEMINATOR OF ANTI-SEMITISM?
A REJOINDER TO JAN BŁOŃSKI 155
Witold Rymanowski

16 THE HIDDEN COMPLEX OF THE POLISH
MIND: POLISH–JEWISH RELATIONS DURING
THE HOLOCAUST 161
Andrzej Bryk

17 ETHICAL PROBLEMS OF THE HOLOCAUST
IN POLAND 184
*Discussion held at the International Conference on
the History and Culture of Polish Jewry in Jerusalem
on Monday 1 February 1988*

Notes on Contributors 233

Index 239

Acknowledgements

This book owes its existence, above all, to the wise counsel and prompting of Rafael Scharf of London. It was he who brought to my attention the significance of Janłoński's article, 'The Poor Poles look at the Ghetto', and who stressed the importance of producing an English version of the ensuing debate. Without his always gentle, if insistent prodding, I doubt whether this volume would have seen the light of day. I am grateful too, to Jerzy Turowicz, editor of *Tygodnik Powszechny*, and to all the contributors for allowing their articles to appear in English. The translators, Teresa Halikowska-Smith, Antoni Bohdanowiiz, Ewa Kalina, Irena Powell and Joanna Hanson worked painstakingly in order to present in English these often complicated and subtle arguments. I was also greatly aided in my editorial work by Veronica Ions. Michael Larkin of Verbatim, and Colette Ritchie of Hampstead Secretarial Bureau were tireless in transcribing the numerous reworkings of the material. Finally we owe a special debt to Edward Roche whose financial support was, in a word often overused, but here totally appropriate, indispensable.

It has been a great privilege to prepare this edition of texts which show individuals wrestling with the awful moral problems posed by the *Shoah*. It is my hope that it will deepen our understanding of the terrible dilemmas faced by individuals and groups confronted by the Nazi policies of mass murder and that it will spur us to create a world in which such atrocities will no longer be possible.

1

INTRODUCTION

ANTONY POLONSKY

No less characteristic of the civilizing process . . . is the development of that peculiar complex of emotions that we call 'shame' or 'embarrassment' . . . The feeling of shame is a specific response, a type of anxiety which is developed in the individual by habit and which is automatically reproduced on certain occasions. It takes on its peculiar colouration from the fact that the person feeling it has done or is about to do something as a consequence of which he comes into conflict with people to whom he is linked in one or other manner, as well as with himself, with that part of his consciousness to which he concedes moral authority. The feeling of shame – fear is not merely the product of a conflict between the individual and the prevailing social opinion: it is rather the outcome of a clash resulting when an individual's behaviour has brought him into collision with that part of himself which reflects this social opinion. It is a conflict with his own personality: he recognises himself as having fallen in his own self-esteem. What he fears is the loss of the respect of others to which he attaches value.

Norbert Elias, *Über den Prozess der Zivilisation*

Let us stop quibbling about extenuating circumstances, let us stop arguing and let us bow our heads.

Ewa Berberyusz, 'Guilt by Neglect' (chapter 5)

The publication in the Kraków-based Catholic weekly *Tygodnik Powszechny* on 17 January 1978 of Jan Błoński's article 'The Poor Poles look at the Ghetto' sparked off what has certainly been the most profound discussion since 1945 of the Holocaust in Poland and, above all, of the vexed question of the Polish

1

response to the mass-murder of the Jews. This had long been a sore point in Polish–Jewish relations. Far from healing the divisions between Poles and Jews, the Nazi Holocaust, carried out as it was largely on Polish soil, considerably strengthened those barriers of suspicion, fear and even hatred between the two communities which had already begun to grow alarmingly in the last years before the outbreak of the war. To the small group of Jews who survived in Poland or who returned from the USSR, Polish behaviour during the war seemed to have confirmed their worst suspicions. It was clear to them that they were not wanted on Polish soil and even that it was dangerous for them to remain in Poland. In their eyes, the Poles had stood aside while the Nazis had implemented their murderous plans. The small amount of assistance provided was, in their eyes, outweighed by the activities of the denouncers and blackmailers, while the attitude of the majority was, at best, indifferent. This feeling of alienation was strengthened by the post-war insecurity and the anti-Jewish outbreaks which culminated in the Kielce pogrom of July 1946 in which at least 40 Jews were murdered. It would probably not be going too far to say that the scarring effects of the Holocaust were so traumatic that they made the establishment of a sizeable Jewish community on Polish soil in the post-war years impossible.

The impact of the Holocaust on the Poles was no less traumatic. It has been well described by the Polish–Jewish sociologist, Zygmunt Bauman:

But the Poles were scarred, too, and scared – by the crime committed on their soil before their eyes. Reactions to the harrowing experience were as if drawn from the psychology textbook. Some tried to talk themselves into believing that the Jews, after all, deserved what they got, brought the hatred upon themselves and hence no-one ought to be castigated for not helping them. Some others tried to shift all the guilt on to the murderers. The odds were overwhelming and nothing we could possibly have done would have balanced them out. Some sought consolation in remembering that they also were on the receiving end of the crime: we all suffered, we all have our dead to commemorate and the Jewish claim that their victims should be treated differently is just another insidious attempt to cast aspersions on their Polish hosts . . . However different the reactions, they were all responses to an unresolved moral problem of suppressed guilt.[1]

Indeed, the divisive effects of the Holocaust greatly complicated any rational discussion of Polish–Jewish relations during the Second World War, as well as making much more difficult any genuine Polish–Jewish reconciliation. The two sides argued not so much with, as past, each other, exchanging mutual recriminations in a tragic dialogue of the deaf. As Bauman has observed:

> Equality in suffering unites and heals; 'singling out' part of the sufferers for special treatment leaves hatred and moral terror in its wake. Far from dispersing the clouds of mutual suspicion and antipathy which hung over Polish–Jewish collaboration, the Holocaust made reconciliation more difficult than ever before.[2]

There were also other factors which inhibited a proper consideration of the implications of the Holocaust in Poland, as well as the wider question of the reasons for the development there in the 1930s of a climate of pervasive anti-semitism and the extent to which this facilitated the Nazis' murderous plans. In the immediate post-war period, before the imposition of a rigidly Stalinist and Soviet-dominated regime, there were a number of efforts to come to terms with these issues. It was at this time that Michał Borwicz and his colleagues at the newly-established Jewish Historical Commission initiated a very valuable attempt to document the events of the *Shoah* and to preserve the testimony of the survivors. Several courageous Polish voices also castigated the evil of anti-semitism. They included the writer Jerzy Andrzejewski who observed in 1947:

> For all honest Poles, the fate of the perishing Jews must have been exceedingly painful, for the dying were people whom our people could not look straight in the face, with a clear conscience. The Polish people could look straight in the face of Polish men and women who were dying for freedom, not in the face of the Jews dying in the burning ghettos.[3]

The Kielce pogrom provoked the sociologist Stanisław Ossowski to write:

3

A more far-sighted, more cynical or more wilful person, or someone with greater historical knowledge might have recalled that sympathy is not the only reaction to the misfortune of others; that those whom the gods have singled out for extinction easily become repugnant to others and are even removed from inter-human relations. He might also recall that if one person's tragedy gives someone else an advantage, it often happens that people want to convince themselves and others that the tragedy was morally justified. Such persons as owners of former Jewish shops or those who harass their Jewish competitors can be included in this group. And perhaps by citing a whole array of historical examples, I could express my doubt as to whether the reaction against the Nazi achievements will, in the short run, root out the influences of the Nazi spirit which, within the course of a few years, attained so much and which led human awareness to become inured to certain offensive slogans because of their frequent repetition.[4]

Already the political climate was exercizing a baleful effect on these attempts to 'overcome the past', as the similar process in Germany has been described. Some of the contributors to the Błoński discussion allude to this with bitterness (pp.54–5, 115–16). In the period 1944–7, Poland was the scene of a sort of civil war, which resulted in the imposition of an unrepresentative communist regime, closely linked with and effectively controlled by the Soviet Union. This regime saw anti-semitism as a useful brush with which to tar its opponents. It was certainly true that this period was disfigured by a number of anti-Jewish excesses (Lucjan Dobroszycki has calculated that these led to the deaths of nearly 1500 people),[5] which were provoked partly by fears that returning Jews would seek to regain their property and partly by the feeling that the regime, in which there were a number of prominent Jewish communists, was the realization of pre-war fears of Judeo-communism ('Żydo-Komuna'). The communists were determined to deny to their opponents any political virtues and to claim that they were the only political force in Poland which had repudiated anti-semitism and its associated fascist doctrines. Thus in the years immediately after liberation, although a Polish 'League for Struggle with Racism' was set up, its activities were soon restricted to protesting about the

4

oppression of blacks in the southern United States. Similarly the role of non-communists in helping the Jews during the war was belittled. This applied particularly to the Council for providing Aid to the Jews (cryptonym *Zegoła*) which was created by the main non-communist underground body the Home Army (*Armia Krajowa* – AK) in 1942 and which was a unique body in Europe. Under these circumstances, a dispassionate analysis of the roots of Polish anti-semitism proved impossible. In the rest of Europe, those right-wing groups which had espoused anti-semitism had been discredited by their collaboration with the Nazis. In Poland, their anti-Nazi record was, for the most part, impeccable, and, now, in addition, they were being persecuted by the communists. They thus retained a degree of legitimacy and respectability which was not to be found elsewhere in Europe.

The situation became still worse when a fully Stalinist regime was established after 1948. The war-time non-communist resistance, and above all the Home Army, was bitterly reviled and many of its members, including those who had set up *Żegota*, like Władysław Bartoszewski, were imprisoned. Anti-semitism, like fascism, was seen as the inevitable consequence of monopoly capitalism and, according to the official ideology, it would only disappear with the abolition of capitalism. The Communist Party of Poland was the only force which had opposed the rising pre-war anti-Jewish tide and the whole of the Polish non-communist camp was hopelessly tainted by anti-semitism and other reactionary vices. At the same time, from about 1952, coinciding with Stalin's growing anti-Jewish paranoia, the number of Jews holding important positions within the regime was considerably reduced. This process went still further after October 1956 when Władysław Gomułka succeeded in establishing a national communist regime as a consequence of the de-Stalinization process within the Soviet Empire.

The Gomułka regime found the Jewish issue an embarrassment. It was determined to establish its national credentials in the eyes of Polish society. It permitted the re-emergence of a number of national symbols and also, partially at least, recognized the role of the Home Army (AK) in the anti-Nazi resistance. Any serious discussion of the Jewish question could only raise difficult problems and could prove to be destabilizing, both because of the sensitive issue of the role played by Jews.in the party, and, above all, the security apparatus, between 1945 and 1953, and because of the presence within it still of a fair number of Jewish cadres. The Jewish issue thus became taboo, emerging only in the period 1967–8, when a younger group of party activists sought to take advantage of the hysterical climate engendered by the Israeli victory in the Six Day War to advance their position by attacking their opponents in the party for 'Zionism' (a Soviet-bloc code-word for Jews). This bid for power by General Moczar and his supporters was unsuccessful, but it did lead to a major anti-Jewish purge within the administration and to the emigration of the bulk of Poland's remaining Jews.

In the 1970s this situation began to change and a new willingness to look again at the thorny and difficult problem of Polish–Jewish relations during the Second World War began to develop. This was, indeed, an inevitable consequence of the growth of interest in the Polish–Jewish past which was a feature of these years. It was increasingly realized in Polish intellectual circles that Poland had been for nearly 1,000 years one of the main centres of the Jewish world. By the time of Poland's partition at the end of the eighteenth century, perhaps two-thirds of the world's Jewish population lived on the lands of the Polish-Lithuanian Commonwealth, and the unique civilization they created outlived the extinction of the Polish state. In the nineteenth and twentieth centuries, it became the seedbed from which grew the major movements which have transformed Jewish life – zionism, socialism, neo-orthodoxy. It was also a reservoir which fed the human flood to Western Europe, North and South America, the Antipodes, and Palestine which has, to a major degree, created the present geography of the Jewish world. The great Jewish historian, Salo Baron, himself of Polish–Jewish origins, has described American Jewry as a 'bridge built by Polish Jews'. As late as 1939, Polish Jewry was still the second-largest Jewish community in the world after the United States and was still a major creative force in Jewish life, in spite of its increasing political and economic difficulties.

In recent years, the importance of the development of this community for Polish life has been widely recognized. Departments of Jewish history have been created at the Jagiellonian University in Kraków, the University of Warsaw, and at the Catholic University of Lublin. Interest in the Jewish past has become surprisingly widespread. Books on Jewish subjects disappear rapidly from the shops, plays on Jewish themes are sold out, and performances of visiting Israeli dance companies or orchestras greeted with rapturous applause. Jewish history and culture were among the subjects studied by the underground 'flying university', in the 1970s. Similarly, the Catholic Church and the opposition have sponsored 'Weeks of Jewish Culture' in a number of cities, during which school children and university students attended lectures on Jewish topics and participated in the restoration of Jewish cemeteries. Catholic monthlies like *Znak* and *Więz* have devoted entire issues to Jewish topics. Ewa Berberyusz was expressing a widely-held view when, in her interview with Stanisław Krajewski, she said:

> I would like to say that the absence of Jews, whom I still remember but who are now gone, leaves me, for one, with a sense of irreplaceable loss. I voice here not just a sentiment in which is enshrined an idealized memory of old Poland, but rather an awareness of the real, manifest impoverishment of Polish culture. Poland has lost a very important creative contribution. (p.108)

As Ewa Berberyusz herself concedes, this interest *is* partly nostalgic in character. Poland, today, is practically mono-ethnic and mono-religious and there is a genuine sense of loss at the disappearance of the more colourful Poland of the past, with its mixture of religions and nationalities. It does, however, have a deeper character. The experiences of the Solidarity years have given the Poles a greater sense of self-esteem. In sharp contrast with the traditional outside view of the Poles as quixotic and impractical political dreamers, in these years Poland astonished the world by its political maturity. A non-violent movement challenged the might of the Soviet Empire for nearly a year and a half and though it was finally crushed, it won a great moral victory. Under these conditions, there was a greater willingness to look at the more controversial aspects of the Polish past and to consider again more critically how the Poles had treated the other peoples alongside whom they had lived, above all the Jews and the Ukrainians. A reckoning with the less admirable aspects of the Polish past was, indeed, seen by important sections of the opposition as a necessary part of the creation of the plural society for which they aimed. This feeling was well articulated in the underground journal *Arka* by Marek Leski (a pseudonym):

> A reckoning with Polish nationalism . . . appears an important task if our society is to become like that of countries characterized by a political culture that respects individual rights and civic freedom and has a plural character. It is therefore injurious and indeed downright harmful to close our eyes to Polish anti-semitism or to diminish its role in our political tradition . . . The one guarantee that we will not make such mistakes again is to remember our past errors and the lost opportunities to make use of the intellectual and social potential possessed by our ethnic minorities, to remember our insensitivity to the achievements of other cultures and the laziness and sloth displayed by the glorifiers of our national past.[6]

Similar preoccupations were voiced by a number of the participants in the Błoński discussion. In the words of Andrzej Bryk:

> The recent Polish search for the lost history of Polish–Jewish relations is not an abstract intellectual exercise. It is morally legitimate and necessary, and long overdue. At stake is the Polish people's choice between freedom, which requires as full a recognition as possible of history, and imprisonment as a people desperately committed to nationalistic myths (p.161).

His sentiments were echoed by the editor of *Tygodnik Powszechny*, Jerzy Turowicz:

> the dispute about Polish anti-semitism . . . is a matter which is much larger [than the mere question of rooting out the remnants of this ideology] . . . It is a dispute . . . over the choice of a model for Polish culture, what kind of culture it is, changing, as does any culture over the ages, and what form it ought to have. (p.219)

Increasingly, too, particularly among the younger generation, there has been a growing feeling of shame over the events of 1968. At the time, the prevailing mood was that this was merely a settling of accounts among the communist elite and that all the factions fighting for power were equally tainted. By the late 1970s however, the realization that one of the consequences of those years had been to deprive Poland of most of what remained of its Jewish intelligentsia and that society had allowed itself to be manipulated by the crude use of anti-semitic slogans led to an increasing feeling of anger. The role of the 1968 crisis in depriving the regime of political legitimacy has, in general, been greatly underestimated.

Another factor stimulating a more critical look at the Polish–Jewish past and, in particular, at Polish–Jewish relations during the Holocaust, was the series of Polish–Jewish historical conferences which began in Columbia in Spring 1983 and culminated in the conference in Jerusalem in February 1988. All points at issue between Poles and Jews were extensively aired and the discussions were often acrimonious, painful and difficult. Of such a discussion at Oxford in September 1984, Jan Błoński writes in his article:

> I recall one moving speech at the Oxford conference, in which the speaker started by comparing the Jewish attitude to Poland to an unrequited love. Despite the suffering and all the problems which beset our mutual relations, he continued, the Jewish community had a genuine attachment to their adopted country. Here they found a home and a sense of security. There was, conscious or unconscious, an expectation that their fate would improve, the burden of humiliation would lighten, that the future would gradually become brighter. What actually happened was exactly the opposite. 'Nothing can ever change now,' he concluded. 'Jews do not have and cannot have any future in Poland. Do tell us, though', he finally demanded, 'that what has happened to us was not our fault. We do not ask for anything else. But we do hope for such an acknowledgement'. (p.45)

Błoński correctly understood this to be a call for Poles to accept some responsibility for the fate of the Jews during the war and it was one of the spurs which led him to write his article.

A final factor in provoking discussion of these thorny issues was Claude Lanzmann's film *Shoah*. When it was first shown in Paris, it was bitterly attacked by the official press as an anti-Polish provocation and the Polish government even delivered a note of protest to the French government which had provided part of the finance for the film. When *Shoah* was finally shown in Poland, as a result of a change of heart by the authorities, reactions were more complex. Most Poles rejected Lanzmann's division of European society during the Holocaust (particularly in Poland) into the murderers, their victims, and the bystanders, largely unsympathetic to the fate of the Jews. Yet many were shocked by his interviews with Polish peasants living in the vicinity of the death camps, which revealed the persistence in the Polish countryside of crude anti-semitic stereotypes. For Catholics, which of course meant the overwhelming majority of Poles, Lanzmann's argument that Nazi anti-semitism was the logical culmination of Christian anti-semitism was also unacceptable. But it, too, forced the re-examination of many strongly-held attitudes. It is striking how many of the participants in the discussion reproduced in this book refer to *Shoah*.

This was the climate in which Jan Błoński's article was written. It was no coincidence that it was published in the weekly *Tygodnik Powszechny*. Since it first appeared 42 years ago, it has established itself as perhaps the most independent newspaper published legally in Poland. (It did not appear between March 1953 and the end of 1956 because it refused to print an obituary of Stalin.) It has a wide following in Polish society, particularly among the intelligentsia, and although its circulation is deliberately restricted to 80,000 it probably reaches at least quarter of a million readers. Heavily censored, it has, since 1981, taken advantage of the new censorship law which allows it to reveal where an article has been cut. (Such cuts can be seen in Ewa Berberyusz's interview with Stanisław Krajewski (chapter 8), where we have been able to reinstate the forbidden passages.) *Tygodnik Powszechny*'s editor, Jerzy Turowicz, has been a consistent advocate of Polish–Jewish and Christian–Jewish rapprochement and many articles on Jewish themes have appeared in the paper, starting with its strong condemnation over 40 years ago of the Kielce pogrom. Ironically, it was the government's press spokesman, Jerzy Urban, himself of Jewish origin, who contemptuously described the paper as 'philo-semitic'.

Błoński gave his article the title 'The Poor Poles look at the Ghetto', taking as his point of departure a poem by the Nobel prizewinner, Czesław Miłosz, written shortly after the destruction of the Warsaw ghetto and bearing the title, 'A Poor Christian looks at the Ghetto'. In the poem, Miłosz imagines the destruction of the ghetto as the first stage in the end of the world, an apocalypse in which he himself will be buried alive. Worse than the fear of this terrible death is another fear. Under the earth, he imagines a mole, the guardian of the underworld, with clearly Jewish features, who makes his way, scrutinizing the corpses he finds. From the spectrograph of his body, he will be able to recognize the poet.

> And he will count me among the helpers of death
> The uncircumcised.

The poem is thus an acceptance of the responsibility of the whole Christian world for the mass murder of the Jews. In his article, Błoński comments that any attempt by Poles to discuss their reactions to this murder, whether with Jews or with other people, very quickly degenerates into apologetics and attempts to justify Polish conduct. The explanation for this, he believes, is clear:

> The reason is that, whether consciously or unconsciously, we fear accusations. We fear that the guardian mole might call to us, after having referred to his book: 'Oh, yes, and you too, have you been assisting at the death? And you too, have you helped to kill?' Or, at the very least: 'Have you looked with acquiescence at the death of the Jews?'. (p. 42)

This fear cannot easily be evaded, even if it is one shared by the Poles with the rest of Europe. It has to be openly faced. The only way for the Poles to calm their subconscious panic, Błoński says, is to stop 'haggling, trying to defend and justify ourselves. To stop arguing about the things that were beyond our power to do, during the occupation and beforehand. Nor to place blame on political, social and economic conditions. But to say first of all, "Yes, we are guilty".'

This guilt consists, in his view, not in the mass murder of the Jews in which the Poles did not participate but in their 'holding back', their 'insufficient effort to resist'. The failure to act, however, is not the central issue. More important is the more distant history:

> if only we had behaved more humanely in the past, had been

11

wiser, more generous, then genocide would perhaps have been 'less imaginable', would probably have been considerably more difficult to carry out, and almost certainly would have met with much greater resistance than it did. To put it differently, it would not have met with the indifference and moral turpitude of the society in whose full view it took place. (p.46)

Błoński employed a powerful analogy:

We did take Jews into our home, but we made them live in the cellar. When they wanted to come into the drawing-room, our response was – Yes, but only after you cease to be Jews, when you become 'civilized'. This was the thinking of our most enlightened minds, such as Orzeszkowa and Prus. There were those among Jews who were ready to adhere to this advice. No sooner did they do this than we started in turn talking of an invasion of Jews, of the danger of their infiltration of Polish society. Then we started to put down conditions like that stated *expressis verbis* by Dmowski, that we shall accept as Poles only those Jews who are willing to cooperate in the attempts to stem Jewish influences in our society. To put it bluntly, those Jews who are willing to turn against their own kith and kin.

Eventually, when we lost our home, and when within that home, the invaders set to murdering Jews, did we show solidarity towards them? How many of us decided that it was none of our business? There were also those (and I leave out of account common criminals) who were secretly pleased that Hitler had solved for us 'the Jewish problem'. We could not even welcome and honour the survivors, even if they were embittered, disorientated, and perhaps sometimes tiresome. I repeat: instead of haggling and justifying ourselves, we should first consider our own faults and weaknesses. This is the moral revolution which is imperative when considering the Polish–Jewish past. It is only this that can gradually cleanse our desecrated soil. (pp.44–5)

He concluded with an appeal to the Poles to imitate the way the Catholic Church has repudiated its anti-Jewish past, whose central feature, he argued, was just such a refusal to excuse past wrongs.

We are also familiar with the Church documents in which –
already at the time of Pope John XXIII – the relationship
between Christians and Jews, or rather, between Christianity
and Judaism, was redefined, hopefully for all time. In the
Pope's speech as well as in these documents one aspect is
immediately clear. They do not concern themselves with
attributing blame nor with the consideration of reasons (social,
economic, intellectual, or whatever) which made Christians
look upon Jews as enemies and intruders. One thing is stated
loud and clear: the Christians of the past and the Church itself
were wrong. They had no reason to consider Jews as a
'damned' nation, the nation responsible for the death of Jesus
Christ, and therefore as a nation which should be excluded
from the community of nations. (pp.43–4)

These were strong words and, not surprisingly, they provoked
strong reactions, both positive and negative. According to Jerzy
Turowicz, speaking in Jerusalem:

When we printed the article, I was, as were my colleagues,
aware that it would be an event to which there would certainly
be a strong reaction. The reaction was greater than anything
known in the course of the forty-two years during which I have
edited that paper. I cannot remember any article which
provoked such a strong reaction on the part of the readers. We
received nearly 200 letters and articles on the subject. We were
able, as you know to publish only a very small part. There
were amongst these, texts and letters which were explicitly
anti-semitic, often anonymous. There was also no shortage of
positive texts which were in solidarity with what Błoński had
written. There were further statements of the kind, 'I'm not an
anti-semite, but . . .' Finally there was often a reaction of
consternation, the consternation of people who could not really
understand how one could, as they understood from Błoński's
article, accuse the Poles of complicity in mass-murder.

I think that no conclusions should be drawn from these
letters, published or otherwise. One cannot generalize about
them. This was not any sort of academic public opinion
research nor a poll. If there were a whole array of voices which
did not agree with Błoński, there is nothing strange in that, as
after all people write to the editor if they do not agree with

something, whereas if they are in agreement they don't usually feel the need to write. None the less, that whole debate disclosed the existence of anti-semitism still in Poland, today more than 40 years after the war. It has shown that it is an attitude which cannot easily be uprooted nor overcome, and one that even at times regenerates itself. However, I do not believe that one should exaggerate the size of this phenomenon. (pp.215–16)

Of the articles printed in *Tygodnik Powszechny*, most, in general terms, supported Błoński's views, though critical on some points. One (by Janina Walewska, chapter 11), which was perhaps most typical of the general reaction of the Polish intelligentsia, simultaneously agreed and disagreed with Błoński. The journal also published a strong attack on Błoński by a veteran opposition lawyer, Władysław Siła-Nowicki, a man who had been imprisoned by the authorities in the Stalinist period and who had defended many accused of political crimes. It also printed two interviews, one with Stanisław Krajewski, described as 'a Pole and a Jew', who has been active in attempts to preserve Jewish life and restore Jewish monuments in Poland, and another with Jan Karski, the Home Army courier who had vainly attempted in 1942 to persuade the Allied governments and Western Jewish leaders to take action to stop the Nazi mass-murder of the Jews. Articles attacking Błoński appeared in the pro-government weekly *Stolica*, in *Przegląd Tygodniowy* and in *Życie Literackie* whose editor, Czesław Machajek, had drawn notoriety to himself in 1968 by printing a number of strongly anti-semitic pieces. The article here, by Witold Rymanowski (chapter 15) even called for the prosecution of Błoński under articles 178 and 270 of the Polish criminal code for 'slandering the Polish nation'. In addition, we have printed an article by a younger historian, Andrzej Bryk, which was intended in a shorter form for *Tygodnik Powszechny* and which was delivered at the International Conference on the History and Culture of Polish Jews held in Jerusalem in February 1988. We have also printed the transcript of a discussion at that conference on 'Ethical Problems of the Holocaust in Poland' which revolves around the issues raised by Błoński. One of the ironic features of this whole debate is that it has been among Catholics, whose Church had been a major factor in the development of pre-war anti-semitism, that the strongest calls for a rethinking of Polish attitudes have been heard, whereas representatives of the communist establishment have indulged in traditional Polish apologetics, which have verged on the anti-semitic (see for instance, the last paragraph of Rymanowski's article, pp.159–60). This development, ruefully commented on in Jerusalem by Professor Jozef Gierowski, is the consequence both of the imperatives of an unpopular regime seeking to justify itself as the defender of the 'national interest' in the eyes of its subjects, and of the change in Catholic thinking on the Jews and Judaism since the Second World War and, in particular, since the papal encyclical *Nostra aetate*.

The general points of division in the debate are very clear and were, indeed, already sketched out by Błoński in his article. Those who agree with Błoński are at one with him in considering that Polish responsibility consists, above all, of an insufficient concern for the fate of the Jews. As a result, the Jews were not included in what Helen Fein has called the 'universe of obligation', 'that circle of persons towards whom obligations are owed, to whom rules apply and whose injuries call for expiation by the community'.[7] This is regarded as a cause for shame. The Poles, as a group, could not have done much to help the Jews, but by their indifference they condemned them to much lonelier and more solitary deaths than they would otherwise have suffered.

Thus, Jerzy Jastrzębowski describes how a member of his family had told him how, during the war the family had been prepared to hide the elderly Jewish friend of his grandmother but had refused to accept him when he asked that they also take in his three sisters. He continues:

> If my family's decision had been different there was a 90 per cent probability that we would have been discovered and executed for hiding Jews. There was probably less than a 10 per cent chance that the family of Eljasz Parzyński could at all be saved *in those conditions*. The person relating this family drama to me said again and again: 'What were we to do? There was nothing we could do!' And yet she did not look me in the eye. She knew I could sense the insincerity of the argument, even though the facts were true. It is about such

moral responsibilities, among other things, that Jan Błoński
writes in his superb article. We must not pretend – we who
survive and remember – that we do not know what this is all
about. (p.120)

In the same vein, Ewa Berberyusz argues that in the eyes of
Polish society during the war:

in the case of the Jews, a kind of turning point, a sort of
threshold, had been reached, beyond which the society
surrounding them, instead of helping, was on the contrary
paralysed and found it was easier to turn its back on what was
happening.

I remember two such cases, when I had looked the other
way, two moments so engraved in my memory that even today
I could draw it all in great detail. It happened twice that a child
from the ghetto found himself within my vision and twice I
pushed away the first impulse to make some contact and simply
to put food into his rag-covered body . . .

If then, when chance brought me those two children, I had
behaved according to my conscience, would that have altered
the fate of the Jews in Poland? The answer 'yes' is not so
unequivocally right, because my desisting in these cases has to
be multiplied by cases of similar behaviour by others. Possibly,
even if more of us had turned out to be more Christian, it
would have made no difference to the statistics of the
extermination, but maybe it would not have been such a lonely
death? (pp.69–70)

In response to Siła-Nowicki's claim that Polish society had
done all it could, Kazimierz Dziewanowski wrote:

If in our country, in our presence and in front of our eyes,
several million innocent people were murdered and we were
not able to prevent it and save them, this is an event so
terrible, a tragedy so enormous, that it is only understandable,
human, and proper that those who survived are somehow
troubled, disturbed, and cannot find peace . . . it is impossible
to prove that more could have been done, but likewise it is
impossible to prove that more could not have been done.
(pp.113, 116)

Polish indifference is linked with pre-war anti-semitism. This issue is sensitively discussed by Jerzy Turowicz:

I am not making the slightest comparison between the responsibility that the Germans must bear and what Błoński calls our shared guilt. This guilt has to do almost exclusively with the fact of Polish anti-semitism. At this point, once again, there is need for a qualification: there is no *direct* connection between Polish anti-semitism and the Jewish Holocaust. It is not true – as we have pointed out many times before in *Tygodnik Powszechny* – that the Nazis located death camps in Poland because the Poles were anti-semites. They were placed there because this was where the greatest concentration of Jewish population happened to be; also, because Poland was separated by the Reich from the West from which Germans were hiding their plans for the extermination of Jews. Those who handed over Jews into German hands (in Poland as elsewhere) need not have been necessarily anti-semitic; they were simple criminals. It is also well known that, on occasions, Polish anti-semites actively helped Jews.

Secondly, the Nazis directed their hatred not only to the Jews, but also to people known to be active Christians, as they were well aware of the link between Christianity and Judaism. Therefore, the anti-semitism of the Nazis, which was racist and pagan in inspiration, was very different from Polish anti-semitism.

All this, however, does not mean that there is no *indirect* connection between Polish anti-semitism and the Jewish Holocaust. Hitler's devilish plan for the physical extermination of the entire Jewish nation was a culmination, the final conclusion of the anti-semitism which had been established for centuries in Europe and elsewhere. This anti-semitism was propagated, we have to admit with regret, by Christian churches, including the Catholic church. Church historians know all too well the long story of discrimination and persecution which Jews were subjected to on religious grounds; they know of the contempt with which Jews had to contend, of the unceasing attempts at their conversion. In fact, the attitude of the Catholic Church to the Jews has effectively changed only in our own century, owing to the efforts of recent Popes and the Second Vatican Council.

Our Polish guilt has, therefore, to do with anti-semitism. Karl Jaspers is reported to have said that, before the Holocaust, anti-semitism was merely a wrong political doctrine; after the Holocaust, it became a crime. Those among us who have never been anti-semites and who may even have fought against it, cannot nevertheless absolve ourselves totally from the collective moral responsibility for the anti-semitism which was so widespread in our country.

If we had not had such anti-semitism in Poland before the war, perhaps we would still have been unable to save many more Jewish lives, but our attitude to their extermination, which was taking place before our eyes, would have been different. We would not have had that sometimes very evident, indifference, or those inhuman and unchristian responses of the type: 'Hitler has solved the Jewish question for us!'

Pre-war Polish anti-semitism did not disappear during the occupation, although the experience of it which was to some extent shared by the two nations, brought forth also attitudes and deeds of solidarity. Tragically, this anti-semitism raised its head again, and quite violently, in the first months after the war, when those few Jews who managed to survive made an attempt to claim back what was theirs. It is horrifying to think that anti-Jewish violence was still possible after the experience of the Holocaust. This anti-semitism, albeit much reduced, is still with us, even though we have practically no Jews left. (pp.140–2)

Błoński's supporters also stress, like him, the unique character of Jewish suffering during the war, something which has been difficult for Poles to accept. In Jerzy Turowicz's words:

Some say that Poles were to suffer the same fate, that they were 'next for the gas'. No, this is not completely true. Undoubtedly, in the event of Hitler's victory, our fate would have been more than grim. Everybody knows that it was Hitler's design to kill off the Polish intelligentsia, and that the rest of the population was to be deported to the territories annexed by Hitler or to be used as slave labour in the service of the *Herrenvolk*. But all this still does not amount to a decision to exterminate the entire nation. Jews are right when they look upon this attempt at the extermination of the whole Jewish nation (and insist that others should also do so) as something unique in the history of mankind. They are right when they divide their own history into the times before and after the Holocaust . . . .

As for the argument: 'We were also being killed.' We must not make an equation between the fate of Jews and the fate of Poles in the Second World War. Nobody is further than I am from the intention of denying or undervaluing the extent of Polish suffering during the years of the German occupation. Poles died by their thousands in concentration camps and in the Gestapo prisons; a great many were shot as hostages. The proportionate losses of the Polish population were, in relation to those of other countries occupied by Hitler, the highest. But the three million Poles who lost their lives during the war were not just victims of the Nazi terror. This figure includes also people who died in battle, in various theatres of war, as well as in the Warsaw Uprising, and those who died at non-German hands. These three million represent about ten per cent of the then Polish population. In contrast, the three million Polish Jews who died as victims of the 'Final Solution' represent more than 95 per cent of the Jewish community of our country.

But it is not the numerical proportions which matter here most; the difference between the fates of Poles and Jews during the war years is also qualitative. If Poles were dying in great numbers as victims of the Nazi terror, it was because of the German desire to subjugate the Polish nation and to crush its resistance. In the case of Jews, it is the entire Jewish nation which was, by Hitler's decree, sentenced to death. Every Jew, whether old man or new-born baby, man or woman, was condemned to death solely because they were Jewish. This decision was systematically implemented: the Jews from the ghettos were gradually transported to the death camps; those who lived outside, in 'freedom', risked their lives every day. (pp.136, 135–6)

One statement of Błoński's from which even his supporters demurred was his claim that the Poles only failed to participate in the mass-murder of the Jews because 'God held back our hand.

Yes, I do mean God, because if we did not take part in that crime, it was because we were still Christians, and at the last moment we came to realize what a satanic enterprise it was' (p.47). According to Jerzy Turowicz, this 'serious accusation' is 'unjust and misguided. I strongly contend that – despite everything – the likelihood of our participation in the crime of genocide did not exist. But this is not to say that the problem of a shared guilt does not arise' (p.139).

Błoński's protagonists also go less far than some Jewish observers who, bitterly and probably unfairly, accuse the Poles of active collaboration in the Holocaust. At the Jerusalem discussion, one of the questions posed from the floor asked whether the Poles' responsibility lies not 'in their indifference but in the prevalence of religious, national, and popular hate. Many people considered the Nazi policies to be an opportunity to remove a national minority which was very embarrassing' (p.222).

Professor Yisrael Gutman, the Israeli historian to whom this question was put responded:

Is this true? I think certainly in part. There is no doubt that there were Poles who said openly or to themselves that it was a good thing that the Jews were disappearing from Poland and the Poles would not have their blood on their hands. I think that was certainly the case. How many such people there were, whether it was general or not it is difficult to say today. That something of the kind existed is, I believe, virtually unquestionable and we can draw the conclusion from documents which we have, that such views were also expressed at the time. But I would like to say now that it was a period of barbarity, as Professor Błoński has said here, that it was easier to hear the voices of evil spirits, that the evil spirits had greater possibilities to flourish and that when we think about the atmosphere, it was one of a certain specific world. I believe that this truth should be stated, but it would not be correct to say, as long as we draw the lessons from it, that the nation always was and always will be like this. (p.222)

This question is also discussed by Teresa Prekerowa. She argues that there were indeed many cases when Jews were denounced to the Nazis by Poles. These 'crimes' she claims, did not, as is sometimes suggested, stem from anti-semitism.

Greed was the motive and anybody sufficiently defenceless could have fallen victim. Nevertheless the lack of sympathetic interest in the fate of the Jews on the part of the surrounding population facilitated the commission of the crime.

There is similar discredit to Polish society in the existence of the blackmailers and *smalcownicy* (extortionists who blackmailed Jews in hiding – they would accost them in the vicinity of ghettos and on the streets of towns). (p.75)

Responding to Siła-Nowicki, who wrote, 'Those who denounced the Jews to the German authorities were sentenced to death and those sentences were carried out by us while running the risk of death ourselves,' she observes:

That's right, but from when? From September 1943, whereas they started their profitable underhand dealings the moment ghettos were closed, and that meant in Warsaw from the autumn of 1940. For three years therefore they could continue to operate undeterred. In the last year – 1943–4 – in all five blackmailers were put to death in Warsaw and a few in Kraków and its environs. There is no doubt that fighting them, and in particular spotting and identifying them, was difficult, but, and I repeat the question, could we really 'not do much more?' (pp.75–6)

Błoński's critics followed the apologetic line already set out and criticized by Błoński in his article. They are concerned that he has blackened the reputation of the Poles. In Siła-Nowicki's words:

published as it was in a journal carrying great weight [the article] may unfortunately be understood as the affirmation and quintessence (unintended of course), of a virulent anti-Polish propaganda campaign conducted endlessly for dozens of years by the enemies not of the government, nor the economic or political system of present-day Poland, but simply of the Polish nation. (p.59)

The Poles did all they could to aid the Jews during the war and therefore have no cause to feel guilt or shame. In Siła-Nowicki's words:

I am proud of my nation's stance in every respect during the period of occupation and in this include the attitude towards the tragedy of the Jewish nation. Obviously, the attitudes towards the Jews during that period do not give us a particular reason to be proud, but neither are they any grounds for shame, and even less for ignominy. Simply, we would have done relatively little more than we actually did. (p.62)

This view was echoed by Kazimierz Kąkol, at present Director of the Main Commission for the Investigation of Nazi War Crimes in Poland.

Resistance, help, rescue initiatives were closely related to the ratio of population – of the persecuted population's needs in relation to the needs of the entire population (which itself was earmarked as next in line for liquidation). The figures were of fundamental significance and we don't need divine assistance to judge how these numerical proportions determined the possibility of help . . . . And they determined them adversely, as did the mass incidence of difference in posture, behaviour, dress, as well as language.' (p.146)

Polish society was itself in danger of total destruction, or as Siła-Nowicki put it 'Both the Jewish and Polish communities were faced with the threat of biological extinction' (p.65), a view which, as we have seen, is echoed by Kąkol. The Jewish failure to resist further reduced the opportunities for providing assistance. According to Siła-Nowicki, 'Passive behaviour – seeking security . . . by accepting German orders – was the first and principal obstacle to the possibility of extending help to the Jews' (p.67).

This accusation of passivity – important in Poland where the tradition of active resistance to tyranny is highly valued and actively cultivated – was rejected with some heat by Błoński's supporters. Turowicz was at his most magisterial:

Several million innocent people, including women, children, and the old, people who were our neighbours, were murdered before our eyes, on our soil, and we were helpless witnesses, unable for the most part to do anything about it. This fact is so horrifying that we cannot ever forget it, nor can we fail to ask ourselves whether this does not still present a moral challenge to us.

And may I suggest that it is at least insensitive – to avoid a stronger term – to accuse the Jews of being passive, when we consider their fate. (p.142)

Teresa Prekerowa points out that the underground functioning of political parties, a clandestine press education and cultural activities were large-scale phenomena in the ghettos and can only be seen as a form of resistance. She also points out that most of Polish society was also 'passive' and that flight to the 'aryan' side was fraught with danger for Jews.

In the eyes of Błoński's critics, the responsibility of the Western allies and of Jews in the west for failing to prevent the mass murder of the Jews was much greater than that of the Poles. According to Siła-Nowicki:

the chances of effectively helping the Jews on a large scale were slim. Jewish organizations in the West, particularly in the United States, had incomparably more such possibilities, and thousands of lives could have been saved simply in exchange for money. But those Jews showed passivity and indifference to the terrible plight of their compatriots in the German-occupied territories. (p.67)

This view, also put forward by Kazimierz Kąkol and Ryszard Żelichowski, is rejected by Błoński's supporters as irrelevant. Kazimierz Dziewanowski observed that what Siła-Nowicki writes about the Western response to the Holocaust is 'true':

I am even of the opinion that the guilt of the Allies, and also of the Jews in the USA and Great Britain, is enormous, immeasurable and second only to the guilt of the Nazis themselves. Although it is difficult to compare, nevertheless, the indifference, stupidity, and unwillingness to believe the truthful and exact nature of the information passed on to them by the Polish government and the emissaries from our country, especially by Karski, are facts which remain incomprehensible and more terrifying than the indifference of the passengers of the famous merry-go-round about which Miłosz wrote. People in the West had ways and means to oppose the evil; the fools on the merry-go-round did not have them. Had they had them, they would have perhaps behaved differently. This is the reason why today it hurts and rouses indignation when those in the West from their comfortable positions dare to pass judgements on the behaviour of Poles here in German-occupied Poland.

This argument, however, though correct, does not matter much to me. It does not concern me or my nation. It concerns strangers. It is a matter for their consciences, not mine. Too often unfortunately in this type of discussion the argument is used that others were no better. The French, for example, had they found themselves in the circumstances which existed in German-occupied Poland, would probably have behaved not any better and possibly worse. Perhaps it would have been so, but it has not been proved, and what is more, I repeat, it does not concern me. I am interested only in my own conscience. (pp.114–15)

Błoński in Jerusalem was less apologetic. He remarked that:

Responsibility, understood in [the] manner [I have outlined], the Poles share naturally with their neighbours, with the whole of Europe, with Christianity. They even, perhaps, share it with American Jews. I know what a tragedy it is for the Jews in the Diaspora, in America, who did not see what happened. I know, I well understand, that tragedy. Yet it is more important to stress that we, unlike them, are not absolved by the fact that we did not know what was happening, firstly because we were on the spot and secondly because the Polish responsibility is greater by virtue of the fact that Jews lived on Polish lands, and we Poles should have known better, understood better, than to make them a scapegoat for our own political and social difficulties. (pp.188–9)

The Jews, claim Błoński's critics, were, in addition, a privileged group in Poland before the war. Thus talk of anti-semitism at that time is greatly exaggerated. Referring to Błoński's statement that 'we did take the Jews into our home, but we made them live in the cellar', Siła-Nowicki demanded rhetorically,

In the cellar, indeed? And in whose hands was the greatest part of the wholesale trade and a great deal of the retail trade in Poland? Who had most capital at their disposal? What was, after all, the Polish majority or the Jewish minority which constituted 10 per cent? Who, on average, had the greater returns from his professional work – the Jew living in 'the cellar' or the Polish occupier of the first floor. . .? (p.64)

Talking of Polish attempts to restrict the number of Jews at universities, he wrote:

> For me it is natural that society defends itself against numerical domination of its intelligentsia – especially pronounced in the medical or legal professions – by an alien intelligentsia. The co-existence of two nations must depend on some balance being observed. (p.65)

And what is one to make of the following statement:

> It is even possible to prove in the most scientific manner that in their veins flows only 1 per cent of the blood of those people who shouted 'Hosanna to the Son of David' and then 'Crucify Him, crucify Him!'; but their nation continues to exist. (p.63)

Similar observations can be found in the article by Rymanowski.

What is really at issue here is what Zygmunt Bauman has called the 'rationality of evil'. The process of mass murder rested on persuading all involved, both victims or bystanders, that it was more sensible to cooperate than to resist, whether by false claims that what was involved was merely resettlement, by holding out the hope that some would survive and by stressing the penalties for non-cooperation.

> By and large, the rulers can count on rationality being on their side. The Nazi rulers twisted the stakes of the game so that the rationality of survival would render all other motives of human action irrational. Inside the Nazi-made, unreal and inhuman world, reason was the enemy of morality. Logic required consent to crime. Rational defence of one's survival called for non-resistance to the other's destruction. This rationality pitched the sufferers against each other and obliterated their joint humanity. This rationality absolved them from immorality. Having reduced human life to the calculus of survival, this rationality robbed human life of humanity.[8]

This is why, as Jerzy Turowicz has observed, the argument between the two sides is 'conducted on totally different planes' (p.138). In Bauman's words:

Siła-Nowicki and Błoński do not argue with, but past, each other. Błoński wrote of the moral significance of the Holocaust, Siła-Nowicki responded with an investigation of the rationality of self-preservation. What he failed to notice was the ethical meaning of the very form such rationality took (or, rather, was forced to assume): the very fact that the Nazi regime set the logic of survival against the moral duty (as a value superior to ethics) was simultaneously the secret of the technical success of the mass murder, one of the most sinister horrors of the event called the 'Holocaust', and the most venomous of its consequences . . .

As far as the substantive argument goes, Siła-Nowicki argues past Błoński's point. Błoński speaks of *moral* shame, not of the shame which in our rational world we use to associate with a botched job or inefficient work. No one calls in question the earnestness and industry of Polish resistance; no one doubts that not much more could *practically* have been done without incalculable cost. This does not mean, however, that moral qualms can be put to sleep. Neither does it mean that a moral person's feeling of shame is unfounded (even if, as could be claimed, it is 'irrational'). To this feeling of shame – our ultimate victory over the pernicious legacy of the Holocaust – the most scrupulous and historically accurate computations of the numbers of those who 'could' and those who 'could not' help, of those who 'could' and those who 'could not' be helped, are irrelevant.[9]

In fact, as Bauman correctly states, the issue is not:

whether the Poles should feel ashamed or whether they should feel proud of themselves. The issue is that only the liberating feeling of shame – the recovery of the moral significance of the joint historical experience – may once and for all exorcise the spectre of the Holocaust, which continues to haunt not only Polish–Jewish relations, but also the ethical self-identity of the Poles and the Jews alike, to this very day. The choice is not between shame and pride. The choice is between the pride of morally purifying shame, and the shame of morally devastating pride.

What perhaps stops Władysław Siła-Nowicki (for all I know

of him, a person of the highest ethical standards) from admitting the moral need of shame, is his conviction that shame, rather than ennobling and purifying, is equivalent to an admission of a 'material guilt' of sorts. That it means confessing to a sinful deed, or worse still – to a base aspect, or a wicked streak in the national character. I do not agree. It was the inhuman world created by a homicidal tyranny which dehumanised its victims, pressing them to use the logic of self-preservation as absolution for moral insensitivity and inaction. No one can be proclaimed guilty for the sheer fact of breaking down under such pressure. Yet no one can be excused from moral self-deprecation for such surrender. And only when feeling ashamed for one's weakness, can one finally shatter the mental prison which has outlived its builders and guards until today.[10]

It is this, too, which gives to the whole controversy a larger dimension. It is not primarily about Polish–Jewish relations, the behaviour of the Poles during the war or even the type of society which one should aim to create in Poland. It is about how and in what conditions resistance can be offered to an all-powerful tyranny.

It is too early to speak in any meaningful way of a 'Jewish response' to Błoński's article and the ensuing controversy. Yet certainly among those Jews involved in Polish–Jewish dialogue the article has been seen as embodying a fundamental change in Polish attitudes. This was clearly reflected in the Jerusalem discussions:

According to Rafael Scharf:

I read Błoński's article, for the first time, with growing excitement and quickened pulse. At one point he makes reference to one of the speakers at the conference in Oxford in 1984, whose words, he said, inspired him to ponder these matters. From the words quoted by him it was clear that he was referring to me. I was startled and also moved to see how one word, a sentence, a thought can strike another man's mind, can germinate there and bear fruit beyond expectation. I was talking then, at least that is how Błoński understood it, to the effect that we Jews no longer expected anything from the Poles but the admission that they have been, in some way, at fault. For many years we listened, waited for a sign – but we heard no voices. In the end, I had thought we would be straining our ears in vain. But now, at last – we hear the voice of Błoński . . .

More than a year has passed since Błoński's voice sounded. I would like to assure all those who feared that it would have a harmful effect on Poland, that quite the opposite has occurred. His article is seen, in itself, as a certain rehabilitation of sorts. When, paradoxically and undeservedly, I am put in the role of an *advocatus Poloniae*, I myself, in many instances, recall this article and those which followed. I maintain that one can no longer speak loosely about the Poles' opinion on the subject without taking into consideration these new voices, which save the reputation of Poland. (pp.197–8)

In Yisrael Gutman's words:

I want to tell you why Błoński is dear to us. Błoński, Turowicz, Bartoszewski, Gierowski, these are people who are perpetuating the most splendid of Polish traditions. Let me quote what Mickiewicz said, perhaps somewhat pompously, of the upholder of Polish ideals: 'The person, who during the revolution inscribed on the banners "For your and for our freedom" had within him a Polish spirit. And he put the word "your" before "our" in spite of past diplomatic logic.' If Błoński's article and Turowicz's summing up and other similar voices appear in Poland, I tell myself and others there is mutual hope. (pp.206–7)

Victor Erlich, son of the Bundist leader Henryk Erlich, murdered by Stalin in 1941, observed:

Today, in the twentieth century, Polish–Jewish relations have taken on the character of a vicious circle. Amongst many Jews, a feeling of distrust was born in relation to the Poles as a result of official or popular Polish anti-semitism, and this behaviour which could be construed as anti-Polish, in conditions of a national catastrophe. Those acts, in turn, added oil to the fire, and fanned a deeply rooted and 'virulent' prejudice. The historical significance of the discussion which was initiated by Jan Błoński's article, a discussion which we are continuing today, rests on the fact that remarks such as those made by Jan

28

Błoński, Ewa Berberyusz, and Jerzy Turowicz help us find a way out of that vicious circle. They help us create the conditions for a Polish–Jewish dialogue devoid of prejudice and misunderstandings, of irresponsible generalizations and self-protective denials, for a dialogue marked by mutual respect and, perhaps more important, respect for what are at times painful facts. We have started that dialogue late, and the path is a long one. Perhaps, however, by a joint effort we will succeed in fulfilling our common duty – and to once again quote Jan Błoński – to confront our past in truth. (p.202)

In addition, partly in response to the belief that Polish attitudes now recognize more sensitively the nature of the Jewish tragedy during the Second World War, and partly, too, as the trauma of the Holocaust diminishes slightly with the passage of time, there has emerged a more balanced attitude on the Jewish side to the awful moral dilemmas of those years.

It was Yisrael Gutman who stated:

Sometimes I hear Jews accusing the Poles of deliberately not helping them even though they could have done so. Such observations are expressions of pain, which eclipse a sensible attitude. More could certainly have been done to save Jews, but the Poles in the conditions of the occupation could not have fundamentally changed the fate of the Jews. The Allies could have perhaps done so, but even that is not certain in the final phases of the murderers' insanity. I shall permit myself to say more – there is no moral imperative which demands that a normal mortal should risk his life and that of his family to save his neighbour. Are we capable of imagining the agony of fear of an individual, a family, which selflessly and voluntarily, only due to an inner human impulse, bring into their home someone threatened with death. Are we capable of understanding the pressure of those fears when a fugitive had to be kept out of sight of neighbours and relations, when a neighbour or friend dare not hear the cough of a sick person nearby, and those hiding the fugitive lived in an unending fear, when all that was needed was one house search for both the hider and the hidden to have an end put to their lives? The Poles should be proud that they had so many just lights, of whom Ringelblum spoke, who are the real heroes of the deluge. And we can never do

29

enough to thank these rare people. But by force of events, such a willingness to sacrifice could have been only a marginal phenomenon. (pp.203–4)

He further observed poignantly:

Once as a young Zionist, I believed that we Jews would never harm another nation, others who lived amongst us, that the lesson of history which the Diaspora taught us would suffice. Today I know I was naïve and that explains and teaches us much. (p.206)

Similarly, a recent issue of the Jewish Anti-Defamation League's quarterly journal *Dimensions* was entitled 'Was there "Another Europe"?' and was devoted to the people who willingly risked death during the Holocaust to rescue nearly 200,000 Jews. According to Dr Dennis Klein, Director of the ADL's International Center for Holocaust Studies, in an implicit rejection of Claude Lanzmann's views:

A desire is growing to understand how and why some people defied anti-semitic mandates or resisted the social pressures to conform to them . . . [There is] impatience with dividing Europe eternally into perpetrators, victims and bystanders . . . Even if resisters and rescuers were numerically marginal, don't their actions bear a historical and moral significance beyond their numbers?[11]

There has also been an increasing realization, similar to that on the Polish side, that what is involved in this discussion is not primarily a Polish–Jewish argument, but something much more fundamental. In Rafael Scharf's words:

With the passage of time it will become clear that the agenda is not about us alone; that our debate and controversy is merely incidental to something bigger and more comprehensive. What is at issue here is a great, common cause of universal significance. The extermination of the Jews on Polish territory was a crucial event in history, marking the crisis of Christianity and the crisis of our civilization (some people regard these concepts as synonymous, but fortunately that is not so). Those events cannot be forgotten or ignored, they will weigh upon the future generations for all time.

What lessons will human beings draw from this, how will
they face up to it, conscious of the enormity of evil which they
are capable of perpetrating; how will they renew their faith in
the basic moral values in a world of which, in Adorno's words,
'we cannot be too much afraid' and where there exist
instruments of destruction which put even the gas-chambers in
shadow? On answers to these questions hang all our
tomorrows. (pp.194–5)

Voices have also been raised criticizing what has been seen as
the excessive Jewish preoccupation with the Holocaust. At the
international Holocaust conference 'Remembering for the Future'
the Chief Rabbi of the United Kingdom, Lord Jakobovits,
remarked:

I have some doubts about the sanctification of the Holocaust as
a cardinal doctrine in contemporary Jewish thought and
teaching. I respect the widely-held view to the contrary, but I
still wonder whether it can be accepted as authentically Jewish,
or even as conducive to healing the wounds inflicted on the
morale and spirit of our people . . .
   The Holocaust and its victims, together with their historic
legacy, must of course be remembered for ever with supreme
reverence. I also recognise that the Holocaust will remain a
major factor both haunting and galvanising Jewish life for a
long time to come. Indeed – I believe, contrary to the opinion
of Ben Gurion and others – that the State of Israel would never
have emerged when it did, were it not for the desperate
pressures and superhuman Jewish energies generated by the
Holocaust.
   But at the same time we must beware against nurturing and
breeding a Holocaust mentality of morose despondency among
our people, especially our youth.[12]

In Jerusalem, Błoński correctly pointed out that the controversy was not primarily about facts. 'There may have been
differences over the facts, but this divergence [between Polish
attitudes and those outside Poland] was too great to be explained
on this basis. It was rather in the understanding of the facts that
the differences lay' (p.186). Yet paradoxically, the articulation of
the moral problems at the centre of the controversy has made

possible a much more effective analysis of the factual problems involved. The study of the subject of Polish–Jewish relations during the Second World War can thus become less the field for emotional exchanges and be advanced by the application of the traditional skills and techniques of the historian. This was the approach of Mrs Prekerowa, who, in her important article, manages to shed considerable light on the vexed questions of how many Jews were saved in Poland during the war (40–60,000 according to her) and how many Poles were involved in hiding and aiding Jews (1–2.5 per cent of the adult population). One may dispute the figures, but her approach is certainly one of the paths we need to follow. A similar set of scholarly imperatives was suggested at Jerusalem by a younger historian, Jan Tomasz Gross.

The articulation of the central moral problems also enables us to move on to another plane in our examination of the Holocaust in Poland and elsewhere. One does not have to share the Chief Rabbi's theological predilections to agree with him that too much attention has perhaps been devoted to the process of mass murder and not enough to what was destroyed. What was at issue here was not only the terrible crime of the cold-blooded murder of 6 million innocent men, women, and children but the destruction of a whole civilization, the civilization of East European Jewry. At the Jerusalem conference Professor Gierowski observed that 'what we are undertaking at the moment is an attempt to save what can still be saved'. This attempt to preserve the memory and values of the 'murdered Jewish nation' to use the phrase of the poet Yitshak Katzenelson, who himself died in Auschwitz, unites both Poles and Jews. It is an investigation of our common Polish–Jewish past, with all its good and bad sides. Its recovery will not be an easy task – the last words should perhaps be left to the poet Jerzy Ficowski:

I did not manage to save
a single life

I did not know how to stop
a single bullet

and I wander round cemeteries
which are not there
I look for words

which are not there
I run

to help where no one called
to rescue after the event

I want to be on time
even if I am too late

The first poem in his 'A Reading of Ashes'

NOTES

1 Review of Irena Hurwic-Nowakowska, *A Social Analysis of Postwar Polish Jewry*, in *POLIN. A Journal of Polish–Jewish Studies*, vol. 3, pp. 440–1.
2 ibid, p. 441.
3 J. Andrzejewski, 'Zagadnienia Polskiego Antysemitizm' (The problem of Polish anti-semitism) in *Martwa Fala* (The dead wave), Warsaw, 1947.
4 Quoted by Yisrael Gutman in the discussion on 'Ethical Problems of the Holocaust in Poland', chapter 17 of this book, pp.184–232.
5 L. Dobroszycki, 'Restoring Jewish Life in Post-war Poland', *Soviet Jewish Affairs*, 1973, 2, p. 59.
6 Marek Leski, 'Glossa do "Zydow Polskich" Normana Daviesa' (Gloss on Norman Davies' 'Polish Jews'), *Arka* 1985, 10.
7 Helen Fein, *Accounting for Genocide. National Responses and Jewish Victimization during the Holocaust*, Chicago, 1984, p. 33, quoted in Bryk, p. 223.
8 Z. Bauman, 'On immoral reason and illogical morality', in *POLIN. A Journal of Polish–Jewish Studies*, vol III, p. 296.
9 ibid., pp. 296–7.
10 ibid., p. 298.
11 *Dimensions A Journal of Holocaust Studies* vol. 3, no. 3, Summer 1988.
12 I. Jakobovits, 'Some personal, theological and religious responses to the Holocaust', in *Remembering for the Future. Papers to be presented at an International Scholars' Conference to be held in Oxford, 10–13 July 1988*, supplementary vol., pp.175–6.

2

THE POOR POLES LOOK AT THE GHETTO*

JAN BŁOŃSKI

On more than one occasion Czesław Miłosz has spoken in a perplexing way of the duty of Polish poetry to purge the burden of guilt from our native soil which is – in his words – 'sullied, blood-stained, desecrated'.[1] His words are perplexing, because one can only be held accountable for the shedding of blood which is not one's own. The blood of one's own kind, when shed by victims of violence, stirs memories, arouses regret and sorrow, demands respect. It also calls for remembrance, prayer, justice. It can also allow for forgiveness, however difficult this may be. The blood of the other, however, even if spilt in a legitimate conflict, is quite another matter but it also does not involve desecration. Killing when in self-defence is legally condoned, though it is already a departure from Christian moral law: Christ ordered Peter to put away his sword. Whenever blood is spilt it calls for reflection and penance. Not always, however, can it be said to desecrate the soil.

What Miłosz means here is neither the blood of his compatriots nor that of the Germans. He clearly means Jewish blood, the genocide which – although not perpetrated by the Polish nation – took place on Polish soil and which has tainted that soil for all time. That collective memory which finds its purest voice in poetry and literature cannot forget this bloody and hideous defilement. It cannot pretend that it never occurred. Occasionally one hears voices, especially among the young, who were not emotionally involved in the tragedy, saying: 'We reject the notion of collective responsibility. We do not have to return to the

---

*This article was first published in *Tygodnik Powszechny*, 11 January 1987.

irrevocable past. It is enough if we condemn this crime *in toto* as we do with any injustice, any act of violence.' What I say to them is this: 'Our country is not a hotel in which one launders the linen after the guests have departed. It is a home which is built above all of memory; memory is at the core of our identity. We cannot dispose of it at will, even though as individuals we are not directly responsible for the actions of the past. We must carry it within us even though it is unpleasant or painful. We must also strive to expiate it.'

How should this be done? To purify after Cain means, above all, to remember Abel. This particular Abel was not alone, he shared our home, lived on our soil. His blood has remained in the walls, seeped into the soil. It has also entered into ourselves, into our memory. So we must cleanse ourselves, and this means we must see ourselves in the light of truth. Without such an insight, our home, our soil, we ourselves, will remain tainted. This is, if I understand correctly, the message of our poet. Or, at any rate, this is how Miłosz sees his duty, while calling upon us at the same time to assume this obligation also.

How difficult this task is can be seen from Miłosz's celebrated poem 'Campo di Fiori'. At the heart of it there is the image of the merry-go-round which was – by chance, but what a coincidence! – built in Krasiński Square in Warsaw just before the outbreak of the ghetto rising. When the fighting broke out, the merry-go-round did not stop; children, youngsters and passers-by crowded around it as before:

> Sometimes the wind from burning houses
> would bring the kites along
> and people on the merry-go-round
> caught the flying charred bits.
> This wind from the burning houses
> blew open the girls' skirts
> and the happy throngs laughed
> on a beautiful Warsaw Sunday.

(translation by A. Gillon)

Miłosz compares 'the happy throng' to the crowd of Roman vendors who – only a moment after the burning at the stake of Giordano Bruno – went merrily about their business as before, enjoying their 'pink fruits of the sea' and 'baskets with olives and lemons' as if nothing had happened. He ends the poem with reflections of 'the loneliness of dying men', who have 'the poet's word' for their only consolation. It is only the word, the poet seems to be saying, which can preserve what can still be saved. It purges the memory by voicing a protest against the passing away and 'the oblivion growing before the flame expired'.

The act of remembering and mourning fixes in the memory the image of the stake in the middle of the market place or that of a merry-go-round on the grave. The success of the poem itself – which is often quoted and has been translated into many languages – is a clear proof of that. In its Hebrew version, the poem may appear as evidence of the hostile indifference of the Poles in the face of the Holocaust. Years later Miłosz wonders 'whether there really was such a street in Warsaw. It existed, and in another sense it did not. It did exist, because there were indeed merry-go-rounds in the vicinity of the ghetto. It did not, because in other parts of town, at other moments, Warsaw was quite different. It was not my intention to make accusations.'[2] The poem, he concedes, is too 'journalistic', allowing one too easily to draw conclusions. It simplifies truth and, by so doing, soothes the conscience. Worse, the poet discovers that he has written 'a very dishonest poem'. Why? Because – I quote – 'it is written about the act of dying from the standpoint of an observer.' So it is; the piece is so composed that the narrator whom we presume to be the poet himself, comes off unscathed. Some are dying, others are enjoying themselves, all that he does is to 'register a protest' and walk away, satisfied by thus having composed a beautiful poem. And so, years later, he feels he got off too lightly. Matched against the horrors of what was occurring at the time, he says, the act of writing is 'immoral'. 'Campo di Fiori' does not succeed in resolving the conflict between life and art. Miłosz adds in his defence that the poem was composed as 'an ordinary human gesture in the spring of 1943' and, of course, we must immediately concede that it was a magnanimous human gesture. During that tragic Easter, it saved – as someone put it somewhat grandiloquently – 'the honour of Polish poetry'. We agree with the poet, though, that the last word on the subject has yet to be spoken.

This agonizing over a poem may perhaps help us to understand why we are still unable to come to terms with the whole of the

Polish–Jewish past. Here then I shall abandon literature and draw directly on my personal experience. Perhaps, on reflection, not even very personal, as almost everybody who has travelled abroad, especially in the West, must have had this question put to him at one time or other: 'Are Poles anti-semites?' Or, more bluntly: 'Why are Poles anti-semites?' I myself have heard it so many times, and so many times I have tried to explain, that I could attempt a thumbnail sketch of some twenty or so of such conversations:

'Are Poles anti-semites?'

'Why do you put your question in this way? There are Poles who are anti-semites, some others who are philo-semites, and a growing number who do not care either way.'

'Well, yes, of course, but I am asking about the majority. Poles have always had a reputation for being anti-semites. Could this be an accident?'

'What do you mean by "always"? Wasn't it true that at a time when Jews were expelled from England, France and Spain, it was in Poland, and not elsewhere, that they found refuge?'

'Yes, maybe, but that was a long time ago, in the Middle Ages. At that time Jews were the objects of universal contempt. But at least since the mid-eighteenth century in Europe, there has always been a problem of Polish intolerance.'

'But it is exactly at that time that Poland disappeared from the map of Europe!'

'Polish society, however, continued to exist and the Jews could not find their place within it. Why?'

'We were under foreign rule; we had to think of ourselves first.'

'This is precisely what I mean. Why could you not think of yourselves together with the Jews?'

'They were too numerous. We did not have sufficient resources. We could not provide for their education, judiciary, administration. Jews didn't even speak Polish: they preferred to learn Russian or German. But there were enlightened people among us who advocated the course of assimilation and strove to bring the two communities together.'

'But why? Why couldn't Jews simply remain Jews? You were also responsible for pogroms, why?'

'It is not true, the first pogroms took place in the Ukraine and they were provoked by the Tsarist police. . .'

And so such discussions continue:

'When you regained independence, the fate of Jews did not improve. On the contrary, anti-semitism became even more vicious.'

'You can't change society in only twenty years, and besides that, was it not much the same elsewhere in Europe at the time? In the aftermath of the First World War we received many Jews from Russia, and after 1934 from Germany.'

'That may be true, but you still treated them as second-class citizens. During the war you saved too few.'

'There is in Israel a place commemorating people who saved Jews during the war. Thirty per cent of the names on that list are Polish names.'

'But the percentage of Jews who survived the war in Poland is low, the lowest in Europe in relation to the total number of the population.'

'In 1942 there were four Jews for every eight Poles in Warsaw. Now, how is it possible for the eight to hide the four?'

'It was indeed the Poles who used to identify Jews and passed them on to the Germans and to the police which was, let us not forget, Polish.'

'In every society there is a handful of people without conscience. You have no idea what the German occupation in Poland was like. To hide one Jew meant risking the life of one's whole family, children included.'

'Yes, that's true, but there were equally brutal punishments for the underground activities, yet a great number of people were involved in them. Following the war Jews did not wish to remain in Poland.'

'Indeed, it was difficult for them to live surrounded by memories.'

'It was difficult for them to live among Poles who did not wish to give them back their houses and shops and threatened and even killed some of them. Have you not heard of the pogroms in Kraków and Kielce?'

'The pogrom in Kielce was a political provocation.'

'Even if it was, so what? It did find a response. Ten thousand
people besieged the Jewish apartment house in Kielce. Ten
thousand people can't be provocateurs.'

'Jews were sometimes a target not for being Jews but for
sympathizing with communists.'

'In 1968, is it because they were communists that they had to
leave Poland?'

And so on, indeed, endlessly. The debates of historians resemble
this discussion. The same arguments and events – only more
carefully documented – appear time and again. There is a vast
body of literature, of both a personal and a documentary nature,
of which we have very little idea in Poland. We should, however,
know it better, because it also refers to us. It contains a wide
range of viewpoints and opinions. There are books whose authors
do not hide that they are motivated by hate. We cannot afford to
ignore them; they are born of personal experiences whose
authenticity cannot be doubted. And, besides, haven't we
ourselves produced a literature abounding in pronouncements
full of hatred, sometimes hysterical hatred, towards Jews?

There are also many books which are cautious and, as far as is
possible, devoid of partisanship. These books carefully remind us
of the intellectual as well as the material conditions of
Polish–Jewish co-existence. They take into account the terror,
unimaginable today, of life under the German occupation and a
certain moral degradation of the society which was a direct result
of life under this enormous pressure. This, in fact, was not a
uniquely Polish experience; it happened also elsewhere.[3] They
make a tacit assumption that tragedies of Eastern Europe cannot
be measured by the yardstick of, say, the English experience.
When the skies are literally falling in, even a kick can be an
expression of sympathy and compassion. The truth, however,
remains difficult to determine and difficult to accept. Two years
ago I attended a discussion in Oxford between some foreign and
some Polish specialists and I must confess that it was a distressing
experience. For us as well as for the Jewish participants, I
suppose. We were a long way from agreeing with each other, but
that is not the aim of such conferences. I was continuously aware
of what was not being said there and what is the main reason why
these discussions – friendly, for the most part – were painful for

all concerned. It was later that I came to the conclusion that this was due to the sense of a kind of contamination, a feeling of being somehow soiled and defiled, which is what Miłosz had in mind in the passage noted above.

And that is why I would like to go back once more to the poet. In 1943 Miłosz wrote another poem about the destruction of the ghetto, a poem entitled 'A Poor Christian Looks at the Ghetto'. It is more ambiguous, perhaps more difficult to understand. It opens with the image of destruction:

> It has begun: the tearing, the trampling on silks,
> It has begun: the breaking of glass, wood, copper, nickel,
>   silver, foam
> Of gypsum, iron sheets, violin strings, trumpets, leaves,
>   balls, crystals,

And later:

> The roof and the wall collapse in flame and heat seizes
>   the foundations.
> Now there is only the earth, sandy, trodden down,
> With one leafless tree.

The city was destroyed, what remained is the earth, full of broken shells and debris. It is also full of human bodies. In this earth, or rather under it:

> Slowly, boring a tunnel, a guardian mole makes his way,
> With a small red lamp fastened to his forehead.
> He touches buried bodies, counts them, pushes on.
> He distinguishes human ashes by their luminous vapour,
> The ashes of each man by a different part of the spectrum.

Who this mole is, it is difficult to say. Is he a guardian, perhaps a guardian of the buried? He has got a torch, so he can see; better, at any rate, than the dead can see. And the poet himself, he is as if among the buried. He lies there with them. He fears something. He fears the mole. It is a striking, startling image:

> I am afraid, so afraid of the guardian mole,
> He has swollen eyelids, like a Patriarch
> Who has sat much in the light of candles
> Reading the great book of the species.

And so this mole has the features of a Jew, poring over the Talmud or the Bible. It seems more likely that it is the Bible, as this alone deserves the name of 'the great book of the species', meaning, of course, the human species.

> What will I tell him, I, a Jew of the New Testament,
> Waiting two thousand years for the second coming of Jesus?
> My broken body will deliver me to his sight
> And he will count me among the helpers of death:
> The uncircumcised.

> (translation Cz. Miłosz)

It is a terrifying poem; it is full of fear. It is as if two fears co-exist here. The first is the fear of death; more precisely, the fear of being buried alive, which is what happened to many people who were trapped in the cellars and underground passages of the ghetto. But there is also a second fear: the fear of the guardian mole. This mole burrows underground but also underneath our consciousness. This is the feeling of guilt which we do not want to admit. Buried under the rubble, among the bodies of the Jews, the 'uncircumcised' fears that he may be counted among the murderers. So it is the fear of damnation, the fear of hell. The fear of a non-Jew who looks at the ghetto burning down. He imagines that he might accidentally die then and there, and in the eyes of the mole who can read the ashes, he may appear 'a helper of death'. And so, indeed, the poem is entitled: 'A Poor Christian Looks at the Ghetto'. This Christian feels fearful of the fate of the Jews but also – muffled, hidden even from himself – he feels the fear that he will be condemned. Condemned by whom? By people? No, people have disappeared. It is the mole who condemns him, or rather *may* condemn him, this mole who sees well and reads 'the book of the species'. It is his own moral conscience which condemns (or may condemn) the poor Christian. And he would like to hide from his mole-conscience, as he does not know what to say to him.

Miłosz, when asked what or who is represented by this mole, declined to answer. He said that he had written the poem spontaneously, not to promote any particular thesis. If this is so, the poem would be a direct expression of the terror which speaks through images, as is often the case in dreams and also in art. It makes tangible something which is not fully comprehended,

41

something that was, and perhaps still is, in other people's as much as in the poet's own psyche, but in an obscure, blurred, muffled shape. When we read such a poem, we understand ourselves better, since that which had been evading us until now is made palpable. As for myself, I have – as probably every reader does – filled in the gaps in my own reading of 'A Poor Christian'. I hope, however, that I have not strayed too far from the intentions of the poet.

Here I return to the hypothetical conversation. It is a simplified summary of dozens of arguments and discussions. What is immediately striking here? In the replies of my fictitious Pole one detects the very same fear which makes itself felt in 'A Poor Christian'. The fear that one might be counted among the helpers of death. It is so strong that we do everything possible not to let it out or to dismiss it. We read or listen to discussions on the subject of Polish–Jewish past and if some event, some fact which puts us in a less-than-advantageous light, emerges, we try our hardest to minimise it, to explain it away and make it seem insignificant. It is not as if we want to hide what happened or to deny that it took place. We feel, though, that not everything is as it should be. How could it have been otherwise? Relations between communities, like the relations of two people, are never perfect. How much more imperfect are relations as stormy and unhappy as these. We are unable to speak of them calmly. The reason is that, whether consciously or unconsciously, we fear accusations. We fear that the guardian mole might call to us, after having referred to his book: 'Oh, yes, and you too, have you been assisting at the death? And you too, have you helped to kill?' Or, at the very least: 'Have you looked with acquiescence at the death of the Jews?'

Let us think calmly: the question will have to be asked. Everybody who is concerned with the Polish–Jewish past must ask these questions, regardless of what the answer might be. But we – consciously or unconsciously – do not want to confront these questions. We tend to dismiss them as impossible and unacceptable. After all, we did not stand by the side of the murderers. After all, *we* were next in line for the gas chambers. After all, even if not in the best way possible, we did live together with the Jews; if our relations were less than perfect, they themselves were also not entirely without blame. So do we have to remind ourselves of this all the time? What will others think of us? What about our self-respect? What about the 'good name' of our society? This concern about the 'good name' is ever-present in private and, even more so, in public discussion. To put it differently, when we consider the past, we want to derive moral advantages from it. Even when we condemn, we ourselves would like to be above – or beyond – condemnation. We want to be absolutely beyond any accusation, we want to be *completely* clean. We want to be also – and only – victims. This concern is, however, underpinned by fear – just as in Miłosz's poem – and this fear warps and disfigures our thoughts about the past. This is immediately communicated to those we speak to. We do not want to have anything to do with the horror. We feel, nevertheless, that it defiles us in some way. This is why we prefer not to speak of it all. Alternatively, we speak of it only in order to deny an accusation. The accusation is seldom articulated but is felt to hang in the air.[4]

Can we rid ourselves of this fear? Can we forestall it? I think not, as it lies, in all truth, in ourselves. It is we ourselves who fear the mole who burrows in our subconscious. I think that we shall not get rid of him. Or at least, we shall not get rid of him by forgetting about the past or taking a defensive attitude towards it. We must face the question of responsibility in a totally sincere and honest way. Let us have no illusions: it is one of the most painful questions which we are likely to be faced with. I am convinced, however, that we cannot shirk it.

We Poles are not alone in grappling with this question. It may be helpful to realize this. Not because it is easier to beat one's breast in company. Not because in this way the blame may appear less weighty. Rather because in this way we shall be able to understand it better. To understand both our responsibility and the reason why we try to evade it.

We read not so long ago about John Paul II's visit to the Synagogue in Rome. We are also familiar with the Church documents in which – already at the time of Pope John XXIII – the relationship between Christians and Jews, or rather, between Christianity and Judaism, was redefined, hopefully for all time. In the Pope's speech as well as in these documents one aspect is immediately clear. They do not concern themselves with attributing blame nor with the consideration of reasons (social, economic, intellectual or whatever) which made Christians look upon Jews as enemies and intruders. One thing is stated loud and clear: the Christians of the past and the Church itself were wrong. They had no reason to consider Jews as a 'damned' nation, the nation responsible for the death of Jesus Christ, and therefore as a nation which should be excluded from the community of nations.

If this did happen, it was because Christians were not Christian enough. The church documents do not state: we 'had to' defend ourselves, we 'could not' save Jews or treat them as brothers. They do not attempt to look for mitigating circumstances (and these can be found). Jews, being monotheists, were 'beyond the pale' already in antiquity. In the Middle Ages what cemented Europe together was religious unity. Let us bear in mind that the Church was, on the whole, more tolerant than the secular rulers. None the less, all this does not change the basic situation and must be put aside. Instead, what has to be stressed is that the Church sustained hostility towards Jews, thereby driving them into isolation and humiliation. To put it briefly, the new Church documents do not attempt to exonerate the past, they do not argue over extenuating circumstances. They speak clearly about the failure to fulfil the duties of brotherhood and compassion. The rest is left to historians. It is precisely in this that the Christian magnanimity of such pronouncements lies.

I think we must imitate this in our attitude to the Polish–Jewish past. We must stop haggling, trying to defend and justify ourselves. We must stop arguing about the things which were beyond our power to do, during the occupation and beforehand. Nor must we place blame on political, social and economic conditions. We must say first of all – Yes, we are guilty. We did take Jews into our home, but we made them live in the cellar. When they wanted to come into the drawing-room, our response was – Yes, but only after you cease to be Jews, when you become 'civilized'. This was the thinking of our most enlightened minds, such as Orzeszkowa and Prus. There were those among Jews who were ready to adhere to this advice. No sooner did they do this than we started in turn talking of an invasion of Jews, of the danger of their infiltration of Polish society. Then we started to put down conditions like that stated *expressis verbis* by Dmowski, that we shall accept as Poles only those Jews who are willing to cooperate in the attempts to stem Jewish influences in our society. To put it bluntly, only those Jews who are willing to turn against their own kith and kin.

Eventually, when we lost our home, and when, within that home, the invaders set to murdering Jews, did we show solidarity towards them? How many of us decided that it was none of our business? There were also those (and I leave out of account common criminals) who were secretly pleased that Hitler had solved for us 'the Jewish problem'. We could not even welcome and honour the survivors, even if they were embittered, disorientated and perhaps sometimes tiresome. I repeat: instead of haggling and justifying ourselves, we should first consider our own faults and weaknesses. This is the moral revolution which is imperative when considering the Polish–Jewish past. It is only this that can gradually cleanse our desecrated soil.

What is easy in the case of words is, however, more difficult in practice. Its precondition is a change in the social awareness of the problem. For our part, we often demand of Jews (or their friends) an impartial and fair assessment of our common history. We should, however, first acknowledge our own guilt, and ask for forgiveness. In fact, this is something that they are waiting for – if, indeed, they are still waiting. I recall one moving speech at the Oxford conference, in which the speaker started by comparing the Jewish attitude to Poland to an unrequited love. Despite the suffering and all the problems which beset our mutual relations, he continued, the Jewish community had a genuine attachment to their adopted country. Here they found a home and a sense of security. There was, conscious or unconscious, an expectation that their fate would improve, the burden of humiliation would lighten, that the future would gradually become brighter. What actually happened was exactly the opposite. 'Nothing can ever change now', he concluded. 'Jews do not have and cannot have any future in Poland. Do tell us, though', he finally demanded, 'that what has happened to us was not our fault. We do not ask for anything else. But we do hope for such an acknowledgement.'

This means for the Polish side the acceptance of responsibility. Here the guardian mole enters for the last time and asks: 'Full responsibility? Also a shared responsibility for the genocide?' I can already hear loud protests. 'How can that be? In God's

name, we didn't take part in the genocide.' 'Yes, that is true,' I
shall reply. Nobody can reasonably claim that Poles as a nation
took part in the genocide of the Jews. From time to time one
hears voices claiming just that. We must consider them calmly,
without getting angry, which might be taken as a mark of panic.
To me, as for the overwhelming majority of people, these claims
are unfounded. So why talk of genocide? And of shared
responsibility? My answer is this: participation and shared responsibility are not the same thing. One can share the responsibility for
the crime without taking part in it. Our responsibility is for
holding back, for insufficient effort to resist. Which of us could
claim that there was sufficient resistance in Poland? It is precisely
because resistance was so weak that we now honour those who
did have the courage to take this historic risk. It may sound
rather strange, but I do believe that this shared responsibility,
through failure to act, is the less crucial part of the problem we
are considering. More significant is the fact that if only we had
behaved more humanely in the past, had been wiser, more
generous, then genocide would perhaps have been 'less
imaginable', would probably have been considerably more
difficult to carry out, and almost certainly would have met with
much greater resistance than it did. To put it differently, it would
not have met with the indifference and moral turpitude of the
society in whose full view it took place.

A question arises immediately whether this could be said not
only of the Poles, but equally well of the French, the English, the
Russians, of the whole of the Christian world. Yes, indeed it can.
This responsibility is, indeed, our common responsibility. But it
cannot be denied that it was in Poland where the greatest number
of Jews lived (more than two-thirds of the world's Jewry are
Polish Jews, in the sense that their forefathers lived in the
territories belonging to the Polish republic in the period before
the Partitions). Consequently, we had the greatest moral
obligation towards the Jewish people. Whether what was
demanded of us was or was not beyond our ability to render God
alone must judge and historians will continue to debate. But, for
us, more than for any other nation, Jews were more of a
problem, a challenge which we had to face.

To refer once more to the realm of literature: nobody
understood this better than Mickiewicz. The thoughts and the

vision of our romantic poet were more far-sighted than that of any of his contemporaries. Unlike the majority of those who were well-disposed to the Jews, Mickiewicz held a deep conviction that Israel, 'the older brother', should not only enjoy the same privileges in Poland as everybody else, but also at the same time retain the right to remain distinct in religion and custom. This was also Norwid's attitude; as far as we can judge, Słowacki was of the same opinion. So, at the very least, our literary greats stood on the side of truth and justice. The thinking of Mickiewicz was indeed visionary: he seems to have been aware that only such a path could save the Jews (if only partially) from extinction, and us from moral turpitude. It would have been a truly extraordinary path to take and one which would have merited the epithet 'messianic' in the proper sense of the word. Reality, unfortunately, took exactly the opposite form to that dreamt of by the poets. It was nowhere else but in Poland, and especially in the twentieth century, that anti-semitism became particularly virulent. Did it lead us to participate in genocide? No. Yet, when one reads what was written about Jews before the war, when one discovers how much hatred there was in Polish society, one can only be surprised that words were not followed by deeds. But they were not (or very rarely). God held back our hand. Yes, I do mean God, because if we did not take part in that crime, it was because we were still Christians, and at the last moment we came to realize what a satanic enterprise it was. This still does not free us from sharing responsibility. The desecration of Polish soil has taken place and we have not yet discharged our duty of seeking expiation. In this graveyard, the only way to achieve this is to face up to our duty of viewing our past truthfully.

NOTES

1 E. Czarnecka, *Prodróżny świata. Rozmowy z Cz. Miłoszem. Komentarze*, New York, 1983, p. 119.
2 ibid., 63–4.
3 The victim cannot accept that he was not only wronged, but also humiliated and demeaned by his persecutor; that he was unable to stand up to the inhumanity of it all. In the years 1944–8, Polish opinion was not able to acknowledge the disintegration of all norms and moral debasement among a large part of our society in the

aftermath of the war. The drastic treatment of these themes by writers such as Borowski and Różewicz aroused indignation. The readers of this journal [*Tygodnik Powszechny*] took exception to J. J. Szczepański's short story 'Buty' ('Shoes'). It was hard to accept the truth of the 'infection with death' (the term coined by K. Wyka). A rather similar attitude was, of course, also to be found among Jews.

4 That is the reason why there are so few literary works that treat the theme of Polish society's attitude to the Jewish Holocaust. It is not only because literature is rendered speechless in the face of genocide. The theme is too hot to handle; writers felt that they came into conflict with their readers' sensibility.

APPENDIX

A. CAMPO DI FIORI

In Rome, on the Campo di Fiori,
baskets with olives and lemons,
the pavement splattered with wine
and broken fragments of flowers.
The hawkers pour on the counters
the pink fruits of the sea,
and heavy armfuls of grapes
fall on the down of peaches.

Here, on this very square
Giordano Bruno was burned;
the hangman kindled the flame of the pyre
in the ring of the gaping crowd,
and hardly the flame extinguished,
the taverns were full again
and hawkers carried on heads
baskets with olives and lemons.

I recalled Campo di Fiori
in Warsaw, on a merry-go-round,
on a fair night in the spring
by the sound of vivacious music.
The salvoes behind the ghetto walls
were drowned in lively tunes,
and vapours freely rose
into the tranquil sky.

Sometimes the wind from burning houses
would bring the kites along,
and people on the merry-go-round

caught the flying charred bits.
This wind from the burning houses
blew open the girls' skirts,
and the happy throngs laughed
on a beautiful Warsaw Sunday.

Perhaps one will guess the moral,
that the people of Warsaw and Rome
trade and play and love
passing by the martyr's pyre.
Another, perhaps, will read
of the passing of human things,
of the oblivion growing
before the flame expired.

But I that day reflected
on the loneliness of dying men,
on the fate of lone Giordano;
that when he climbed the scaffold
he found no word in human tongue
with which to bid farewell
to those of mankind who remain.

Already they were on the run,
to peddle starfish, gulp their wine;
they carried olives and lemons
in the gay hum of the city.
And he was already remote
As though ages have passed,
and they waited a while
for his flight in the fire.

And those dying alone,
forgotten by the world,
their tongue grew strange to us,
like the tongue of an ancient planet.
And all will become a legend –
and then after many years
the poet's word shall stir revolt
on the new Campo di Fiori.

Warsaw, 1943 (translation A. Gillon)

B. A POOR CHRISTIAN LOOKS AT THE GHETTO

Bees build around red liver,
Ants build around black bone.
It has begun: the tearing, the trampling on silks,
It has begun: the breaking of glass, wood, copper, nickel,
  silver, foam
Of gypsum, iron sheets, violin strings, trumpets, leaves, balls,
  crystals.
Poof! Phosphorescent fire from yellow walls
Engulfs animal and human hair.

Bees build around the honeycomb of lungs,
Ants build around white bone.
Torn is paper, rubber, linen, leather, flax,
Fibre, fabrics, cellulose, snakeskin, wire.
The roof and the wall collapse in flame and heat seizes the
  foundations.
Now there is only the earth, sandy, trodden down,
With one leafless tree.

Slowly, boring a tunnel, a guardian mole makes his way,
With a small red lamp fastened to his forehead.
He touches burned bodies, counts them, pushes on.
He distinguishes human ashes by their luminous vapour,
The ashes of each man by a different part of the spectrum
Bees build around a red trace.
Ants build around the place left by my body.

I am afraid, so afraid of the guardian mole.
He has swollen eyelids, like a Patriarch
Who has sat much in the light of candles
Reading the great book of the species.

What will I tell him, I, a Jew of the New Testament,
Waiting two thousand years for the second coming of Jesus?
My broken body will deliver me to his sight
And he will count me among the helpers of death:
The uncircumcised.

                    Warsaw, 1943 (translation Cz. Miłosz)

51

C. DEDICATION

You whom I could not save
Listen to me.
Try to understand this simple speech as I would be ashamed of
    another.
I swear, there is in me no wizardry of words.
I speak to you with silence like a cloud or a tree.

What strengthened me, for you was lethal.
You mixed up farewell to an epoch with the beginning of a new
    one,
Inspiration of hatred with lyrical beauty,
Blind force with accomplished shape.

Here is the valley of shallow Polish rivers. And an immense
    bridge
Going into white fog. Here is a broken city,
And the wind throws screams of gulls on your grave
When I am talking with you.

What is poetry which does not save
Nations or people?
A connivance with official lies,
A song of drunkards whose throats will be cut in a moment,
Readings for sophomore girls.
That I wanted good poetry without knowing it,
That I discovered, late, its salutary aim,
In this and only this I find salvation.

They used to pour on graves millet or poppy seeds
To feed the dead who would come disguised as birds.
I put this book here for you, who once lived
To that you should visit us no more.

1945 (translation Cz. Miłosz)

3

THE DEEP ROOTS AND LONG LIFE OF STEREOTYPES*

STANISŁAW SALMONOWICZ

These remarks arose from reading the bitter but greatly needed article by Professor Jan Błoński, 'The Poor Poles look at the Ghetto' [chapter 2]. The subject of Polish–Jewish relations – and this is something of which the great majority of the Poles who never go abroad for other reasons than to buy a sheepskin coat in Istanbul are totally unaware – defines to an enormous extent Poland's image in the eyes of Western, particularly Anglo-Saxon, public opinion. As a historian, I have taken an interest in these matters for years and it is a bitter, very bitter, subject.

As a foot-note to Jan Błoński's observations, I would like to touch upon a few questions concerning the Polish–Jewish dialogue. What I write could be documented in detail with historic and contemporary materials, which does not mean that my utterances will evoke enthusiasm on anybody's part. It is a subject so full of all sorts of taboos, so packed with distortions and at the same time of emotions, true, false, or fabricated, that any lucid pronouncement is unpopular in the widest sense of the word and also usually – if for various reasons – unpopular in both camps, so to speak. Equally, some of Błoński's pronouncements will probably meet with criticism from various quarters. I have to admit that on the whole I am a pessimist in what concerns the effects of a dialogue in the short run, because the fight against antiquated stereotypes, particularly if they continue to be guarded by suitably powerful institutions manipulating the mass media, is rather futile. Even so the battle must continue –

*This article was first published in *Tygodnik Powszechny*, 8 February 1987.

53

anyway, there is no other choice. Another indication that the situation is difficult is the hostility which met some of the pronouncements in the USA of the eminent expert on Polish affairs, Professor Norman Davies, who wanted to view Polish–Jewish affairs comprehensively and without prejudice. What is worse is that on the Polish side the fight against some stereotypes is belated by something nearer a hundred years than forty.

Let us start, however, with our own backyard. The Jewish problem in Poland ceased to exist a long time ago. The great majority of the younger generation (people under forty) have most probably not seen an authentic Jew in their lives. The mythology, however, lives on. The tragedy of the Holocaust encumbers us, it would seem, with certain moral obligations; in any event it should incline us to some sort of decent deportment in this sensitive issue. . . However, that is not so! As even in the France of today – the cradle of democracy and fraternity – where anti-semitism still persists, the relics of anti-semitism still survive in Poland. In France, however, the Jewish community is a meaningful presence. In Poland only the myth has remained.

Anti-semitism, it can be imagined, as it is difficult to judge those things unequivocally, is a marginal issue. It is, however, a characteristic phenomenon also among some groups of young people, particularly those of country or small-town origin. Why? This is a subject for sociological studies. In any case, stereotypes are long-lived. In stating that fact and not justifying it in any way, it must also be said that anti-semitism is alive and well in the world, and also in places, it would seem, ideologically different from ours. In our case, is it just the poisoned tradition dating from the National Democratic (*Endek*) ideology, or is it mainly a reminiscence of the sometimes horrific economic struggle carried on in pre-war, overpopulated Poland? There are undoubtedly many reasons for it. We cannot, however, deny that the phenomenon, even if only marginal, does exist.

The post-1945 period with its subjects unmentionable in the climate of the immediate years after the war has not passed without leaving its mark. Positive, multi-national traditions in the more or less tolerant Republic were most often unnecessarily considered to be embarrassing. The greatest mistake of the last thirty years has been a peculiar silence. We well remember the times when even publications detailing the not inconsiderable extent of Polish help to the Jews during the occupation got into publishing and other difficulties. I myself know how much effort – wasted as a rule – it took in the sixties to point out the dangers inherent in the formulation – in which we were not involved – of an image in foreign publications of the extermination of the Jews in Europe in which usually excessive good will towards Poland or knowledge of its affairs was not to be found. So the important fact – which may one day be studied by historians – is that difficulties have been created and that in the end we did very little, and what we did was usually too late and met with no response, to present our point of view, in a dialogue. Jan Błoński is right, of course. No statistical disputes or part-achievements on our side can obscure some very bitter truths. Let me add a proviso here that only the interested party can accuse himself or herself before their own conscience of the feeling of passive powerlessness, or be aware that one somehow did not measure up to the extreme challenge of this grim period. Even his or her descendants who are not in their situation cannot judge them. I do not see that any other parties have the right to make the charge that an individual or a community as a whole lacked heroic qualities. Can one expect heroics from ordinary people who found themselves in extraordinary circumstances? Is not heroism indeed an exceptional phenomenon?

In raising these questions, I must add at the same time that not only should those manifestations of heroism be discussed openly and loudly, but so also should the ugly side of Polish society brought forth (or revealed) by the German practice of extermination, which was carried out before our eyes. We have talked too seldom of the role – incidental, but bitterly remembered by those of its victims who survived – of a greedy Polish peasant here or of a hateful *petit bourgeois* there, let alone of the infamous role of the police (particularly in the provinces). Of course, it is a sad and peculiar paradox that in the West the main grievances are often not addressed to those who at that moment in history were smiling or gathering scraps from the Nazi loot. It is easy to beat someone else's breast. We cannot, however, deny that such an idiotic smile, such a material profit, were in the highest degree a morally poisoned form of consent *sui generis* to what was taking place before our eyes. This is why I am ready to put up stoically with quite a number of exaggerations and feelings of resentment

from survivors whose ordeal does not incline them to un-
emotional, objective reporting and who remember the evil rather
than the good done to them.

All this needs to be understood. It is a different matter,
however, when pronouncements of this kind are deliberately and
with bad faith generalized and utilized. The trouble is that
opinions about Polish behaviour during the Second World War
have fallen on well-prepared ground. Negative opinions about
Poland and the Poles, often connected with some Jewish circles
in the Anglo-Saxon countries or in France, are by no means new.
They were formed in general at the end of the nineteenth and in
the first quarter of the twentieth century. For lack of space, let
me provide just a few important statements and hypotheses
which show us that in the same way as there is an anti-semitic
stereotype of the Jew and that this stereotype appears to be alive
even after the Second World War, so on the other hand there are
– mostly in the Anglo-Saxon countries – anti-Polish stereotypes
which have their origin in eighteenth-century Prusso–Russian
propaganda justifying the Partitions of Poland.

As far as the participation of Jewish circles in this propaganda
is concerned, again there is a peculiar paradox in that, in my
view, the authors and main propagators of this stereotype most
often had nothing in common with the Jewish communities who
lived in Poland for generations. In spite of resentments dated
from the war and pre-war times, it is not the Jews of Polish origin
who are the chief bearers of anti-Polish opinions, but groups who
have never seen an authentic Pole in their lives. Nostalgia for
Poland and Polish culture is quite frequent among Jews of Polish
origin (apart from the Orthodox), as has been beautifully
described by Andrzej Chciuk.

Of course, quite diverse Jewish groups lived in the pre-
Partition territories of the former Republic. On the Prussian
territories, the Jews quite quickly identified with the great
German culture, in return for the right to assimilate. Numerous
Jews in the Russian Empire reacted similarly, particularly when
they lived in Lithuanian, Ukrainian or Byelorussian territories.
On the whole, in the second part of the nineteenth century the
process of identification, the tendency – often futile – to identify
with the country where they lived, prevailed. Thus the apparent
paradox that it is not the Polish Jews who are or were the

propagators of the derogatory opinions about the Poles, but Jews from milieux connected with German or Russian culture: they adopted the stereotypes formulated and propagated about Poland and the Poles by Prussian literature and Prussian historiography (for instance, by G. Freytag, Treitschke and hundreds of their imitators).

These anti-Polish stereotypes were a threat to Polish national interests as early as 1918–21. Naturally, one cannot possibly enumerate in this brief article all the various and many-sided historical reasons and sociological patterns which influenced the propagation of those stereotypes. It is beyond doubt, for instance, that the first generation of Polish migrants to the United States, coming mainly from rural, backward places, supplied ample evidence to support the one-sided and on the whole negative image of Poland, as perceived, largely to this day, by general American 'public opinion'. This is not an image of an elegant spendthrift nobleman, or a gallant light-cavalryman, heroic yet reckless, but on the contrary – an uneducated, greedy simpleton, a brute if not a gangster – a drunkard and an anti-semite. Stereotypes therefore do exist and getting away from them is particularly difficult.

Can any practical conclusions be formulated, and is it worth it? I think there is a need for a long-term fight, with no guarantee of instant success, to be carried on – to use a currently fashionable military term – on two fronts. On the one, anti-semitism should be fought and written about; and why it came about (including the enormous and infamous role of the Christian churches which is admitted today), and particularly why anti-semitism is inadmissible in the civilized world. At the same time, the complicated history of the Jewish Diaspora in Poland, which includes positive aspects as well as negative elements, should be written about – the Diaspora which played a vital role in the history of the Jewish nation which fell victim to an unparalleled extermination. The second front is the attempt at a matter-of-fact dialogue with the Jewish communities (much has been achieved in the last few years) to encourage them to cease their completely unfounded and unjust attacks and accusations, to call for a bilaterally objective look at our common history which was far from idyllic, but shared. But then, before the time of Western democracy and liberalism, what was a good place for the Jews?

It should be particularly stressed that spontaneous, modern anti-semitism in Poland, the legacy of National Democracy, fails to recognize the unique achievements of the Jewish communities made possible by the toleration of the Polish–Lithuanian Commonwealth in the sixteenth and seventeenth centuries. It is after all on Polish territories (Kraków, Wilno, and so on) that the greatest achievements of Jewish culture took place. This should not be forgotten by both sides.

Finally, one more remark in the style of Kisiel's very justified lament addressed to the West.[1] Today we know well (from W. Laqueur and others) that in the years 1941–4, when much could have been done to save at least some of the Jews in Europe, influential British and American quarters, as well as the governments of the neutral countries, did practically nothing to stop the Germans from carrying out their plans. Those same circles, particularly in the USA, lead the way today in accusing Polish society of a lack of heroism or humanism. Is this not typical Anglo-Saxon (a stereotype!) hypocrisy?

NOTE

1 Stefan Kisielewski (pseudonym Kisiel) is a member of the editorial board of *Tygodnik Powszechny* and its regular commentator on social and political issues.

4

A REPLY TO JAN BŁOŃSKI*

WŁADYSŁAW SIŁA-NOWICKI

In the second issue of *Tygodnik Powszechny* in 1987, that of 11 January, an article appeared entitled 'The Poor Poles Look at the Ghetto'. The article, signed by Jan Błoński, published as it was in a journal carrying great weight, may unfortunately be understood as the affirmation and quintessence (unintended of course), of a virulent anti-Polish propaganda campaign conducted endlessly for dozens of years by the enemies not of the government, nor the economic or political system of present-day Poland, but simply of the Polish nation. This article is in my view a very dangerous propagandistic enunciation, and it is regrettable on two scores. One, that it was written by an eminent specialist in literature, and two, that it appeared in a leading Catholic socio-cultural Polish paper. How the words 'Father, forgive them, they know not what they do' spring to mind!

The article starts with an analysis of two poems by Czesław Miłosz. Yet even though this eminent poet states – with sincerity, it seems, and in a most authoritative manner – that the poem 'Campo di Fiori' is journalistic and therefore too unequivocal, that it is immoral because it describes death from the point of view of an observer, and that it originated as an ordinary human gesture in the spring of 1943, Błoński gives it the character of a moral and political judgement and formulates on its theme several vague and sometimes even incomprehensible thoughts, for example that shedding the blood of other than your own people weighs the most heavily, which is a peculiar view of fratricide or of the murder of a mother or a father. In his

*This article was first published in *Tygodnik Powszechny*, 22 February 1987.

deliberations, Błoński accepts at face value pronouncements which are often quite obviously divorced from reality and at the same time deeply hostile to Poland. The author quotes those pronouncements and engages in polemics with them in a way which raises grave doubts as to whether he does not agree with them in the first place.

Alas, often he simply does agree with them. Because in answer to the statement 'When you regained independence, the fate of the Jews not only did not improve. On the contrary, anti-semitism became even more vicious', he does not just say that this is not true, or at least that this is an inadmissible generalization. His reply is that society cannot be transformed in twenty years, and anyway wasn't it the same in the rest of Europe, which is accepting that the charge was justified?

A litany of imaginary charges and answers to them may find approval with anybody hating Poland either on this or on the other side of the Atlantic. And the comment is likely to be: 'Well, if even a Polish paper of this calibre writes in this way about Poles in their historic capital. . .'

But it is not just that. In an imaginary dialogue even an obvious lie is not simply called an untruth.

And what can one say about the author's own statements, such as: 'There are books whose authors do not hide that they are motivated by hate. We cannot afford to ignore them; they are born of personal experiences whose authenticity cannot be doubted. And, besides, haven't we ourselves produced a literature abounding in pronouncements full of hatred, sometimes hysterical hatred, towards Jews?'

These are very odd words coming from a Pole and appearing on the pages of *Tygodnik Powszechny*. Am I so totally ignorant of Polish literature that I have never in my over seventy years come across this 'abundance of pronouncements' full of that hysterical hatred? It did not exist before the war. Perhaps today some irresponsible arguments of small, totally unrepresentative, groups could be seen as examples of this hatred, but on no account could those statements come under the heading of Polish literature. Or perhaps Adolf Hitler's *Mein Kampf* belongs to Polish literature? Because, as a matter of fact, in many countries the Germans are viewed in a more favourable light than the Poles as far as anti-semitism is concerned. And this is despite what was going on in the years 1933–9 in the uncultured and madly anti-semitic Poland and in the deeply cultured and humanitarian Third Reich, and later on the territories of the thousand-year-old Reich and of the General-Government [German occupied Poland].

Jan Błoński writes about the 'terror, unimaginable today, of life under the German occupation'. I belong to a generation – and the same could be said about people ten years younger than myself and still fully active – who do not need to imagine anything, because we still remember it all extremely well. But his next statement, that this intense terror produced 'a moral degradation' into barbarity of Polish society is an inadmissible and outrageous use of the principle *pars pro toto*. And in our case the *pars* was quite insignificant.

And surely the heroism of Poles during that cruel time of intense terror under occupation should not be forgotten. As a nation we need not be ashamed of our attitude in the terrible years of occupation. And it would be difficult, probably, to find a nation in the whole of martyred Europe which could look down on us on this score and lecture us about our moral duties.

The extensive and complicated deliberation on Czesław Miłosz's poem 'A Poor Christian Looks at the Ghetto' are totally irrelevant. They can be compared to those extensive nineteenth-century tracts on the subject of who Adam Mickiewicz had in mind when he gave his hero of the future the name Forty-four. Again, what strikes one here is that the interpretation is quite different to that given by the author. Miłosz said that he wrote the poem on the spur of the moment and not as his credo, but for Błoński this means nothing. The poet refuses to give his work propaganda value? So what! It is the critic's job to work out the poem's credo and to tell its author what he had in mind! Poetry and prose can go hand in hand, even without agreeing on joint action! Why ask the poet, when one knows better than him what he actually wanted to say in his poem to the 'Polish nation which had degenerated into barbarity'!

And finally, the last part, the summing up, the essence of this message to the Polish nation, to the poor Poles. The author talks first about fear, continually using the first person plural: we, we, we. We do not want condemnation, we want to rise above condemnation, we are afraid. But, forgive me, who are 'we'?

Everybody has got the right to speak in his own name when he feels called upon to thunder and to lecture – but let him speak in his own name and not in the name of this nation, the people whose degeneration into barbarity he has perceived, while failing to notice its suffering and heroism; not in the name of the people he addresses as one of them – undoubtedly in good faith, but in a language which in its contents is the language of its deadly enemies and slanderers. And if Jan Błoński is afraid, this is a matter for him. I am not afraid and neither are, rightly, millions of Poles, though of course none of us is without fault because only God is perfect. But understanding one's imperfections, faults, breakdowns and the inevitable human frailties, which befall even the greatest heroes, let alone ordinary people, is quite different from the feeling of shame for the behaviour of the entire nation. Jan Błoński, writing about the extermination of the Jews in Poland, is ashamed of his people. I am proud of my nation's stance in every respect during the period of occupation and in this include the attitude towards the tragedy of the Jewish nation. Obviously, the attitudes towards the Jews during that period do not give us a particular reason to be proud, but neither are they any grounds for shame, and even less for ignominy. Simply, we would have done relatively little more than we actually did.

The statement by the author of the article that 'if only we had behaved more humanely in the past, had been wiser, more generous, then genocide would perhaps have been less "imaginable", and 'almost certainly would have met with much greater resistance' is in terms of life under occupation the equivalent of the conviction held by many British people that had Great Britain been occupied, the Germans would have had to leave those isles very quickly, simply because they would not be sold anything in the shops there. England is a country lucky enough to make such views coming from an Englishman only very ridiculous. When they come from a Pole, however, they are dangerous and harmful.

The author who is unfamiliar with the realities of those times, not having lived through them as an adult, is also unfamiliar with the complexities and difficulties of the Jewish problem in the years 1919–39. The Jewish people are amazing and incomparable with any other in terms of the strength of their national bond!

What is left of the representatives of other nations of the world after a few generations had grown up away from their native land? Mostly nothing or very little. Nostalgia, a distant memory, a kind of special feeling – at best. How often, in the American melting-pot, for instance, did one find outright dislike, a desire to forget, attempts to cut oneself off, to merge with the rest, not to be different from this majority which broke away from the nationality of its ancestors? It is tragic how, at its leadership's meetings, the problems of such an enormous group as the Polish community, in spite of the enormous number of people having thousands of links with their ancestors' former homeland, are discussed in English, and even the prayer ending a national holiday celebration is recited in English.

The Jews survived as a people for centuries, driven out from the countries of Western Europe where so much is now talked about Polish anti-semitism; they escaped to Poland and found a home here. Driven out from their homeland, they went to different countries in the world. They survived, broken up into small groups, and everywhere they were able to make contact with each other. In the great majority they remained Jews, not just in Poland and in Europe, but also on the American continents. It is even possible to prove in the most scientific manner that in their veins flows only 1 per cent of the blood of those people who shouted 'Hosanna to the Son of David' and then 'Crucify Him, crucify Him!'; but their nation continues to exist. After the terrible national tragedy of the Second World War, engulfing all the territories where they lived, which found themselves under the boot of the Germanic invader, they recreated a Jewish state in the place of the Christian Kingdom of Jerusalem, a Jewish state which like centuries before was surrounded by a hostile sea of Arab people, a state which has probably got a better chance of survival than the states of Godfrey of Bouillon, Baldwin and their successors.

But to survive for centuries in a hostile environment, among people of a different faith, with different customs, they needed to keep their separateness. The guests could not grow to be like their hosts. They had to create their own community in the community in which they lived. Creating their community was hard work because the laws of a community can be harsh. And from necessity, to survive, they had to love that community more than that of the host, and to put the interests of their own, inner, community first. And they created that community everywhere, by means of the amazing strength of their national bond which has already been mentioned.

By creating their own community and keeping up the ties among them, the Jews gave and continue to give the people on whose territories they live eminent scientists, great artists, intellectuals, politicians, great financiers, economists, administrators, poets, excellent writers. The difficult conditions in which they worked, not having their own country, induced extra-hard intellectual efforts drawing on their centuries-long cultural traditions, and no nation in the world has produced such a high percentage of eminent people. And those people very often, it could be said as a rule, kept some sort of bond with the Jewish community.

But the problem of living a separate life on somebody's else territory, within a state of a different nation, became particularly apparent in Poland. Precisely because, as a result of tolerance dating from time immemorial, we had in this country the highest percentage of Jewish population in the world. Moreover, this population lived almost exclusively in towns, which had further consequences and created inevitable difficulties of nobody's making.

Jan Błoński says: 'We did take Jews into our home, but we made them live in the cellar.' In the cellar, indeed? And in whose hands was the greatest part of the wholesale trade and a great part of the retail trade in Poland? Who had the most capital at their disposal? What was, after all, the Polish majority or the Jewish minority which constituted 10 per cent? Who, on average, had the greater returns from his professional work – the Jew living in 'the cellar' or the Polish occupier of the first floor, and that in spite of the existence of a large Jewish proletariat? Because in that respect the differences between the rich and the poor were much more pronounced among the Jews than among the Poles, but this surely is not to the Poles' discredit; Jan Błoński must remember that the Jews in Poland were also human, with human frailties. And this is not altered by the fact that the Jewish proletariat in towns dwelt, admittedly not in cellars, but in basements, very often in conditions even worse than the Polish proletariat.

I always felt disgusted by the anti-Jewish incidents at the Polish universities, the noisy demands for a *numerus clausus*, or the inadmissible postulates of the 'ghetto benches' rule by which Jewish students sat separately during university lectures. But all these were child's play in comparison with what was going on at that time, in the mid-thirties, in Germany. After all, the perpetrators of anti-Jewish incidents in Poland could expect to be hosed down or to spend a few hours in jail which, admittedly, was not a terrible punishment, but it was still unpleasant. Those incidents were occurring not just because of a growing wave of nationalism, but also because the Jewish population – living mostly in towns – had easier access to schools and the percentage of Jews leaving schools and entering universities was much higher, proportionately, than the percentage of the Polish population getting their school leaving certificates and going on to universities. For me it is natural that society defends itself against numerical domination of its intelligentsia – especially pronounced in the medical or legal professions – by an alien intelligentsia. The co-existence of two nations must depend on some balance being observed. Assimilation is something Jan Błoński writes about with reluctance, if not actually distaste.

This vast Jewish population in Poland, which was of great importance and weight in Polish life, as being very diverse both in its attitudes and economic well-being, lived, however, as an independent entity. It had its own life, lived largely alongside that of the Polish population. The consequences of this was that it was much easier for the Germans to carry out their gigantic genocide, which in spite of the deliberations of *Mein Kampf*, in spite of crimes already committed, in spite of Dachau, Gross Rosen, Buchenwald, Auschwitz and Majdanek, was totally unimaginable to the Polish people. It also came as a total surprise to the Jews, almost until the very last moment.

The Germans managed to concentrate the Jewish population in ghettos with relative ease, in the great majority of cases setting them up in the areas where the Jews used to live before. The conditions of life in the ghettos got gradually worse, while terror was growing in all the occupied countries, though in very diverse ways. Both the Jewish and the Polish communities were faced with the threat of biological extinction. However, finding itself – in spite of all the horrors of occupation – in incomparably easier conditions and probably to a large extent also because of that, the Polish community took up a much more active struggle against the occupier. From the very start and at the cost of many lives, a vast underground organization was set up, active resistance operations were carried out, thus forcing the Germans to maintain large armed forces on the occupied territories. At the time when the Germans began their mass murder of the Jewish population, German-occupied Poland was one of the most explosive spots in the German 'New Order' and Warsaw was beginning to be compared to a jungle. The Germans were being shot at in the streets of Warsaw – but this almost never happened in the ghettos. Similarly, members of the Jewish police, incomparably more ruthless and brutal towards their compatriots than the Polish police, were almost never shot at in the ghettos.

In the tragic moments in its history, every nation is guided by instinct. This instinct can sometimes be right, but it can also fail. It seems that the Jewish population's instinct failed it as it lived in the terrible conditions of the ghetto, worsening gradually from the beginning of the war, but still for over three years, in spite of a high mortality rate, allowing the great mass of population to survive and live – the poor in utmost poverty, the rich even in comfort. This mass and the individuals within it saw their salvation in passivity. It could be that the sometimes extremely hard experience of hundreds, even thousands, of years weighed most heavily here. Because, after all, that experience did not include the terrible genocide which the twentieth century had in store for them.

And in the spring of 1943 the war was more than halfway through. To seek salvation in passivity and to bear the pressures at all costs might have seemed the logical thing to do.

To us Poles, it often seemed amazing to see the population of a few thousand of one or other small town led along a route at least a few kilometres long to the railway station, guarded by a few, sometimes six, sometimes four guards, armed with ordinary guns. This is how it happened in German-occupied Poland and on the eastern territories of the Second Republic. And nobody escaped, even though it would have presented no particular difficulties, at least for reasonably fit people. It could have been because of a herd instinct, orders by their elders, a fear that if those able to escape would do so, this might bring reprisals against the remaining old people, women, and children. And yet escaping would have given a chance to survive.

Passive behaviour – seeking security by staying with the group and by accepting German orders – was the first and principal obstacle to the possibility of extending help to the Jews.

This is not a criticism. This is an understanding of human motivation. Herman Levi, an elder in the Jewish community in Kielce and the father of my school friend, sent his sons to a Polish school while adhering to the Jewish religion. I knew him personally. As an elder he co-operated with the occupier, but undoubtedly saw in it a chance of survival for his compatriots. He was shot dead by the Germans, together with his two sons, my friend Aleksander Levi and his older brother. All three shouted 'Long live Poland!' during the execution and on the third or fourth time their cries were cut short by a volley of German shots. . .

And then, total surprise at the tragic finale. Surprise which only allowed for the last tragic act of the uprising in the ghetto, when there was nothing left to lose. But can one blame the Jews for not starting the uprising earlier? The impressive gesture which was the Warsaw Uprising could and did rely on immediate help from the Soviet troops. An earlier uprising in the ghetto just would have been an act of mass suicide; as it was, the people living there could hope that at least a large part of them would survive the war.

But even if similarly to the Poles aiming for active resistance, the Jewish national instinct had not seen its chance to survive solely in passive surrender to the occupant's order, the chances of effectively helping the Jews on a large scale were slim. Jewish organizations in the West, particularly in the United States, had incomparably more such possibilities, and thousands of lives could have been saved simply in exchange for money. But those Jews showed passivity and indifference to the terrible plight of their compatriots in the German-occupied territories. And it was in protest against the attitudes of such people and not against the alleged indifference of the Poles that Shmul Zygielbojm, a member of the Polish National Council in London, committed suicide in a most horrific way, explaining in detail the reasons for what he did in his suicide note.

And we ourselves, what more could we have done? We

witnessed the shame of Majdanek and Auschwitz, we watched people on our land being driven through the gate with the mocking inscription *Arbeit macht frei* and the cremation ovens smoking on our native soil, in which the bodies of thousands of our compatriots and people of other nationalities were being burned, with a feeling of powerless despair and of terrible anger. But what were we to do? To attack those camps with the forces available to us, at an enormous cost and ensuring that all the people who had a chance to survive would perish too? Because of the good of the nation and to save people, we had to conduct our fight sensibly.

Let no-one talk to us, our people, our nation, who fought at the time of the German occupation, about our supposedly unfulfilled moral obligations. Let the author not write at the end of his deeply unjust and totally untrue article that we ourselves were about to commit the crime of genocide, only at the last moment God had stayed our hand. Even those few who, carried by the wave of pre-war nationalism, shouted 'Jews, go to Madagascar!' never, even for one moment, had genocide in mind. Those who denounced the Jews to the German authorities were sentenced to death and those sentences were carried out by us while running the risk of death ourselves. I knew a sixteen-year-old Jewish girl who was kept in hiding by a Polish couple in their home, thus putting the lives of their entire family at risk. The girl had been manually pulled out of a crowd, which was being driven to the Majdanek crematorium, by a policeman who had first glanced at the SS guard to make sure he was looking the other way. The policeman pushed her towards a group of people watching from the pavement. And she did not perish among those strangers, even though the policeman, as well as everybody else involved, risked at least their own lives: and none of these people have got their tree in Israel.

5

GUILT BY NEGLECT*

EWA BERBERYUSZ

In spite of the passing time, the Polish–Jewish issue, wherever it appears, creates in us Poles, particularly in those of us who witnessed the extermination of the Jews, a peculiar state of aggressiveness mixed with apprehension. This proves just how deeply that something described in Jan Błoński's article [chapter 2], a subconscious secret feeling of guilt about what had happened to the Jewish people on our land, is ingrained in us. Błoński talks explicitly about guilt by neglect.

I was ten when the war broke out. My father, an officer in the army, went into hiding; if he had been found out, his life would have been in danger. We were not safe at home, we were cold and hungry. I had chilblains on my hands and feet from wearing old shoes and gloves which were too small for me. And yet, however unhappy and uncertain my own fate was, it was totally incomparable with the fate of the Jewish children of the same age in the ghetto, who were passing furtively through the streets on the 'Aryan side' of Warsaw in search of food. The desolation and the hopeless situation of those children could not be compared with anything, not even the fate of the children from the Zamość province who had been snatched from the Eastern Station platform and taken to various Warsaw homes, to save them from Germanization. I daresay that in the case of the Jews, a kind of turning point, a sort of threshold, had been reached, beyond which the society surrounding them, instead of helping, was on the contrary paralysed and found it was easier to turn its back on what was happening.

*This article was first published in *Tygodnik Powszechny*, 22 February 1987.

I remember two such cases, when I looked the other way, two moments so engraved in my memory that even today I could draw it all in great detail. It happened twice that a child from the ghetto found himself within my vision and twice I pushed away the first impulse to make some contact and simply to put food into his rag-covered body. Was I afraid? Yes, I was afraid – it was all taking place so publicly and the Jewish child looked so doomed (not so much by his semitic features as by his 'inhuman', Job-like condition). I was therefore afraid of the consequences of aiding him, but was that all? Was it not that he had found himself beyond that turning point which let me decide that he was beyond the frontier of human solidarity? Because, normally, we children looked after the Jewish children playing with us in our courtyard and we would warn them if we saw a German approach. Yes, but those children were like us, they lived on the Aryan side of town; we were not so terribly different.

I remember that when I once saw someone giving food to a child – which was not such an unusual occurrence – from the ghetto on the steps leading to the cellar in our house, I felt not so much ashamed for my behaviour as relieved that there was someone in our society who acted as one should. And when I once saw my own mother doing it, my morale soared again. It is interesting that we never talked about it at all. Was it just fear? Or was it just shame that nothing more was being done?

If then, when chance brought me those two children, I had behaved according to my conscience, would that have altered the fate of the Jews in Poland? The answer 'yes' is not so unequivocally right, because my desisting in these cases has to be multiplied by cases of similar behaviour by others. Possibly, even if more of us had turned out to be more Christian, it would have made no difference to the statistics of the extermination, but maybe it would not have been such a lonely death?

I remember Easter 1943 in Warsaw. I was walking with my father to Orla Street where we were invited to Easter breakfast. We stopped, watching the thick smoke over the ghetto, my father let go of my hand and stood looking there for a long moment. His usual despondency gave way to a kind of paralysis, and he was unable to move his legs.

In my recollections of my father in those days (he was killed in the Warsaw Uprising), I remember most of all his feeling of hopeless powerlessness, so different from the image of a resistance fighter as presented in literature – but was this not nearer to our inner attitude in those days?

I shall never know how my father would have reacted to Jan Błoński's article. I am grateful to the author that by his article he made me see with greater clarity my share of guilt by neglect. I do not feel exonerated by my young age in those times. I therefore accept the message of the article: let us stop quibbling about extenuating circumstances, let us stop arguing, and let us bow our heads.

6

THE 'JUST' AND
THE 'PASSIVE'*

TERESA PREKEROWA

Each period in the history of Polish–Jewish relations has had its own specific character; each has created its own problems and conflicts. The observations made by the lawyer Siła-Nowicki and published in *Tygodnik Powszechny*, on 22 February 1987 [chapter 4] relate to two periods in particular: the interim years between the two World Wars and the years of occupation. In both cases they are controversial and some observations are clearly unacceptable. As I am surely not going to be the only participant in this discussion, I would like to confine my comments to the period I am more familiar with – that of 1939–45.

Among other things Siła-Nowicki writes: 'I am proud of my nation's stance in every respect during the period of occupation, and in this I include the attitude towards the tragedy of the Jewish nation. . . Simply we could have done relatively little more than we actually did.'

This is a strong statement. And although the author indicates clearly that he is expressing his private opinion, his article can only inspire or strengthen in some social circles the mood of self-appeasement and self-satisfaction to which, as far as Polish–Jewish relations are concerned, we have a strong inclination anyway. The article creates an impression that help was commonly extended to Jews within the limits permitted by the conditions of terror under the occupation. Yet if one were to take a closer

*This article was published in *Tygodnik Powszechny*, 29 March 1987.

look, what was the situation like in reality?

It is of course impossible to present it in terms of exact numerical data, yet one may be forgiven for attempting some kind of estimate. The number of Jews whose lives were saved in the Polish territories of 1939, who survived the war by hiding on the 'Aryan' side (that is not in camps and not among partisans), should be the starting point in this calculation. As one can only partially rely on the incomplete register compiled in Poland in 1945 by the Central Jewish Committee, the historians vary considerably in their estimates, which range from 40,000 to 60,000.

Naturally not every Jew seeking rescue on the 'Aryan' side succeeded in surviving the war. Reports seem to suggest that more or less half managed to save their lives. The numbers in hiding, therefore, would run between 80,000 and 120,000 people.

And how many Poles were helping them and providing shelter? It is a most difficult task to settle on even an approximate figure here. The difficulties are multiplied by the fact that on the one hand those in hiding rarely spent the whole period of occupation in one place. Much more commonly they had to, as a result of a variety of circumstances, change their abode more than once, thus involving new people in the rescue-chain. On the other hand an individual Pole would sometimes help several refugees from the ghetto. Furthermore, many Jews hiding 'on Aryan papers' survived exclusively owing to their own efforts – having 'good looks' and an opportunity for employment. Generally speaking it seems that an average figure of 2–3 people helping one Jew would not be too far from the truth.

This kind of calculation will allow us to estimate – very roughly – the figure for people helping on the 'Aryan side' (Poles, and in the East, Byelorussians and in a few cases, Ukrainians) as ranging from 160,000 to 360,000 people.

To some degree, much smaller though, help was also given to Jewish partisans by village people. But on the whole the relationships in this area were far from satisfactory and the number of those who offered a night's lodgings or food to the Jewish units from the forests would change the above estimate only very insignificantly.

What proportion of the population was composed of those who were helping? The figure for the population on the Polish territories at the time is equally hard to establish. It is known to have reached about 35 millions in 1939. One has to subtract from this number the 3 million murdered Jews and about 3 million murdered Poles, and about 4 million Poles who had been deported beyond the borders or sent to camps or who were living abroad. Also unable to help the Jews was the population (around 4 million Poles) living on the territories incorporated into the Third Reich. The Jews were removed from those territories in 1940 and no ghettos were established there. One must also discount about 6 million children and young people below the age of 18. Having deducted all these categories of population, we would arrive at a figure of about 15 million people who could offer help. Those who were actually helping constituted, therefore, about 1–2.5 per cent of that number.

All the elements in this calculation are only very roughly estimated and may undergo modification when a more exact examination takes place. However, one is not aiming at some precise figure – which is no longer possible to achieve today anyway – but at defining the order of magnitude, at showing the approximate degree to which the action of saving Jewish lives was spread among the adult Polish population. Does the final figure – the participation of about 2 per cent of society – permit the statement that 'we would have done relatively more than we actually did'? I doubt it very much. My doubts are also increased by the fact that a proportion of that help (an estimated one-fifth) was rendered for a payment. Although Emanuel Ringelblum stated that 'there is no such money in the world which could have recompensed the sacrifice made by the protectors', nevertheless payment which exceeded the cost of keeping the person concerned – a condition of rendering help – lowers the moral status of such help. Yet it was that help, in whatever form it came, which was most important. We were powerless against the Nazi plans for the total annihilation of the Jews. Effective saving of lives could have been carried out only by individuals, with or without the support of political parties, or aid-organizations like the Council for Aid to Jews (Rada Pomocy Żydom). Contrary to the opinion of Siła-Nowicki, I think that it could have been much more widespread than it was.

Public opinion outside Poland sometimes contrasts the 'just', who were giving help, with the common criminals who, driven by greed, committed crimes with complete impunity. Polish literature on the whole keeps silent about them. One can, however, find many concrete accusations in the numerous Jewish Memorial Books relating to individual cities and townships. These books, published by the Jewish associations of compatriots, contain accounts and recollections of persons who survived. They do not mince words. They talk directly, mentioning the names, of Polish peasants, shopkeepers or policemen who, according to the authors, would first take from the Jewish fugitives their money and then they would drive them out to a certain death or, as the case may be, give them away to the gendarmerie or themselves murder those whom they had robbed.

It would not be right to consider every one of these accounts to be fully trustworthy. They were written many years after the war, in most cases recreating events which the authors had merely heard about (or, less commonly, had observed from a hiding place), often while they were still very young. The interpretation of the remembered facts and accounts was undoubtedly influenced by later events (as, for example, the pogrom in Kielce) and by the opinions held in their present-day surroundings which are unfavourable to Poland. But assuming even those recollections – whose exactness is impossible to ascertain – are in parts exaggerated and inaccurate, one cannot just discard them. There are hundreds of them. They could not have been created out of nothing.

The crimes mentioned here did not, as is sometimes suggested, stem from anti-semitism. Greed was the motive and anybody sufficiently defenceless could have fallen victim. Nevertheless the lack of sympathetic interest in the fate of Jews on the part of the surrounding population facilitated the commission of the crime.

There is similar discredit to Polish society in the existence of the blackmailers and the *szmalcownicy* (extortionists who blackmailed Jews in hiding – they would accost them in the vicinity of ghettos and on the streets of towns). Siła-Nowicki writes: '*Szmalcownicy* were sentenced to death and those sentences were carried out by us while running the risk of death ourselves.' That's right, but from when? From September 1943, whereas they started their profitable underhand dealings the moment ghettos were closed, and that meant in Warsaw from the autumn of 1940. For three years therefore they could continue to operate undeterred. In the last year – 1943–4 – in all five blackmailers were put to death in Warsaw and a few in Kraków and its environs. There is no doubt that fighting them, and in particular spotting and identifying them, was difficult, but, and I repeat the question, could we really 'not do much more'?

Between these two social extremes there was an enormous majority of the population which did not interfere in 'Jewish matters'. Its attitude towards Jews varied. There certainly was a group which was predominantly well-disposed towards them. Yet for a variety of reasons their feelings never took the concrete form of help: not everyone's circumstances would allow it; not everyone felt morally entitled to risk the lives of those nearest to them, for whose safety they felt responsible first of all; not everyone was able to overcome their own fear – which is also human and understandable; not everybody's feeling of friendliness was strong enough to propel them into action; finally not everybody encountered the problem of how to help Jews or found themselves in a situation in which his active help would be called for. Moreover, if one did not have the right contacts and acquaintances, the search for a Jew to protect proved under the circumstances of occupation almost as difficult as the search for a protector if one was a Jew.

Side by side with the friendly Poles there were those who, although sympathetic on the humane level, separated themselves from the existing situation by stating that 'it is not our business'. And then there were those whose animosity and antipathy towards Jews was not mitigated by their tragedy. Unfortunately, those who were friendly to Jews, and particularly those who were actively engaged in helping them, had to keep silent, while the anti-semites, often coming from the lowest social strata, did not feel inhibited from voicing their opinions aloud even in public – in trams, trains or work places. It was also they who would rush into the emptied ghettos to grab ex-Jewish property, that is, property that belonged to nobody. It is impossible to establish what proportions of the population held these differing attitudes. Naturally we would like in our estimates to increase the numbers of those who were friendly. But one cannot be surprised that the Jews see these proportions differently. Many of them hiding as 'Aryans' heard those sneering and derisive remarks and must have felt them painfully. To them it was precisely those loud anti-semites together with the blackmailers that formed the 'climate' of the streets.

Friendliness which is not expressed by deeds does not constitute a cause for pride. Whereas expressing (if only in words) anti-semitic views at the time of the extermination of the Jewish nation deserves unequivocal condemnation. While defending ourselves against accusations which often go too far, we must not lose sight of the fact that, as far as our attitude towards Jews is concerned, our history during the occupation contains some beautiful pages but also many dark ones.

The second element in the views of Siła-Nowicki which is unacceptable is his appraisal of the attitude of the Jews. It is described with one adjective: passive. The author states: 'Passive behaviour – seeking security by staying with the group and by accepting German orders – was the first and principal obstacle to the possibility of extending help to the Jews.'

It is an obscure statement: who wanted to help the Jews and was prevented from doing so by their passive behaviour? The Polish population? The Polish underground? And what sort of help was it meant to be?

The charge of passivity represents a very strong accusation in a society which values resistance against force very highly and considers it also to be a feature of its national character. Siła-Nowicki is naturally not the first to level this criticism against the Jews. It had been thrown at them already during the occupation by some of the underground press, and as can be seen, for example, from the textbooks for the eighth form, similar views are instilled in schoolchildren today.

Everyone wanting to describe the attitudes of the Polish population during the occupation could list without hesitation various forms of armed resistance as well as various types of civil resistance: underground functioning of political parties, clandestine press and education, underground cultural activities, and so on. And rightly so. The resistance has long since stopped being identified with armed conspiracy alone. But in the analogous situation when it comes to the Jews there is always a stereotyped answer: the Jews were passive, always and everywhere passive until, when they had nothing to lose any more, they started an uprising first in Warsaw and then in Białystok.

This assumed 'passivity' is so deeply embedded in our social consciousness that it makes us blind to the fact that every single form of the above-mentioned civil resistance existed also in the ghettos. In many of them the major pre-war political parties re-established their conspiratorial activity, as did probably all youth organizations. These groups published in the Warsaw ghetto itself about forty newspapers (this number was smaller in other ghettos). The Jewish female couriers kept the communication lines open by travelling on 'Aryan papers' to even the furthest ghettos carrying dispatches and publications; the young people attended underground courses and took final exams in private homes; under the cover of the officially permitted sanitary courses the curriculum of the medical school was also studied (one of the lecturers was Professor Ludwik Hirszfeld). Scientific research was being carried out on the disease of starvation, among other subjects; unofficial concerts and theatre perform-ances were being organized, and the secret archives created in Warsaw and Białystok had no equivalent on the 'Aryan side'. Does this wide-ranging underground activity prove the 'passivity' of the Jewish community? Is this, which we consider to be a proof of resilience and resistance in Polish society, of no significance in the ghettos?

Obviously not all the Jewish population was involved in conspiracy. But was every Pole a conspirator? The enormous majority of the population even in Warsaw, in this heart of underground Poland, to say nothing of the inhabitants of the tens of smaller cities and towns and the hundreds of villages, thought only about ways to survive the war, to stay alive. The peasants 'passively' submitted their levies (because they had to). Every morning the town population 'passively' went to work in order to support themselves and their families. Their everyday lives were filled by commonplace activities which helped to make living under the occupation bearable.

Siła-Nowicki paints a very vivid picture of a crowd of several thousand Jews 'of one or other small town' being driven to a railway station by just a few guards. Why did none of the young and fit ones try to run? Poles in their place would have done so.

It is not such a clear-cut matter. The above procedure was used in the years 1940–2 to resettle the inhabitants of smaller ghettos into the larger ones which were already in existence and densely populated. The Jews knew that the living conditions there would be very difficult and that one would have to fight hard for a roof over one's head and for a piece of bread. Could then those 'young and fit' abandon their children or old parents and run? And would escape give them a bigger chance of survival than life in a ghetto, even if they were starving there (mass extermination had not been foreseen then)? A fugitive Pole would have a chance to disappear in urban crowds or in a remote village. A Jew did not. Semitic features or a poor knowledge of the Polish language might have meant a death sentence for them, and it would have been unwise to count on the unlikely event of coming across someone belonging to those 2 per cent of population willing to give them shelter.

The Jewish population was certainly less involved in the armed resistance and only began engaging in it much later. But did they have the same possibilities as we did? It is a large subject, too large to discuss here. It should, however, be obvious without lengthy explanations that from people closed behind walls one cannot demand the same as one can from those who enjoyed incomparably greater freedom; one cannot blame them for shooting less at the representatives of the machinery of oppression. The ghetto in Warsaw, not to mention the one in Łódź, was from the start a kind of camp, and from autumn 1942 almost exclusively a labour camp. And as in any camp armed action had no chance of success there. It could only become what it did in fact become in April and May 1943. 'A nation which was going to its death had in its last moments a guard of honour', as it was beautifully expressed by the historian (and at the time a partisan from Białystok), Szymon Datner, when writing about the Białystok uprising.

And yet, the shots fired in April and August by the 'passive' Jewish population were the first manifestation of armed resistance on such a scale in occupied Europe (with the exception of Yugoslavia). The armed revolts, culminating in mass break-outs which were organized in the extermination camps of Treblinka and Sobibór, as well as the revolts of the *Sonderkommandos* in Auschwitz and in Chełmno on the Ner, belong to the biggest actions of this kind in occupied Europe.

Perhaps one should therefore revise the stereotype of the 'passive Jew'. The liberal use of this accusation of 'passivity' sometimes gives the impression that we are trying to justify ourselves: 'We did not help because they did not want to avail themselves of our help. They were passive.'

7

THE MISSION THAT FAILED:
A Polish Courier who Tried to Help the Jews*

MACIEJ KOZŁOWSKI

Jan Karski, proper name Jan Kozielewski, was born in Łódź, Poland, in 1914. He has lived in the United States since 1944, and is now a professor of government at Georgetown University. (Those who saw Claude Lanzmann's film *Shoah* will remember that during his interview Karski was so overcome with emotion that he had to leave the room to compose himself before returning to continue.)

Before the war he graduated from Jan Kazimierz University in Lwów and began his career in the Polish Foreign Service. In 1939 he was drafted into the army as a second lieutenant in the mounted artillery. Taken prisoner of war by the Soviets, he managed to escape and, after many adventures, returned to Warsaw, where he joined the Polish underground.

In December 1939 he was sent, as one of the first couriers, to France, where he briefed the new Polish government-in-exile about the situation in occupied Poland. A few months later, following the same route through Hungary and Czechoslovakia, he returned to Poland bringing instructions and nominations for the leaders of the underground. A few weeks later, he was sent to France again, but this time his mission failed, and he was arrested by the Gestapo in Slovakia. He was tortured but did not betray any secrets.

Following an abortive suicide attempt in his prison cell, he was rescued in a daring action by a commando for the Polish underground. After his recovery he worked in the Kraków

*This interview with Jan Karski was first published in Polish in *Tygodnik Powszechny*, 15 March 1987. The English translation, with all non-English names transliterated, was published in *Dissent*, Summer 1987.

section of the Union of Armed Struggle, the military underground organization preceding the Home Army. Afterwards, he worked in Warsaw in the Bureau of Information and Propaganda.

In the autumn of 1942 'Witold' (his conspiracy pseudonym) was charged with a mission to London. I have talked with Professor Karski about this mission and particularly about the part connected with the Holocaust of Polish Jewry.

Maciej Kozłowski: Your mission was to carry a report to the Polish government in London and to the representatives of the political parties on the situation in occupied Poland. Part of this report was to be an account of the tragic situation of the Polish Jews. You were also charged with relaying the demands of the leaders of the Jewish underground to the Allied governments and the public opinion in the West. Who was the initiator of this part of the mission?

Jan Karski: The Jews. When the leaders of the two most important Jewish underground organisations, the Bund and the Zionist organisation, learned that 'Witold' was going to London, they asked the government delegate in Poland if they could use his services in the same way as the other underground political parties. The delegate, Cyryl Ratajski, called me and presented me with this proposition, adding, 'I think, Witold, you should do it'.

It was mid-September 1942. At this time I had completed the political preparations for the mission. I had instructions from the government delegate and the League of the Political Underground Parties, as well as opinions and views of some important political leaders. I was waiting for the technical preparations to be carried with the documents of one of the French workers who was employed by the Germans in Poland, and who was to go on a holiday to France in October. I was waiting for the documents.

M.K: How was the meeting with the Jewish leaders organized?

J.K: The meeting took place in the late afternoon, in one of the half-ruined buildings in the suburbs of Warsaw. Two people came and introduced themselves with pseudonyms, saying they represented the Bund and the Zionist organization. Later, after the war, I learned that the Bund representative had formerly been a lawyer, Leon Fajner. I still do not know who the Zionists' representative was. According to some sources, it was Adolf Berman, the representative of the left wing of the *Poalei Tsion*, who was at that time living outside the ghetto. Walter Laqueur, in his book *The Terrible Secret* (London and Boston, 1980), claims it was Menachem Kirschenbaum. In 1982, when I was in Israel to receive the Yad Vashem medal, in a kibbutz made up of former inhabitants of the Warsaw ghetto, I heard that this man's name was Guzik. I never had any further contact with those men.

Both men were in despair. They were fully aware that the deportations from the Warsaw ghetto as well as from other ghettos in Poland would lead to the extermination of the Jewish people. They knew that the Jews were being transported to extermination camps (those were their exact words) although they did not know the details of the operation. They both stressed that unless dramatic, extraordinary measures were immediately put into effect, the entire Jewish people would perish. I remember the exact words of the Bund representative: 'You Poles are also suffering; many of you will die. But after the war Poland will be restored, your wounds will slowly heal. But by then, the Polish Jews will no longer exist. Hitler will lose this war, but he will win the war he declared against the Polish Jews.'

When the two learned that my mission covered meetings not only with the Polish authorities in London, but also with the highest circles of the Allied governments, they asked me to transmit a number of specific demands. First they summed up the situation in more or less this manner: The systematic extermination of the Jews in occupied Poland is not motivated by military needs connected with the war. Hitler plans the extermination of the Jews before the end of the war regardless of its outcome. The Polish Jews are helpless. They have no country of their own, nor representatives in the high Allied command. They cannot count on the Polish underground or Polish society as a whole. The Poles can save some individuals but they are unable to stop or even postpone the extermination. Therefore, the entire historical responsibility rests on the Allied governments, which must take extraordinary measures. They demanded that the governments do the following:

1 Announce publicly that prevention of the physical

extermination of the Jews will be part of the overall Allied strategy.

2 Inform the German nation through radio, leaflets, and other means about the government's crimes against the Jews. All names of the German officials taking part in this action, as well as specific facts and methods used, should be publicly denounced.

3 Make formal public appeals to the German people to exert pressure on their government to stop the extermination.

4 Declare that if such pressure is not exerted and the extermination continues, the responsibility for the crimes will be placed on the German nation as a whole.

5 Make formal public announcements that if the extermination is not halted, the Allied governments will take unprecedented steps:

a Chosen targets in Germany will be bombed. The German people will be informed that the bombings are in retaliation for the Nazi crimes against the Jews.

b German prisoners of war who, having been informed about their government's crimes, still profess loyalty to the Nazi authorities, will be held responsible for those crimes.

The representatives of the Polish Jews in London, Shmul Zygielbojm and Dr Ignacy Szwarcbart, were to be charged to make every possible effort to bring these demands to the Allied governments. I also had a special message for the President of the Polish Republic, Władysław Raczkiewicz. It was an appeal to Pope Pius XII to use every means, excommunication included, to stop the crimes against the Jews.

The next demand was to be presented to Prime Minister Władysław Sikorski and the Interior Minister Stanisław Mikołajczyk. The Jewish leaders wanted the Polish government to issue strict orders that Poles blackmailing, or informing on, Jews in hiding be sentenced to death by the Polish underground. The identity of those punished and the nature of their crimes should be made public through the underground press. In order to avoid any risk of anti-Polish propaganda, I was forbidden to discuss this point with any non-Polish Jews.

I was also urged to appeal to governments, representatives of public opinion and political leaders for technical and financial aid. Hard currency was needed to bribe the German officials. some Jews would be able to leave Poland if blank, genuine foreign passports were provided. Provision had to be made that those Jews who succeeded in leaving Poland would be accepted abroad. Money, medicine, food and clothing were needed for survivors in ghettos as well as for Christians hiding the Jews.

Finally, the two leaders told me about the preparations for the armed uprising in the Warsaw ghetto. The younger elements there were planning a 'Jewish War' against the Third Reich. They had turned to the Home Army for weapons and been denied. The Jews were Polish citizens. They had a right to fight the common enemy regardless of the outcome. They demanded that General Sikorski, commander-in-chief of the Polish armed forces, change the attitude of the command of the Home Army.

M.K: Did you agree to transmit all these demands?

J.K: Not fully. I was deeply moved by what I had heard, but I tried to explain that their demand that German POWs be punished in retaliation was unrealistic. No democratic government could do that. It would be against international law. The Allies could not use the methods the Nazis used. 'I know English people,' I explained, 'they would not do that.'

M.K: How did the Jewish leaders react?

J.K: They told me, 'Try to understand us. We are desperate, we are dying. We are putting forward these demands to stop the extermination. We cannot judge what is and what is not realistic. You have to determine that.'

M.K: What were your other reservations?

J.K: I refused to carry the message to General Sikorski. I told them, 'I understand you and your situation, but I am a soldier in the Home Army. I cannot carry such a message behind the back of the Home Army Commander, who is my superior, unless you authorize me to my commander in person. I will inform him of your complaints and ask for his comments.' Both Jewish leaders heartily agreed. I started seeking contact with General Grot. It was not easy, as I was only a lieutenant. Because I was working in the Bureau of Information and Propaganda (BIP) I asked for a contact from Jerzy Makowiecki, my immediate superior. He sent me to his superior, Colonel Jan Rzepecki. I did not tell them why I wanted to see General Grot, but only that it concerned my mission to London. After further efforts, I finally obtained permission to contact General Grot.

M.K: Did you talk alone with him?

J.K: No. Colonel Rzepecki was present. At first General Grot praised my attitude, but then he said he was astonished that the Jewish leaders asked me to conduct such a mission behind his back. He knew them and was in touch with them. It was true that the Jews had asked him for weapons. He had given them something, but not much. He himself did not have enough weapons. He had to give arms to the units of diversion and sabotage, and the partisans fighting in the forests. Commanders of all the districts asked him for weapons. In most cases, he was unable to give them arms, but instead he issued money, because weapons could be bought from the Germans in the black market. He ordered his own subordinates to acquire weapons themselves. Moreover, as Commander of the Home Army, he had specified duties to fulfil. Apart from diversion, sabotage and the current struggles, the most important task of the Home Army was to build reserves of human forces and weapons so that at a critical moment, difficult to foretell, they could plunge a knife into Germany's back. He was a military commander. All his actions had to make military sense. An uprising in the ghetto did not make such sense. The Germans would deal with it, I remember his words well, 'in a few hours'.

M.K: We know today how wrong he was. The uprising in the ghetto lasted for over three weeks and the Germans sustained heavy losses.

J.K: That is true. But at the time I understood his arguments as I did those of the Jews. At the end of our conversation, the general said that he was a well-disciplined soldier and if he received an order from London to transfer a specific number and kind of weapons to the ghetto, he would carry out that order. But handing out weapons in the amount the Jews asked for was beyond his capability. The decision had to be made by the commander-in-chief.

M.K: You carried this message to General Sikorski. What was his reaction?

J.K: This message, like all the other messages, I repeated as accurately as possible, first to Szwarcbart and Zygielbojm, and then to General Sikorski. But I am unable to say anything about the Polish government's reaction because I simply do not know. I was only a courier. My duty was to transfer information. Nothing else. I could not ask the commander-in-chief what his opinion was about this or any other question. Any messages to relay to Poland would be given shortly before I left. Such was the practice. And as you know, I did not come back, although it had been planned that I would.

A. WITNESS FOR THE JEWS

M.K: Let us go back to Warsaw and to your talks with the Jewish leaders. They had an unusual proposition for you?

J.K: They wanted me to see with my own eyes at least part of what I had heard from them. They understood as well as I that in my future talks with the Western statesmen I would be much more convincing if my report were backed by eyewitness testimony. The extermination of the Jews was without precedent in the history of mankind. No one was prepared to grasp the atrociousness of what was going on. It is not true, as sometimes has been written, that I was the first one to present to the West the whole truth of the fate of the Jews in occupied Poland. There were others. The news was being transmitted through the underground radio, which was controlled by the Chief of Civil Struggle, Stefan Korboński. There were some Jews who managed to escape. The tragedy was that these testimonies were not believed. Not because of ill will, but simply because the facts were beyond human imagination.

I experienced this myself. When I was in the United States and told Justice Felix Frankfurter the story of the Polish Jews, he said, at the end of our conversation, 'I cannot believe you'. We were with the Polish ambassador to the US, Jan Ciechanowski. Hearing the justice's comments, he was indignant. 'Lieutenant Karski is on an official mission. My government's authority stands behind him. You cannot say to his face that he is lying'.

Frankfurter's answer was, 'I am not saying that he is lying. I only said that I cannot believe him, and there is a difference'. I met with disbelief many times.

M.K: You saw the Warsaw ghetto in its last days. You were also taken to the Bełżec extermination camp. How were these undertakings conducted? Were they very dangerous?

J.K: Getting into the ghetto was quite easy. At that time it was divided into four smaller zones. Streetcars ran between them. There were passages through basements, through sewer systems, and guards could be bribed. In the ghetto there was no danger. The trip to Bełżec was much riskier.

M.K: Did your superiors agree to that risk? Apart from the Jewish problem, you had an important mission to carry out. You were a soldier, under orders.

J.K: You do not understand my role in that damned war. I was a nobody. In all four of my missions, I acted as a mailbox or a gramophone record, hurried from one side of the front to the other. Everybody had me swear that I would tell what I heard to authorized persons only. I knew that if something happened to me the Jews would take responsibility and inform the government's delegate. I did not even think about asking anybody. Besides, whom was I to ask? Colonel Rowecki? The Alliance of Political Parties? Any one of them or all together? Also, at that time, in the autumn of 1942, my personal situation was not very clear. I was working for BIP and it was not clear if my superiors were military or civil authorities. I carried my mission for the civil authorities only. The Home Army was responsible for the technical matters, but I was a political courier, not a military one. General Grot made that very clear during our conversation. Therefore, I had to make the decision myself. Actually, the Jews were making it.

M.K: How was the Warsaw ghetto when you saw it?

J.K: I was in the ghetto twice. The Bund representative accompanied me. I saw terrible things. Not only did I witness starvation and misery. I witnessed a 'hunt'. I saw boys from the *Hitlerjugend* shooting into a crowd of running people. I have remembered these scenes all my life.

M.K: How did you get into the Bełżec camp?

J.K: A guide contacted me. He appeared to be a Jew, but of course I cannot say for sure. We did not introduce ourselves and we did not talk. We went together to Lublin, changed trains, and arrived in Bełżec. It was the middle of October. The guide took me to a hardware shop. Several hours later a man arrived. He spoke perfect Polish and was very matter-of-fact. He had an Estonian guard's uniform for me. I knew that the Germans never used Poles in the death camps. The extermination was to be kept secret. The man gave me precise instructions: 'You will follow me. You must not speak to anyone. You speak neither Polish nor German. I will take you into the camp, but once inside you will be on your own. As far as I know, you want to see the camp. After a while, I will give you a sign, and we will leave together.'

We entered the camp without any trouble. My guide was well known there, and after showing some documents, we were allowed in. The camp was enclosed, partly with barbed wire, partly by the wall. On the right side I saw a railway sidetrack. I was standing close to the main gate through which the Jews were being taken out. For many years I could not understand it. I thought that Bełżec was a transit camp. It was after the war that I learned that it was a death camp. During the trials of the German war criminals in the late 1940s, some Polish railwaymen who co-operated with the underground were cross-examined as witnesses. They explained the scene I saw.

By German standards, Bełżec was run very inefficiently. In fact at that time its commander, SS Captain Gottlieb Hering, was on trial before an SS court. The extermination in Bełżec was done by exhaust gases from engines salvaged from Soviet tanks. It was a very ineffective way of killing. The engines over-heated, and the whole process of killing lasted for a long time. Sometimes one transport had not been completed by the time a new one arrived. In such cases the new transport was directed to Sobibor, where the death machine was running much better. I witnessed such a scene. The Jews were being transported from Bełżec to Sobibor. I could not see the gas chambers; they were, as I learned later, deeper inside the camp, on the other side of the mass of people being directed into the cars.

I would like now to mention some events that were taking

place at the same time but were fully revealed only after the war. In August 1942 a certain German officer, Kurt Gerstein, arrived in Bełżec. He was to put things in order, that is, to instruct the inefficient commander as to the virtues of Cyklon B gas compared with exhaust gas. He fulfilled his duty, but he must have had some conscience still alive within him. Returning, he met a Swedish diplomat on the train and told him the whole story. He told about the exhaust gases, the collapsing tank engines, the whole story about the extermination of Jews in the Bełżec camp. The Swede made a report and sent it to Stockholm. But the Swedish authorities, in an effort not to antagonize the still powerful Germans, kept this report secret. An entire year passed before the report reached London. It didn't mention Gerstein, of course. The Polish government learned about the report and made an uproar. But by now it was 1944. The 'Jewish question' in occupied Poland was solved. After the war Gerstein was caught by the French. He made a detailed report, and committed suicide.

M.K: That means that the information you transmitted to the West was not complete, but even so it was horrible enough the people could not believe you?

J.K: I saw terrible things in Bełżec. I wrote about them in my book, *Story of a Secret State*, (Boston, 1944). I broke down right there. My guide noticed that I was not behaving normally and he shouted over the Jewish crowd, 'Folge mir, folge mir! (follow me, follow me)' We both left by the same route. I spent less than an hour in the camp. I was sick, vomiting blood. I saw terrible things. Unbelievable. You would not believe what I saw either! Even today, although over forty years have passed, I cannot forget the scenes I witnessed there.

M.K: You left Warsaw with the documents of a French worker. Your itinerary took you through Germany to Paris, through the Pyrenees to neutral Spain, and from the port of Algeciras you took a boat to a waiting British ship, which in turn took you to Gibraltar. You arrived in London in the middle of November.

J.K: I remember that date because my trip broke a record: twenty-one days from Warsaw to London. No other courier made this trip in such a short time. When I was in Paris, I delivered some reports, among them the report about the situation of the Jews, to the commander of the Polish underground in France, Aleksander Kawalkowski. He sent them to London. The Jewish report, made by three men from BIP – Henryk Woliński, Ludwik Widerszal, and Stanislaw Herbst – was over forty written pages, put on microfilm, hidden in a specially designed key.

When I arrived in London, I stayed with Paweł Siudak, an associate of Stanisław Kot and Stanisław Mikołajczyk in their contacts with occupied Poland, and kept under cover. I was to come back with another mission.

On the first day after my arrival I met General Sikorski. I did not make a detailed report because the general told me that he was leaving. Later I learned that he was going to Washington to meet President Roosevelt. The general told me only that I would receive the highest Polish Order of Merit, the Virtuti Militari Cross. For a month after this conversation I was allowed to see only a small group of Poles. It was after Sikorski's return that I was able to see some Britons. I had a chance to speak with four members of the highest authority, the War Cabinet. I saw the Foreign Secretary Anthony Eden, the Conservative leader Lord Cranborne, Arthur Greenwood from the Labour Party, and the President of the Board of Trade Hugh Dalton. I also spoke several times with Lord Selborne, who was responsible in the British government for the contacts with underground movements in occupied countries. I also saw the British and American ambassadors to the Polish government, the influential member of parliament Ellen Wilkinson, and many other people.

For every meeting I prepared scrupulously. I knew that I had to be brief because at any given moment the person I was talking with could close the meeting. Usually I prepared a twenty-minute briefing. Four or five minutes of the briefing were devoted to the fate of the Jews.

M.K: What were the reactions to this part of your report?

J.K: They varied. Eden, for instance, stopped me short saying, 'We already received Karski's report. Matters will take their due course.' At the time, I did not understand this statement. After the war, I learned from Martin Gilbert's book, *Auschwitz and the Allies* (London, 1981), that a detailed report had been prepared, based on my revelations to Professor Kot as well as on microfilms that had been sent from Paris. Professor Kot, by the way, was deeply concerned about the fate of the Jews. This report was presented to A. L. Eastermann, a liaison man between the Jewish Congress and the British Foreign Office. According to Gilbert, who used British archives opened thirty years after the war, this report was handed to Under-Secretary of State Richard Law on 26 November. When I spoke with Eden in mid-February, he may have already read the report, and perhaps that was the reason why, among many questions, he asked none concerning the Jewish question. Lord Selborne was more interested in the fate of the Jews, but he told me very frankly that the demands made by the Jewish leaders could not be met. According to him, the main task of the Allies was winning the war, and therefore anything not strictly of a military character was regarded as a side issue.

M.K: Shmul Zygielbojm met with the same attitude and therefore he committed suicide a few months later to protest against it.

J.K: Zygielbojm was a tragic figure. His suicide, which was to have been a dramatic cry of protest, did not affect the fate of Polish Jews in any way.

M.K: Let us come back to your mission. Apart from talks with officials, you were asked by Jewish leaders from Poland to influence public opinion. How did you fulfil this part of your task?

J.K: I attempted to reach the most influential people in cultural and artistic milieus. I met Arthur Koestler, who tried to do whatever he could. Acting on Lord Selborne's suggestion, he wrote and read several speeches for BBC radio, speaking as Karski. My voice would not be recognized, and Lord Selborne said that Koestler spoke with the same bad accent as I, so he could act a courier from Poland.

I also broadcast from the 'Świt' station. It was a station that broadcast from Britain but passed as broadcasting from occupied Poland.

My meeting with H. G. Wells, whom I met through the Polish writer and poet Antoni Słonimski, was very different. The only comment Wells made after my briefing was, 'I wonder why in every country where there are Jews, there is anti-semitism. Some research should be done about this problem.'

I had many meetings with journalists, and before my trip to the United States I collaborated with Thomas Mann and Aleksei Tolstoy on a booklet of Nazi crimes against the Jews. Thousands of copies were published. Its title was *Fate of the Jews* (reference unavailable).

M.K: When did your trip to the United States take place?

J.K: In the summer of 1943. I went with a false diplomatic passport as Jan Karski because I was still supposed to go back to Poland. That was the origin of my present name, because later, when I applied for US citizenship, these false papers were the only ones I had. When I explained the story to the US officials, they said that Karski was easier to pronounce than Kozielewski, and so I became Karski. My mission in the United States had the same purpose as in London. I was to meet government officials, representatives of public opinion, and church dignitaries.

M.K: And as in London, you were met with disbelief?

J.K: I already told you about my meeting with Justice Frankfurter. I also met President Roosevelt. It was a great experience for me. You must understand that people such as Roosevelt or Churchill, men who held the fate of the world in their hands, appeared like gods to a young soldier like me. It is understandable that I was intimidated. Roosevelt was very friendly. He asked many questions concerning the political situation in Poland. Knowing that I was supposed to return to Poland, he tried to convince me that the Polish eastern border had to be changed and that Poland would obtain compensation in the west. Altogether the conversation lasted for one hour and twenty minutes. As I mentioned above, I was under the spell of the President. He radiated power and dignity.

Today I see this conversation in a different light. Apart from polite generalities, he said nothing important, either on Poland or on Jewish questions. He said only that Poland had a friend in the White House and that the Nazi criminals would be punished after the war.

M.K: So the American part of the mission was completely

fruitless?

J.K: Not completely. A few years ago I read an account of John Pehle's press conference. He was the first director of the American Refugee Board, an institution set up to take care of the refugees from occupied Europe, mostly Jews. During that conference Pehle said, 'Karski's mission really shocked the president. He changed his attitude and the attitude of the State Department. Roosevelt at once asked for the creation of the American Refugee Board. We started our work in February 1944. But it was too late, then.'

M.K: What was the attitude of the Americans you met to the other dramatic demands of the Polish Jews?

J.K: Once again, I cannot say. Wherever I could, I presented these demands. Some people, like Rabbi Stephen Wise, the leader of the American Jews, were interested in some details. For instance, he asked me about the blank passports. But as in London, I was not informed about the results of my mission.

M.K: At the end of 1943 you were supposed to go back to Poland. Why did you not return?

J.K: When I got back to London I learned that the Germans knew about my trip to the United States. German radio broadcasts claimed that a certain Karski, a Bolshevik agent paid by American Jews, was slandering the Third Reich, presenting false, fabricated stories. Because of these Mikołajczyk decided that my return to Poland would be too risky. I was marked by the scars on my wrists. To tell the truth, the Polish government did not know what to do with me. I knew too many secrets. Finally, I found myself in the United States as a member of the Polish Embassy staff.

B. ASSESSING THE MISSION

M.K: As far as I know, you did not return to your war adventures until you agreed to be interviewed by Claude Lanzmann for his film *Shoah*. But the entire interview was not shown on the film. You did not say anything about the results of your mission. What can you say now, forty years later, about the results of the 'Karski Mission'?

J.K: As to the Jewish part of my mission, it was an obvious failure. Six million Jews died and no one offered them effective help. Not any nation, not any government, not any church. The help they did receive, heroic help, was provided only by individuals.

M.K: After the war, when the full extent of Nazi crimes became well known, there were many voices expressing surprise. Facts that had been revealed were generally regarded as sensational fabrications. But these facts should have been known. They were described in your book. You presented them personally. How can we understand that?

J.K: Hypocrisy. Everybody who wanted to know about German crimes against the Jews could have known and not only through me. There were many other sources. But this truth could not get through. This was not only because of ill will. The Holocaust, the systematic extermination of an entire nation, happened for the first time in the history of mankind. People were not prepared for such truths. And that is why these truths were rejected, even subconsciously. The most trustworthy witnesses were rejected. There are things which minds and hearts refuse to accept.

M.K: After the war, after publishing your book, you disappeared from the public scene. Many people thought you had died. You came back to this part of your life in Lanzmann's film. Why did you decide to speak up after so many years?

J.K: I was persuaded by Claude Lanzmann. He is a difficult man, very emotional and obsessed with his film. He spent eleven years making it. At first I refused. But Lanzmann persuaded me. He told me that it was my duty to speak. And finally, I consented.

M.K: Did you regret it after seeing the film? *Shoah* aroused much controversy. Lanzmann was criticized for presenting a biased view and for distorting historical truth by the selective way he chose those he interviewed.

J.K: I do not agree with such opinions. Lanzmann made a great film. But a large part of the Polish press, both in Poland and abroad, did not understand his intentions. It is a film about the Holocaust. About it alone and nothing else. Even the war is merely mentioned in it. There are no political issues. Lanzmann told me he was interested in interviewing three categories of people: the Jews who lived through the Holocaust, those who were instigators, and the witnesses. Most of those who saw the Holocaust were Poles. And they were not intellectuals, city-dwellers and educated persons, but peasants and people from small cities who lived close to the death camps. And it is not Lanzmann's fault that they are presented the way they are. He does not speak Polish. He did not instruct them how and what to say.

M.K: But among witnesses there were also decent people, without resentment against Jews. There was a special cell in the Home Army, 'Żegota', concerned only with helping the persecuted Jews. There were hundreds of Poles who helped Jews at the risk of their own lives. They could help only individuals, there was no other choice.

J.K: You do not want to understand either. Lanzmann made a film about the mechanism of the Holocaust. Not about the Poles' – or any other nation's – attitude towards the Jews, not about the attempts to help. Therefore, he took only a part from my interview, which lasted for many hours, my testimony from the ghetto and Bełżec. He was not interested in what Karski or anyone else did to help the Jews. I regret that my interview was shortened, but I have no grounds for complaint. The second part of the interview, from the point of view of the film-maker, was not to the point.

The film is a masterpiece. It was a sensation not only in the United States, but in the whole world. Even among Poles, after their first hysterical reactions, after trumped-up charges and exaggerated figures concerning help given to Jews during the war, some sobriety was evident, especially among those who had seen the entire film. It was evident in the press, both in Poland and abroad.

This film will shape the consciousness of millions of people. It will teach the results of intolerance, anti-semitism, racism and hatred. The Pope underlined this, praising the film and its director. But critics of the film preferred to ignore the Pope's remarks.

One may regret, as I do, that Lanzmann did not mention in his film the problems involved in helping the Jews in Poland, France, Hungary, Holland, Denmark or Bulgaria. Therefore, I see the necessity of making another film, one as great and powerful as *Shoah*, a film that would also shape the consciousness of mankind. So let the churches, governments, international organizations, and people of talent and good heart, find a way to cooperate in the production of such a film. Let this new film show the endeavours of millions of Europeans who risked their lives or freedom to save the Jews.

Such a film becomes important because *Shoah* is so powerful. Above all, it is truly necessary that those generations that did not live through the Holocaust, that did not witness it, Jew and Gentile alike, do not lose their faith in mankind. After all, it is not true that the Jews were totally abandoned. Over half a million Jews survived the Holocaust in Europe. Someone helped them: nuns and peasants, workers and underground organizations. This film, which has yet to be made, should show what love for one's neighbour means, how powerful a force it can be. Because, I repeat, the Jews were not totally abandoned. They were abandoned by governments, social structures, church hierarchies, but not by ordinary men and women. The organized structures fell short of expectation, but not the ordinary people. And there were millions of such people. In this is hidden a sense of optimism, and this optimism should be passed on to those generations for whom the Holocaust is only a page from a history textbook.

8

'THE BLACK HOLE':

Conversation with Stanisław Krajewski, 'a Pole and a Jew in One Person'*

EWA BERBERYUSZ

Ewa Berberyusz: I have just uttered the word 'Jew' and it grated on the ear. You winced yourself. Why is it that every time Jews and Poles come together, there is immediately tension in the air? I feel that the person facing me wonders whether I am an anti-semite. This feeling is like a paralysis; I am choking on this word: 'Jew'.

Stanisław Krajewski: Yes, unfortunately, this seems indeed to be so. A great majority of Jews, especially abroad, when they meet a Pole, assume that they have before them an anti-semite. On the one hand, this is very distressing to me, since I consider this idea to be a silly cliché; on the other hand I cannot dismiss it as totally unfounded. The history of our mutual relations is so muddied that it is difficult to get into clear water on the subject. It may be pure thoughtlessness but the word 'Jew' is still used as an insult, especially by children. It tells us something about the general climate but it also testifies to the history of our mutual relations. Besides, there are hardly any Jews left in Poland; those who have decided to stay do not wish to have anything to do with Jewishness. For those people, any references to their origins, even in a positive spirit, are perceived as threatening.

E.B: On one occasion I said in conversation, with the best of intentions if perhaps little knowledge, that Jews make good husbands. What I got as a reply was: 'Oh, yes, so you are an anti-semite. . .'

*This article was first published in *Tygodnik Powszechny*, 5 April 1987. Deletions by the censor are marked in square brackets.

S.K: That's right. However, in the situation when the Jewish person you are talking to is reassured that the intention behind such a comment is not anti-semitic, that it comes from a well-wisher, it usually brings a pleasant surprise.

E.B: But generally speaking, what does Poland today mean to the world Jewry?

S.K: It represents something important to them, in a positive as well as a negative sense. What is positive is the sentiment for the realities of the country: the landscape, the horse-cart, the cooking and the customs. The Polish folk dance ensemble Mazowsze was greeted with tears in Israel, where even the Prime Minister himself came to see it. At the same time, however, Jews also have negative associations with regard to Poland which is – in the view of some – a cursed place, a black hole. The place where yesterday the Jewish culture was thriving only to come to a tragic end. What has been left is a gnawing void. Looking at it in this way, Poland deserves to be put out of mind. A finished chapter. Underneath, however, the sentiment persists and with some it takes the upper hand: they decide to come to Poland for a visit. Often, they are pleasantly surprised; Poland can be intriguing. For others, however, this attitude of 'giving up on Poland' hardens: they don't want to know. . .

E.B: What about the young?

S.K: That Poland is anti-semitic is something they take for granted. This is hardly surprising given the experience of their parents and grandparents: those people who may have been frightened to walk across the Saxon Garden in Warsaw dressed in a gabardine in fear of being beaten up. But this is not the whole story. The full glory of the old Jewish culture in Poland appears more and more important. After all, the achievements of Jewish religious thought, all the contemporary Jewish cultural and political movements, can be traced back to Poland. Polish surnames, those of specific localities, crop up all the time when you think of Jewish history of the last two centuries. Some of these names do not mean very much to the Poles themselves: a good example here might be Rymanów, the place of residence of the famous Rymanower *tsaddik*. In consequence, the place became a centre of the Jewish world, a place of pilgrimage for Hasidic Jews, while remaining totally unimportant for Poles.

E.B: For us it is just a small spa town in south-eastern Poland. But this is just one small example. Could you give me an example of something for which Poles and Jews may have diametrically opposed associations?

S.K: Yes, indeed. One such example may be the General Haller's army, so highly regarded by Poles. In the collective memory of Jews Haller's soldiers are remembered as people who went about shaving off Jewish beards. What is important here is not facts themselves, but the way in which they have been seen and are remembered. But as soon as we have said this we must remember that Jews during the last hundred years were not a homogeneous group; their views were far from uniform. Therefore, we have those who never bothered about Poland, those who felt at home in it and those who identified themselves completely with Polish aspirations. One could quote endless examples. . .

E.B: Perhaps you could give us an example from your own life?

S.K: For me Polishness was simply a fact of life. I did not have to come to it; I was brought up as a Pole. It was my Jewish tradition that I had to regain. But I think that my Jewish identification is today sufficiently strong for me to understand other Jews and entitles me to express a Jewish point of view on the Jewish experience in Poland and beyond.

E.B: What made you identify with Jewishness?

S.K: Probably March 1968. In reaction to the suspicion that 'they' (the authorities) meant me harm solely on the account of my being Jewish, I suddenly came to see a positive value in Jewishness and that is how, after a long time, I have come to identify with it. I was never personally threatened either in my career or in my job as I was only a student then, but I nevertheless took this attack against Jews as directed against myself. I decided I belonged to the same category of people. It was then that the feeling of being Jewish grew in me.

E.B: Let me tell you what happened to me in March 1968. I had not been a student for a long time then but I identified myself with the students' protest. The University area and Holy Cross Church across the road became places I spent a lot of time in. I was beaten once or twice; the tear gas made me weep. At the same time, I laughed at the then popular joke: 'Who is the persecuted Jew?' 'The Deputy Minister'. I thought then that there is a straight correlation between being Jewish and being in power. And we needed History to intervene to show us that the mechanism was really different. I am afraid that there were many people in Poland at that time who thought similarly. Whereas for the generation younger still, like, for example, for my son, then 12 years old, the March events kindled a new interest. It inspired him to do such reading as not only the *Diary of Adam Czerniaków*, but also the Old Testament.

S.K: Yes, March 1968 did indeed stimulate different lines of enquiry wider in implication than the Jewish question alone. It all happened to coincide with developments on a much wider scale. As the cliché has it: the twilight of the ideological era, the crisis of scientific outlook on life, the realization of the limits of science. As for me, the crisis led me to religion. By various routes I have come to identify myself with Judaism in which I have rediscovered my roots. But to be absolutely honest, I have no idea why it happened: what I have said so far is simplification. I value the two things equally – my Jewishness and my Polishness – and I know only this: my place is in Poland. Here I feel at home, also as a Jew.

E.B: And you feel safe here?

S.K: I can say with a clear conscience that I do not feel threatened in Poland. I have never met with a concrete threat. To give you one example: my wife and I have been travelling all round Poland for years photographing Jewish cemeteries, and not once have I felt threatened. I often tell this to my contemporaries, Jews from the USA, who have been told by their parents that a trip to Polish countryside presents a mortal danger. I do not feel physically threatened on account of being Jewish, but – this said – I feel my answer is too simple. Anti-semitism has not disappeared and one can never be sure when it may again rear its head. And, indeed, could it be that being Jewish presents a problem *per se*? Being Jewish is something abnormal in the normal state of affairs. But perhaps this in itself is something valuable and one need not run away from it?

E.B: What I would wish is that encounters between Jews and Poles could be more normal, by which I mean that the two parties could at least speak to each other in a simpler and more natural way.

S.K: Unfortunately, here everything becomes more complicated. The situation is much simpler with the Germans. They are responsible for the Holocaust and they do not deny it. Both parties have by now reached the stage of being able to talk about it directly. This point has not, however, been reached between Poles and Jews, even though Poles were not guilty of the genocide of Jews. There is an enormous barrier on both sides. Poles, for the most part, exhibit a defensive attitude. They find themselves unable to admit the fact that the fate of Jews during the war was different from their own, insisting that it was just the same. This is the attitude expressed in the recent article by Siła-Nowicki in this journal [*Tygodnik Powszechny,* chapter 4]. I am not claiming that it was anti-semitic; it simply was insensitive to the fate of Jews, while being entrenched in the defence of Polish honour, the honour of the Home Army and the whole resistance movement. He is saying in effect: 'We were doing all that was possible in the circumstances, therefore we are blameless.'

E.B: I confess that I can't share his idea of honour. . .

S.K: Poles perceive themselves as victims of history. They cannot tolerate the thought that someone else might have suffered even more. It is they who are victims and that is the end of the argument. So, firstly, Jews could not suffer more than we did, and, secondly, we could not conceivably have added to their suffering, because a victim cannot cause suffering to others. This idea stems from the philosophy of Polish messianism, which dictates two points of view in relation to Jews: they can be perceived either as allies or as enemies. If we choose to look upon them as enemies, one can look back to the tradition, by no means completely extinct, of the threat of Judaeo-masonry, and so on. A friend of mine has a saying: 'How can there not be anti-semitism (in Poland) – there is no room for *two* chosen nations in the same land.' If, however, one chooses to look with favour on Jews, then they can be seen as Mickiewicz saw them, as the elder brother among the chosen nations. As God is king for Jews, so Poles have elected Mary their queen. In both cases the monarch is of a special kind: they both reign in heaven. Inscribed on the Gdańsk Memorial is the quotation from Psalm 29:11: 'The Lord will give strength unto his people'. I daresay most Poles apply these words to themselves.

E.B: For me, the 'people' in that quotation are meant to signify all those suffering – not necessarily Poles.

S.K: It is interesting that you think so, as my impression is that most Poles consider themselves God's people. Perhaps, indeed, it is a legitimate interpretation, and one somewhat close to my heart, even though, understandably, I treat it with greater ambivalence than someone who has no Jewish roots. Therefore if we are to look upon Poland as a victim who is suffering and who, through this suffering, may perhaps save the world, then everything which stands in the way of this suffering fades into the margins of one's vision. Put in more concrete terms: there is a reluctance in Poland to accept the fact that during the German occupation a Jewish child's chance of survival was one in a thousand, whereas for a Polish child it was incomparably greater.

E.B: It is not that this fact is being denied, but that one immediately starts talking of one's own suffering. I was myself trapped by this argument for years: 'After all, we were next for the gas.' It was only after having read the article by Jan Błoński (chapter 2) (which preceded that of Siła-Nowicki, which you referred to earlier) that I was able to recognize the futility of this type of defensive attitude. By the way, the social response to the Błoński article was a litmus paper for a certain kind of mentality; it brought into relief its complexes, its xenophobia, the lack of tolerance. I, who have written a short personal reflection which was published alongside (chapter 5), was accused of Pharisaism and of fouling my own nest.

S.K: The article by Jan Błoński is a complete novelty precisely because it acknowledges the Jewish point of view and the Jewish experience. He did not try to gloss over the difference in the fate of the two nations. In this way he was able to pinpoint the reasons for this morass which bedevils Polish–Jewish relations.

E.B: And in no way did he tarnish the Polish image abroad; on the contrary, he did much to improve it! You have mentioned Polish messianism as a possible additional aspect of anti-semitism. Can you see any difference between Polish and German anti-semitism?

S.K: German anti-semitism reached the stage of genocide; Polish anti-semitism did not. Nobody in Poland would have conceived of the idea of extermination. But it seems to me that anti-semitism has also its metaphysical aspect – at the root of it lies the conviction that Jews personify all the evil of the world; that a Jew is the devil incarnate.

E.B: In this case how are we to understand Polish anti-semites hiding Jews during the war?

S.K: This is a curious paradox. When it came to killing Jews, it proved too much even for good Polish anti-semites. The well-known appeal of Zofia Kossak-Szczucka to Poles during the war is very characteristic here. It speaks of the Jew who is an enemy but at the same time our neighbour who is to be helped in the event of a threat to their life. It was apparently her conviction.

E.B: I think not. She is said to have explained that she had written this in order to make her appeal more effective.

S.K: So much more telling!

E.B: How much of that atmosphere has – in your opinion – survived to this day?

S.K: I cannot really tell. But do take note that the word 'Jew' still functions in the society. [Someone's Jewish origins are underlined when he is part of the opposing camp, and obliterated when he is 'one of us'.]

E.B: Can one observe a difference between generations in this respect? Don't the young, who do not remember the war, look on these matters differently?

S.K: In this respect, I must confess, my ideas are not fully supported by my personal observations. Among my friends, there are people who are not only well-disposed, but also genuinely eager to understand. Is it merely because I am not in the habit of befriending anti-semites? My conviction is, however, that the majority of Poles see these matters in an entirely different light. The young, as a whole, are marked by a certain innocence which stems from ignorance. They are not prepared to accept that Poles may be guilty in this matter; the accusations levelled against them are taken as proof of the anti-Polish campaign; the merits of the case are not examined. The prevailing feeling that Poland is a victim seems to be coupled with an assumption that Poles could not do harm to Jews, and especially so after the war. This sense of being a victim is linked in their minds with the conviction that Jews had it too good in Poland. Therefore to talk about Polish anti-semitism is to invite scepticism and a dismissive wave of the hand. Of course, they admit that there were poor Jews in Poland, but – they add – if their lot had been so intolerable, Jews would have left long ago. To sum it up, it appears that the difficulty in understanding the Jewish experience is fairly common in Poland, irrespective of age and social class.

E.B: How can this be changed? Through increased contacts?

S.K: Yes, except even then it seems that genuine understanding as well as a natural way of relating to each other seems to elude us. These encounters often arouse mixed feelings and the sense of embarrassment which you mentioned in the beginning. However, if mutual contacts are to be the basis of the 'therapy', perhaps it is only natural that they should go through this inflamed stage? Let me tell you a story which happened recently: a young American Jew, on a visit to Poland, had a chance meeting with a Pole who introduced himself as a member of PAN [the Polish Academy of Science] and who, on hearing that the visitor from America represented the Wiesenthal Centre, exclaimed: 'Oh, it is you who track down war criminals, isn't it? I imagine you might think me a criminal, too!' This conversation may have taken place after several vodkas, but a strange joke, just the same, don't you think?

E.B: Yes, like the one which could be heard during the occupation, that Hitler deserves a memorial for having settled the Jewish problem. I guarantee, however, that not a single one of those who circulated that 'joke' would have acted upon it. These bloodthirsty and cynical jokes were just a way of releasing tension at that time.

S.K: [Yet at the same time there was relief that an insoluble problem had disappeared as a result of outside intervention.] And besides, how might a Jew who was in hiding on Aryan papers take this joke? Or someone just returning from Russia?

E.B: One other point is that it was quite unthinkable to say that sort of thing aloud without it being taken as an affront to Polish patriotism. I recall here what I have been told by a friend who had been researching the press of the Grey Ranks (*Szare Szeregi* – a scout movement). In the columns of this underground press, which was very sensitive to moral issues and which was concerned with the moral education of the young generation of Poles, Jews were totally absent! Not that the underground press was hostile to them; the whole issue was simply not mentioned there! At the same time what was going on 'behind the wall'? Extermination.

S.K: The specificity of the Polish case lies exactly in this. In other countries anti-semitism was connected with pro-German feeling, but in Poland it was possible at the same time to be an anti-semite and to fight the Germans; everywhere else this would be scarcely imaginable. This one thing seems to have remained unchanged: it is still possible to be a good Pole and an anti-semite. I am of the opinion that anti-semitism in Poland is a very complex phenomenon. One speaks sometimes about anti-semitism without Jews and there is something in that.

S.K: But since everything here is bound to be more complicated, one cannot deny that there also is in Poland a fascination with Jews, a very zealous philo-semitism. On the other hand, there is in the Polish consciousness this mental block which renders impossible an understanding of a point of view different from their own. The fixed view of the past held by the Poles makes it very difficult for them to take an imaginative leap towards a changed consciousness.

E.B: The Church has just made such a leap.

S.K: The theological changes which the Church has introduced are revolutionary indeed. They represent a 180 degree turn.

According to the traditional dogma, Jews were blamed for the sin of deicide, of which their subsequent sufferings were but a consequence. The Second Vatican Council, however, validated a contrary view which – even though it has never completely disappeared – has only now become part of the official teaching of the Church. It holds that Jews not only were, but, in religious terms, still *are* the chosen nation and that the crime of deicide must not be regarded as their collective responsibility, therefore their sufferings can in no way be justified. The representation, from the pulpit, of Jews as the chosen nation is something new for Poles, as it is a complete *novum* for the Church also. It is, incidentally, interesting that, in theological terms, we are beginning to view the state of Israel as something new in God's design for the world.

E.B: But popular opinion in Poland takes no account of this view!

S.K: You are right. This new theological view of Jews is difficult to accept, especially for people of the older generation who have preserved memories of concrete persons and situations. This type of thinking about Jews, however, even if it has not yet gained currency, has had a great impact on the attitudes of people of my own generation. None the less, let us have no illusions: such fundamental changes will take a long time to work through.

E.B: No chance of speeding up this process?

S.K: Is one thing which could perhaps bring about such a change the shock which comes through reliving the experience of Jews? It may be a silly idea, but I think that a tragic story, a report or a film which a hearer/viewer can identify with, might have the deepest impact. . .

E.B: Lanzmann's *Shoah* has not achieved such an effect, I think, because it pursued a 'thesis'. But since we are on this subject, let me ask, do you share the opinion that the Poles represented there seem to have been glad of the fate which had befallen Jews? As for me, I think that even if their reactions may appear a little primitive, they were genuinely concerned. I shall never forget the tragic eyes of that engine driver. The Poles in that film seem to me to contrast rather favourably with the well-composed and over-polite Germans.

S.K: I completely agree. There was no sense of gladness in the Polish reaction, only horror and the acceptance of fate.

E.B: Volumes have been written about this film, therefore I do not propose to discuss it here. I would rather touch on something which I personally feel very acutely and which has a bearing on our subject. I would like to say that the absence of Jews, whom I still remember but who are now gone, leaves me, for one, with a sense of irreplacable loss. I voice here not just a sentiment in which is enshrined an idealized memory of old Poland, but rather an awareness of the real, manifest impoverishment of Polish culture. Poland has lost a very important creative contribution.

S.K: It sounds like music to my ears, but I must say that I have an impression that, by idealizing the old Poland, the young simply express their dissatisfaction with things as they are now. One is inclined to think sentimentally of old times and, curiously, Jews have come to symbolize them. Jews have suddenly become a symbol of the old Poland, the better Poland. This view seems to me as widespread as anti-semitism.

E.B: It was not sentiment that has led me to mention this, but the conviction that it may be worth while to start building on this as a way to improve Polish–Jewish relations at the present time. We seem to be continually coming back to this, as it appears to be the root of all good as well as all evil. When we are contemplating the negative image of Jews which has formed in the Polish consciousness, we cannot ignore a strongly held conviction that Jews support each other and eliminate non-Jews. There is a strong belief in the theory of a Jewish conspiracy. In our time this conviction seems to date back to the Stalinist era. I myself recall a university friend who was making life difficult for me, because I was not a member of any political organization. The situation became dangerous for me; luckily, just at that time I contracted TB and had to be removed from 'the inner circle'. Among my acquaintances, she was the only one who behaved like that, therefore she alone became the target of my hostility, but there were a great many people who were ready to use the plural in such cases so that 'Jews' were blamed. In this way, Jews came to be seen as the root of all evil in Poland. Do you not agree that this attitude had a lot to substantiate it in those times?

S.K: Certainly. With the small reservation that Jews who did not like the system left Poland as a rule. And those who decided to stay were victimized later. [Because later many people thought that the system would be not bad, if only it could be 'de-Jewed'. But perhaps subsequent developments have discredited this view.]

E.B: Indeed! But the conviction that there is a Jewish lobby, particularly in the arts, television and the press, has remained. I have been told by some people I know in the musical circles, violinists in this case, that they know it for a fact that a non-Jew will never be allowed to 'make it to the top' in that profession. . .

S.K: I do not know how things may stand with violinists. My view on this subject is this. It is an undeniable fact that Jews are present in many important places. But they are also divided among themselves; you can find them in every camp. Take this example: all those involved in the celebrated Rosenberg trial in America were Jews: the defendants themselves, the prosecutor, the counsel for the defence and the judge. Cliques exist everywhere, of course, but it is usually the Jewish involvement which becomes the subject of a myth. In addition, to prove the point, often non-Jews become Jews in these stories. What is quite another matter is that if a Jew were in a position to decide about the career of someone whose views he knows to be anti-semitic, he would, of course, have some difficulty in that decision. . .

E.B: But how is one to prove that one is not an anti-semite? How is one to react to insinuations to that effect? Is one expected to make declarations? We are returning here to our point of departure: in our encounters with Jews we always feel gagged. Despite the fundamental difference in historical circumstances, despite the profound shift in the Church's attitude, there exists between us a black hole.

S.K: In order to bring about some change, one must will it and work for it. For my own part, I see my role in challenging the clichés on both side of the divide: to make Poles more aware of the Jewish experience and to persuade Jews that anti-semitism is not of the essence of Polishness.

9

DO NOT SPEAK
FOR ME, PLEASE*

KAZIMIERZ DZIEWANOWSKI

After having read in the 11 January number of *Tygodnik Powszechny* the article by Jan Błoński entitled 'The Poor Poles look at the Ghetto', I had the experience of being faced simultaneously with two contradictory feelings. The first was a sense of relief and satisfaction: at least someone had expressed the thoughts which for a long time had been troubling me as well; at last someone had called a spade a spade and had done what should have been done ages ago and had not got entangled in what is typical for Polish journalism on the subject, the painstaking building-up of defensive walls which obstruct the view of the problem itself. The second feeling was less heartening. It was easy to imagine that Błoński's article would be attacked by his adversaries from various sides. It was easy to foresee what arguments they would use, and how they would strive to prove that we Poles are beyond reproach, and if anybody saw as much as the slightest blemish, such a person could only be our mortal enemy.

One did not have to wait long. Already in the issue of *Tygodnik Powszechny* dated 22 February there appeared an article [chapter 4] by a man who one might have expected to have revealed a deeper understanding of the tragic and confused nature of Polish–Jewish relations, and a better comprehension of what complex ethical problems we touch upon when we attempt to analyse them thoroughly. A man who went through a lot himself, and who, on that score as well as on the score of his

*This article was first published in *Tygodnik Powszechny*, 5 April 1987.

activity up to the present, is held in high esteem by the people. Władysław Siła-Nowicki, however, started his article ('A Reply to Jan Błoński') in the following fashion:

The article, signed by Jan Błoński, published as it was in a journal carrying great weight, may unfortunately be understood as the affirmation and quintessence (unintended of course), of a virulent anti-Polish propaganda campaign conducted endlessly for dozens of years by the enemies not of the government, nor the economic or political system of present-day Poland, but simply of the Polish nation. This article is in my view a very dangerous propagandistic enunciation, and it is regrettable on two scores. One, that it was written by an eminent specialist in literature, and two, that it appeared in a leading Catholic socio-cultural Polish paper.

Actually, after such an introduction, one does not feel like reading the rest. I have quoted it, therefore, not for its polemic value, but out of sadness. It is sad when an eminent counsel for the defence, a man who during his career engaged in many a good cause, uses language which suits him ill. It is not a good phenomenon. But worse is to come as the famous advocate gets entangled in his argument in a manner which now and again goes against the grain of logic, and the style of his utterance becomes difficult to follow. This happens for instance when he strives to explain to us, against logic and all that is obvious, that Miłosz did not write what he wrote, or rather that although he did write it, he did not intend to say what he did say. Not willing to condemn Miłosz as well and count him among the enemies of the Polish nation, barrister Siła-Nowicki tries to convince us that he knows better what the poet had in mind and what he hadn't. The argument gets here rather confused (if I may say so) and this in itself is not surprising, as it is difficult to explain that black is white. I would like to ask the barrister why, if the way in which the normal readers interpret the two poems of the great poet ('Campo di Fiori' and 'A Poor Christian Looks at the Ghetto') is so mistaken and so conflicting with the intentions of the poet, has he been agreeing all these years to have those poems included in all his anthologies? Why did he write them at all? Why did he not exclude them?

Siła-Nowicki writes: 'what strikes one here is that the

interpretation is quite different to that given by the author. Miłosz said that he wrote the poem on the spur of the moment and not as his credo, but for Błoński this means nothing.' Putting aside the question of style, for which one could possibly blame the proofreaders, I would like to ask what it all means. It obviously means only that Miłosz wrote both poems under the pressure of the moment, motivated emotionally, reacting to what he saw, heard and felt. He wrote spontaneously as opposed to sitting at his desk with an intellectual concept and credo in mind. But does this mean that the poems do not express what they do express? And why should we not quote them? If the poet did not wish it, he would have withdrawn, destroyed, or renounced them. But he did not do so. Therefore, I suspect that Siła-Nowicki, in persuading us about Błoński's bad intentions, parted for a moment with common logic.

This, however, is only a side-issue. The essence of Siła-Nowicki's opinions comes to light in two or three other places. He writes:

> Jan Błoński, writing about the extermination of the Jews in Poland, is ashamed of his people. I am proud of my nation's stance in every respect during the period of occupation, and in this include the attitude towards the tragedy of the Jewish nation. Obviously, the attitudes towards the Jews during that period do not give us a particular reason to be proud, but neither are they are grounds for shame, and even less for ignominy. Simply, we could have done relatively little more than we actually did.

Here again the argument does not commit the sin of clarity. Is Siła-Nowicki proud or isn't he? Piling up negatives does not help towards the understanding of his thought. But let's shut our eyes to that. With a little bit of effort, one can draw the conclusion from his text that yes, he is proud, feels good about it and has inner peace. My objection comes from the fact that I do not feel good about this whole matter, nor do I have that inner peace. I simply have not got it. I am of the opinion that too much happened, that the whole thing is too tragic, complicated and ambiguous to feel calm about. Naturally I am only talking about myself. The annihilation of Jews on the Polish territories and the attitude of Poles to that annihilation are problems which I still haven't come to terms with. They trouble me, disturb me and haunt me.

Side by side with Siła-Nowicki's article was placed a very brief and deeply moving text by Ewa Berberyusz, who partly expressed what I mean and did it beautifully. I also saw the same things as she did and felt like she did. When Warsaw was the stage for the events we are talking about, I was first eleven and then twelve years old. I could then, with even more justification than Siła-Nowicki, say that nothing depended on me, that I could do nothing. Nevertheless I am not saying it because I am not fully convinced. Perhaps I could have done something, even a tiny little bit?

If in our country, in our presence and in front of our eyes, several million innocent people were murdered and we were not able to prevent it and save them, this is an event so terrible, a tragedy so enormous, that it is only understandable, human, and proper that those who survived are somehow troubled, disturbed, and cannot find peace. This is why the calmness and good feeling demonstrated by the author of the article who is arguing with Błoński does not satisfy me.

He does not present any convincing arguments, either. At one point he writes that anti-semitism and hatred towards Jews was just a fabrication: 'It did not exist before the war. Perhaps today some irresponsible arguments of small, totally unrepresentative groups could be seen as examples of this hatred.' I dare to be of a different opinion. The largest pre-war political grouping openly included anti-semitism in its programme. Bandying 'national' slogans, they did not understand and did not want to understand that consolidating in world opinion an image of Poland as a country of anti-semites most severely damaged Polish national interests. Remnants of writings from that period, although Siła-Nowicki denies it, exist in every serious academic library in Poland and abroad. I have some also at home: the writings of Roman Dmowski, the declarations of the leaders of ONR, Falanga and related organizations. These remnants are being reanimated also today, a fact that everybody in Warsaw who takes an interest in the matter knows well. It is true that today it really is a product of a defined group, and does not elicit a wide social response. Nevertheless people who engage in these activities count on attracting a response to their 'works', such as used to be the case in the past. It is also a known fact that it was not all that difficult to find in the Polish underground press during the occupation period statements to the effect that although we Poles did not co-operate with the Nazi 'Final Solution' policy, nevertheless Hitler was accomplishing with his own hands what should perhaps be accomplished. The historians of this period have no difficulty in pointing out such publications.

Siła-Nowicki employs yet another argument which in itself is correct and justified, yet does not concern the subject under discussion. He writes:

> the chances of effectively helping the Jews on a large scale were slim. Jewish organizations in the West, particularly in the United States, had incomparably more such possibilities, and thousands of lives could have been saved simply in exchange for money. But those Jews showed passivity and indifference to the terrible plight of their compatriots in the German-occupied territories.

That is what Siła-Nowicki writes and it is true. I am even of the opinion that the guilt of the Allies, and also of the Jews in the USA and Great Britain, is enormous, immeasurable and second only to the guilt of the Nazis themselves. Although it is difficult to compare, nevertheless the indifference, stupidity, and unwillingness to believe the truthful and exact nature of the information passed on to them by the Polish government and the emissaries from our country, especially by Karski, are facts which remain incomprehensible and more terrifying than the indifference of the passengers of the famous merry-go-round about which Miłosz wrote. People in the West had ways and means to oppose the evil; the fools on the merry-go-round did not have them. Had they had them, they would have perhaps behaved differently. This is the reason why today it hurts and rouses indignation when those in the West from their comfortable positions dare to pass judgements on the behaviour of Poles here in German-occupied Poland.

This argument, however, though correct, does not matter much to me. It does not concern me or my nation. It concerns strangers. It is a matter for their consciences, not mine. Too often unfortunately in this type of discussion the argument is used that others were no better. The French, for example, had they found themselves in the circumstances which existed in German-occupied Poland, would probably have behaved not any better and possibly worse. Perhaps it would have been so, but it has not been proved, and what is more, I repeat, it does not concern me. I am interested only in my own conscience.

There is one more argument, which is often used in this kind of discussion, though Siła-Nowicki does not employ it: namely, that in the great reckoning of consciences which should take place between the two nations, between the Poles and the Jews, there is no way in which one can omit the fact that blame lies on both sides. It is a fact that everybody in Poland (except for the youngest perhaps) knows the names of Berman, Rozański and Feigin. And we all know what they meant. We know that it happened more than once that the Poles who sacrificed everything to fight the Nazi occupier and to offer help to the persecuted Jews were later accused of co-operating with the Gestapo by people like the ones mentioned above. We know it all, but in my opinion it does not contribute anything to the discussion of the subject as undertaken by Błoński. Firstly, the events which I mentioned above took place later. Secondly, it is a matter which the Jews themselves should account for, and not a matter which should clear our Polish conscience. The reckoning up of the wrongs and the guilt is not a game with a zero sum at the end. One guilt or one wrong does not cancel out another. In such a reckoning each and every one of them must be examined, weighed, and judged. One cannot explain and justify one by another.

I think therefore that Błoński had the right – and even the duty – to write his article. Like him, I also think that in Poland the Jewish Holocaust and our attitude to that Holocaust were not subjects which we ever discussed through to the end. That we never discussed them to the end was partly our fault and partly not ours. I think it was mainly due to the circumstances in the first years after the war that such a reckoning of conscience should have been attempted but, for various reasons, proved impossible. It was not at all possible at the time to speak the whole truth about the occupation and the war years. Had it been possible then to tell the whole truth of those years, had we been able to speak out with a clear voice, then this matter as well would have been illuminated and discussed fully. This would have been a cleaner and better alternative. But it was not to be. On the contrary, much was done to deepen the mistrust and the bad blood between the two nations. From that time a full understanding came to be more difficult.

Siła-Nowicki attacks Błoński by writing:

> The author talks first about fear, continually using the first person plural: we, we, we. We do not want condemnation, we want to rise above condemnation, we are afraid. But, forgive me, who are 'we'? Everybody has got the right to speak in his own name when he feels called upon to thunder and to lecture – but let him speak in his own name and not in the name of this nation, the [Polish] people.

And I would be willing to agree with Siła-Nowicki if not for what follows. Two sentences further he continues:

> And if Jan Błoński is afraid, this is a matter for him. I am not afraid and neither are, rightly, millions of Poles, though of course none of us is without fault because only God is perfect.

So now let me have my say: I beg your pardon, Sir, but what is the situation? Is everybody to speak for himself, or are there some who are exempted, who have a right to make pronouncements in the name of millions of Poles? I accept: you are at peace, you are not afraid. But I am not. I know, understand, and feel that in this matter which we are discussing, it is impossible to prove that more could have been done, but likewise it is impossible to prove that more could not have been done. Hence my disquietude and fear, which I share with Błoński and also with Ewa Berberyusz, whose article was available to the readers in the same issue. So perhaps there are not only three, but more of us? Nothing to hide – I know that there are things to hide, but I will not refer to them as I cannot prove them. I suggest, however, that you too speak only in your own name and not in that of the millions. In any case, do not speak for me. I feel quite competent in this matter and you must not speak for me. You are a brilliant and worthy defence lawyer, but in this matter, please, do not defend me. Leave it to me.

You write: 'Let no one talk to us, our people, our nation, who fought at the time of the German occupation, about our supposedly unfulfilled moral obligations.' Here you went even further, you speak not only in the names of millions but in the name of the whole society and nation. So also in this respect I suggest politely that, for the sake of principles which you yourself established, you take a more humble stand: speak for yourself. And I will speak for myself.

10

DIFFERING ETHICAL STANDPOINTS*

JERZY JASTRZĘBOWSKI

For a variety of reasons I have high regard for Władysław Siła-Nowicki. But I disagree with the conclusions to his article 'A Reply to Jan Błoński' in *Tygodnik Powszechny* (chapter 4). I agree with most of the arguments put forward by Jan Błoński in 'The Poor Poles Look at the Ghetto' (chapter 2). Speaking with a member of *Tygodnik*'s editorial board I did not hesitate to describe Professor Błoński's article as 'a breakthrough'. Such a breakthrough is nowhere in sight in Siła-Nowicki's interpretation of the subject: undeniable facts, rational arguments, all lead – in my opinion – to missed points. Missed, because he argues from a standpoint which has little to do with Błoński's reasoning as I understand it. Siła-Nowicki argues like a pedigree staff officer who knows that a million people have sometimes to be sacrificed in order for two million to be saved. If, in addition, those million people remain passive and do not seek their own salvation in flight, then why even mention our, Polish, fault? In terms of his own standpoint Siła-Nowicki is right.

The remarkable barrister clearly fails to understand the ethical stance proposed by Jan Błoński. He does not understand that one Judge and one alone will judge the sins which stick like thorns in the consciences of many Christians, and not only in Poland for that matter. Is the misunderstanding caused perhaps by Siła-Nowicki's persistent thinking in terms of 'us Poles'? And not once in terms of 'us Christians'?

*This article was first published in *Tygodnik Powszechny*, 5 April 1987.

It emerges from Siła-Nowicki's argument that his conscience is clear with regard to the tragedy of the Polish Jews during the occupation. I do not question the truth of his statement. Everyone has the right to speak for himself, and so have I. My conscience is not clear although – having been barely five years old at the critical moment – I would not have been able to save 'my Jew'. Since the present young generation reads the discussion following Błoński's article as a spooky take beyond belief, I should like to bring into sharper focus the issue of this half-guilt/half-innocence by citing a personal reminiscence.

I was born two years before the war into a family of hesitantly *Endek* sympathies,[1] a family that would have been outraged if anyone had described it as anti-Semitic. Its dislike of the Jews was merely pragmatic; indeed, it was pragmatic to the point where it accepted without misgivings the ever-present friend of my widowed grandmother as a friend of the household. Eljasz Parzyński had the looks of a *Polish* nobleman with a bushy grey moustache, he spoke beautiful Polish with an eastern accent, spoke German like a Viennese (he had attended a school of commerce there) or like a Swiss gentleman (he had graduated from an institute of technology in Switzerland). He was my family legend: he would recite *Pan Tadeusz*[2] off the cuff, he taught me – a two-year-old toddler – Brzechwa's[3] poems. And if only he had agreed to be baptized he would have been absolutely *comme il faut*. He supported three sisters. Besides them and us he had nobody else.

It must have been 1941 or 1942 when the Warsaw ghetto was being packed to capacity and when only incorrigible optimists could delude themselves as to what fate awaited its inhabitants. One afternoon Grandpa Eli came to our house with the news that he had an hour to decide: either he vanishes from sight on our side or . . .

The conversation, apparently, was brief but dramatic. I know about it from the reluctant disclosures of a long-departed member of the family, many years after the war: 'Of course we agreed to hide him. But he insisted that he could not leave his sisters behind; either they came with him or he went with them to the ghetto.' And as for those sisters, one wore a wig, and all spoke with a giveaway Yiddish accent.

Grandpa Eli stood in the door for a while, then turned away

119

and walked in the direction of the ghetto. We never saw him again. All that remains is a small dog-eared photograph in a family album.

If my family's decision had been different there was a 90 per cent probability that we would have been discovered and executed for hiding Jews. There was probably less than a 10 per cent chance that the family of Eljasz Parzyński could at all be saved *in those conditions*. The person relating this family drama to me said again and again: 'What were we to do?' There was nothing we could do!'. And yet, she did not look me in the eye. She knew I sensed the insincerity of the argument even though the facts were true. It is about such *moral* responsibilities, among other things, that Jan Błoński writes in his superb article. We must not pretend – we who survive and remember – that we do not know what this is all about.

The late Cardinal Kominek would often say that at the Last Judgment the chief sin to be tried will be that of omission because that is the most common sin in the life of the human kind.

If one accepts as correct my assertion that Siła-Nowicki and Błoński pursue their arguments from differing ethical standpoints then my disagreement with the conclusions contained in Siła-Nowicki's article could end right there. There are, however, three other points which I should like to address. I believe that leaving them without rectification would obscure the picture for the reader of *Tygodnik Powszechny*.

1 Siła-Nowicki calls Błoński's dialogue between the imaginary Jew and Pole 'an imaginary dialogue even an obvious lie'. I disagree. I have lived long enough in North America to know that similar dialogues occur every day: in the United States, in Canada, and also in Israel. I know full well that the Pole – unless he wants simply to break off such a dialogue – is unavoidably pushed onto the defensive although a wealth of facts speaks for him. He is pushed there not because he does not know how to argue the points but because such is the power of the *moral* reason.

2 Siła-Nowicki comments on Jan Błoński's essay: 'This article is in my view a very dangerous propagandistic enunciation, and it is regrettable on two scores. One, that it was written

by an eminent specialist in literature, and two, that it appeared in a leading Catholic socio-cultural Polish paper.' Then he goes on to accuse Błoński of speaking 'undoubtedly in good faith but in a language which in its content is the language of Poland's deadly enemies'.

I do not know on what studies of the subject or on what discussions with representatives of world Jewry Siła-Nowicki based these shocking assertions. From fragmentary information in my possession it would appear that the World Jewish Congress, which does not have executive powers but whose voice carries enormous authority precisely because of that, has long been waiting for a convincing signal from Poland, and with no intention whatever of making propaganda capital out of it. Does Siła-Nowicki imagine that a signal – any signal for *moral* reconciliation – would be more convincing if it appeared in *Trybuna Ludu*? And as for 'the language of deadly enemies', Błoński's article and *Tygodnik Powszechny's* initiative do not have to find, or even look for, recognition among the leaders of the Jewish Anti-Defamation League, B'nai B'rith, or the bigoted popular press. This initiative, as I understand it, is designed to find a way to the consciences and hearts of Poles. Only when that happens will we have the right to shrug off anti-Polish attacks with equanimity; only when that happens, not sooner! I express the hope that it is precisely Jan Błoński's article that will set this process in motion by inaugurating the initial phase in a *sui generis* reconciliation of two communities – and more recently two nations as well – which were never at war with each other. I am convinced that the inception of this process will in time take all the wind out of the sails of the 'virulent anti-Polish propaganda' as Siła-Nowicki quite rightly describes this sad phenomenon. Let's not waste the opportunity.

3 In Siła-Nowicki's statement and posture I note an aspect of capital importance, something that in its negation is, in essence, constructive. He writes: 'forgive me, but who are "we"? Everyone has got the right to speak in his own name . . .'.

Siła-Nowicki is right. In a society fighting for the recognition of pluralism, not just in opinion, it is a view that must not be disregarded. It is an indicator that a publicist, however talented, or an editorial team, however competent and credible, will not be strong enough – if acting alone – to carry a cause so responsible and so sensitive as that of Jewish–Polish reconciliation. It is clear that the author or authors of *Tygodnik Powszechny's* excellent initiative are under no illusions. In future the participation of a greater collective moral authority will be needed in this work. There has been a precedent. It caused a storm at the time but the initiative developed favourably. Can the reconciliation of Jews with Poles be more difficult than the reconciliation of Poles with Germans? Who knows . . .

NOTES

1 Endek, from Endecja – a nationalistic right-wing anti-Jewish party.
2 Pan Tadeusz – a Polish national epic.
3 Jan Brzechwa – an immensely popular author of children's poems.

11

IN A SENSE I AM AN ANTI-SEMITE*

JANINA WALEWSKA

Having read Jan Błoński's article, I intended to write a letter to the Editor, but now, having read the subsequent contributions to the discussion, in particular by Siła-Nowicki and Ewa Berberyusz, I have resolved to write an article, even at the risk that it will contain no revelations. Yet, perhaps I shall manage to say something of essence, since I have thought about these matters a great deal and for a long time.

In a sense, I am an anti-semite. This is not my fault; it is how I was brought up. I still cannot understand how those nearest to me, endowed with sincere and strong beliefs, are unable to perceive the moral aspect of this issue, but see exclusively its socio-political context. For the greater part of my life, I was also blind to this moral aspect. I never thought about it thoroughly or in any depth and I excluded it from my mind. Yet some years ago I came to understand. From that time on, I began to struggle against anti-semitism within myself and within others (though I am not sure whether this struggle of mine has been fully sincere and uninterrupted).

I am 'torn' in two and I conduct a continuous discourse within myself. I am divided between two attitudes, one close to the attitude of Siła-Nowicki and the other to that of Błoński. On the one hand, I think that the Jews, as an entity, a nation, a national minority (the Great Quantifier!) have on their conscience many sins against the Polish people and that this has been a

*This article was first published in *Tygodnik Powszechny*, 5 April 1987.

123

contributing factor in the frequent eruption of Polish anti-semitism. (If anti-semitism can be considered in the words of Siła-Nowicki: 'For me it is natural that society defends itself against numerical domination of its intelligentsia. . . by an alien intelligentsia'.)

On the other hand, I well understand and accept the moral side of the problem (in a sense against myself) and the views of Jan Błoński and like-minded people on our Polish guilt and moral responsibility. In the innumerable debates on this question, I take first one side then another. More often, I take Błoński's position, because it is deeper and more Christian, though such an attitude is, probably, not fully sincere and is something of an imposition upon myself. Taking part in these discussions, my words are extreme, as I try to be as convincing as possible in expressing the view that we shall never solve the questions of Polish–Jewish relations and anti-semitism without putting them on the moral plane. Probably, we will not solve them at all, just as, till the end of the world, we will not solve the question of evil. I know that I should add: 'We will not solve them without God', but I am not enough a Christian to prevent such words sounding artificial.

In general, I encounter debaters who are also blinded by passion and that prevents us from coming to a true understanding of the matter. I am either condemned for anti-semitism when I try cautiously to air my doubts, or I am ridiculed for my 'idealism' when I attempt to take an attitude close to Błoński's. Only rarely and with very few persons am I able to talk quietly. This shows how painful and controversial the subject is.

Mostly, however, I carry out a debate within myself, though in the knowledge that there is no common ground for debate between the two attitudes, both quite sincere: that which I symbolically call Błoński's attitude, founded on a spiritual, moral and very Christian plane; and the other, here symbolically called Siła-Nowicki's attitude, based on a legal–sociological foundation, which, of course, does not make it an immoral attitude.

And more: I do believe that Błoński is able to understand Siła-Nowicki, as he adopts a standpoint which is above haggling over details and looking for mitigating circumstances, which makes his standpoint broader and deeper. Siła-Nowicki, however, is quite clearly incapable of understanding Błoński, as he proceeds from a legal–factual starting point. I would not dare to make charges against Siła-Nowicki, knowing what a righteous, honest and uncompromising man he is. Insignificant and cowardly as I am, I do not feel I have the right to criticize. But, on the other hand, Siła-Nowicki is not alone in his views. I remember a discussion on the film *Shoah* in the Warsaw KIK.[1] It took place after the debates on television and after the appearance of the judicious review by Jerzy Turowicz in the columns of *Tygodnik Powszechny*. A member of the discussion panel, Father Jacek Salij, spoke words which were fully consonant with the spirit in which Jan Błoński's article was written: for him the significance of the Polish (or, rather, as I would argue, anti-Polish) fragments of the film was unimportant in comparison with the shocking meaning conveyed by the film as a whole. He so deeply moved by the work itself and its theme, the destruction of the Jewish people, that in his view all our charges and reproaches against the makers of the film must be set aside.

I am aware that my summary of Father Salij's views is clumsy, but that was exactly its sense. I personally trust Father Salij without any doubts, and all his words are 'holy' to me. Consequently, I have repeated them with admiration, in front of persons more 'factually' inclined, and I have had to face their anger. They hold that every Pole has the duty to defend the truth and fight against unjust accusations. Hence, if the attitude of Father Salij is different, his attitude is 'anti-Polish' and he himself becomes a 'controversial personality'. These are the same accusations that Siła-Nowicki directs against Błoński. It proved impossible for me to convey to my opponents the view that their line of reasoning rests on a different plane from that of Father Salij.

As the editors of *Tygodnik Powszechny* have confirmed, Błoński's article has given rise to much controversy. I have witnessed this on a number of occasions. In one discussion, where calm and good will prevailed, questions were asked: why should we ask Jews for forgiveness; for what reasons; would this not be excessive? My answer to these questions was that we should, perhaps, say, in the spirit expressed by Primate Wyszyński in his memorable letter to the German bishops in 1965: 'We forgive and ask for forgiveness'. That was before I learned the contents of Błoński's article. Having read it, I came to the conclusion that I was wrong. We can only say: 'We ask for forgiveness'. Nothing else. Because it is we who want to be cleansed and, therefore, if we do feel guilty (as I do, independently of my other 'I' that keeps reminding me of the Jewish wrongs), we must ask to be forgiven. My anti-semitism somehow revolts against this view, but that which revolts in me is always worse and inferior and is opposed to the clear commands of Christianity. How can one justify that, while we have said to the Germans, 'we forgive and ask for forgiveness', to the Jews we must say: 'we ask your forgiveness'? Because the wrongs which we suffered at the hands of the Germans were incomparably greater than those done to us by Jews. There is, therefore, a great deal to forgive the Germans for. What about the Jews? Well, wrongs had been committed by both sides and the correlation is not so simple as in the case of Germans. To put it simply, there are many reasons for not remembering the wrongs committed against us by the Jews, even in the form 'we forgive'. The Germans are not such a tragic nation as the Jews. The Jewish people have suffered a terrible destruction, have been branded with the mark of martyrdom. This should produce among us a state of inhibition and even fear, which should prevent us from airing our sorrows and grudges and should make us feel their impropriety. It is easier to forget about them in the face of human beings, and a nation, that have gone through so much suffering.

Towards the Germans our guilt is, first and foremost, hatred. This, surely, is an evil that destroys more those who hate than the hated. But our hatred of the Germans has expressed itself in words rather than in deeds. It was also, as I see it, more of a spontaneous, uncontrolled reaction to German crimes than 'cold hatred'. It was a desire for retaliation and revenge. This is supported by many facts. For example, during the Warsaw Uprising wounded Germans were placed in the hospitals of the Polish insurgents. That hatred played a role as an element of struggle; it was a stimulus to fight.

Our sins against the Jews are certainly much greater and more terrible: a great deal of hardened malice, burdening the Jews with responsibility for all the evils affecting Poland, contempt, indifference – all having a share of responsibility for the persecution of the Jewish people. This is the responsibility which

Błoński refers to and it is primarily moral in its nature; though at times it manifested itself in brutal facts: for example *szmalcownictwo*,[2] or the pogrom in Kielce in the post-war period.

It is clear that this did not affect all, but only some Poles. It is also clear that some extreme occurrences, for example participation in the murder of Jewish people, were exceptional. However, if we treat the Jews as an entity, Poles too must be treated in the same way.

These are very difficult and sad matters. Our mutual wrongs result from a centuries-old, swollen and painful knot of historical, sociological and religious factors. This knot has been fairly and honestly described in Siła-Nowicki's article. It is no longer possible to establish 'who started it', 'who is the guilty party', or who is responsible for what had happened. However, if we desire to break that vicious circle, we must suppress our sorrows; considering our consciousness of the terrible fate which has befallen the Jewish people, we must ponder upon our own guilt and we must ask for forgiveness.

There is one more aspect to this question, in a sense a 'practical' one. I remember the indignation of many people directed against Primate Wyszyński after his letter to German bishops: 'For what are we to apologize?' 'How does the Primate dare to speak in the name of the whole nation?' Yet that letter began the renewal of Polish–German relations, characterized by honesty and based on a spiritual foundation. It was a turning point, which broke the ice. Something has changed from the inside. Therefore we have at our disposal a tangible fact (for the 'Polish–German thaw' is a fact), a 'practical' consideration which justifies an appeal as unpopular as 'let us ask for forgiveness' – at a time when our own hearts and heads were overflowing with sorrow and grief.

Yes, Błoński's article is marvellous in its Christian grasp of these difficult matters. As far as I am personally concerned, I found in this article many of my own reflections and feelings, not yet formulated, perhaps still hidden in my subconscious. Possibly Błoński exaggerated at some points, pitching his writing at the 'high diapason' in which it was composed. Siła-Nowicki points out a number of such exaggerations. It is clear that Siła-Nowicki and persons thinking like him have the right to raise painful and difficult problems in which Polish–Jewish relations have abounded, if only for the sake of historical truth.

Siła-Nowicki reproaches Błoński for his acceptance of the indictment of 'vicious' Polish anti-semitism. But Błoński is right. There existed in Poland, and still exists, an anti-semitism which manifested itself quite frequently, too frequently: a 'virulent' variant and an innocent, mild variant. Jokes, nicknames such as *Żydek*, *Żydówa*, *Żydy*, and so on. Seemingly of no importance, they are an expression of a hurtful contempt. It is the case that people who used such expressions before the war sometimes risked their lives during the German occupation to save those very *Żydki* they ridiculed. But Jews, those who were protected and saved, found it hard to forget the contempt shown to them in the past. I know from experience the bitter taste of help, rendered with utmost risk, but seasoned with aversion, ridicule, irritation, and other similar 'ingredients'.

We Poles reproach the Jews: 'How is it that we, the Polish people taken as an entity, tried to save Jewish people, taking risks, dying for you, and yet we are censured because we saved only a few, because we are anti-semitic, because of this and that?' Yes, this is our bitterness and we are not able to free ourselves from it. This is psychologically most comprehensible. However, we must also try to understand the sorrows and bitterness of the Jews, which are also psychologically comprehensible. Błoński raises exactly these points. In my view, studies should appear which will throw light on these matters from various angles. (An example of such a study is Turowicz's review of *Shoah* in *Tygodnik Powszechny* on 10 November 1985.) This must be done for the sake of discovering historical truth and for the sake of refuting unjust accusations.

It is also my view that we have the undisputed right to repudiate accusations which are the product of political or propagandist aims and which are clearly malicious. In particular, we might instance accusations that come from abroad and from people who have never been in Poland and do not know these matters, at least not from the inside.

But we should not fight back against people who reproach us out of genuine feeling, those who still suffer from old wounds, those who despite the many reproaches against the Polish people still retain feelings of loyalty and, despite all, friendliness. Let me quote a particular example: Dr Marek Edelman. I remember a meeting with him in the Warsaw KIK. There was a lot of noise, arguing, questions flying, badly formulated views aired from the 'Polish side'; grudges hanging in the air. I remember my own irritation at much of what he said. And, yet, he expressed what he felt at the time: 'I was young, I wanted to fight, I was in a rage that the AK[3] would not give us arms.' That is also how this man feels now; he is still incapable of cool analysis.

My remarks above are only loosely connected with the question of anti-semitism in Poland, because I do not consider that when Jews accuse Poles of not rendering help or even of taking part in the murders, and when this meets with Polish resentment, that this resentment should be described as anti-semitism. It is just another link in the fatal chain of Polish–Jewish relations. (Besides, not all the Jews accuse us: the book by Bartoszewski and Lewin, *Ten jest z ojczyzny mojej* provides ample proof.[4]) Nevertheless, I have made the above observations to achieve a fuller picture.

It is an undeniable fact that anti-semitism continues to exist and that there are publications, lectures and pronouncements filled with hatred, or at least aversion; they are often deceptive, full of stupidity and narrow fanaticism. This does exist; I have experienced it myself, despite what Siła-Nowicki claims. It is possible that the groups of people involved are really small and that they are detached from the bulk of the nation, that these nationalist circles are deprived of influence on the wider strata of the population and find no echo. But is such a diagnosis correct? From my own observation, the methods of activity of these 'small groups', as Siła-Nowicki calls them, and of these circles are thoroughly premeditated, their manner of action is ingenious and cunning, and I am not certain that they are not echoed more widely, in particular among the younger generation.

Did Polish society at the time of occupation descend into 'savagery'? Błoński writes: 'the terror, unimaginable today, of life under the German occupation and a certain moral degradation of society . . . not just Polish [society]'. This is probably an exaggeration, at least in the region of *facts*. Not everybody became 'degraded'; perhaps the *szmalcownicy*, but not the nation as a whole. There were people who drew material advantages from hiding Jews, yet who would not deliver them into the hands of the Germans. They were not acting in accordance with the

Christian command of loving your neighbour; but could that be branded as 'savagery'? *Szmalcownicy* were the rare exception. I wish to stress that I am here discussing the sphere of facts and acts and not that of moral, internal attitudes. In this latter sphere, matters were worse and I admit that Błoński is partly in the right; but only partly. From whatever angle one looks, the 'savagery' thesis does not apply to the whole Polish society, as one might infer from Błoński's words. In this respect, Siła-Nowicki is right in his insistence that we ought not to take *pars pro toto*, as this would amount to a lie. This is an unintentional wrong which Błoński has done the Polish people. It is a very serious and unjust accusation, directed by a Pole at other Poles, of whom so many perished in defence of Jewish people.

Siła-Nowicki is indignant at Błoński's view that the Poles came close to the crime of genocide. Siła-Nowicki may be right. Possibly, considering that deeds did not follow words, Błoński attaches too much weight to the pre-war fanatical anti-semitic pronouncements. In Błoński's view, the Poles came to their senses only at the last moment. In my view, it is not that Poles 'at the last moment came to realize what a satanic enterprise it was', but that Nazi crimes made them aware what anti-semitism could lead to. They had no intention in their hearts, either before the war or, even less, at the time of the occupation, of exterminating Jews. The frightful fate of both peoples during the occupation persuaded many to acts of solidarity with Jews, because they were still Christian in some measure, and were perfectly aware of the Nazis' satanic methods. And there were many Poles who were 'very' Christian, risking their lives and perishing in defence of Jews. Of course, if all Poles had always been 'very' Christian, anti-semitism would not have existed, nor indifference towards the Jewish tragedy, nor the division into 'them' and 'us'. Nor would there have existed that state of moral savagery, described by Błoński, which though only expressed minimally in participation in acts of extermination, affected many Poles on the spiritual plane. In this respect Błoński is right: we are Christian, on the whole, but only 'a little' Christian.

However, Błoński's fear that we came close to the crime of genocide, much too grave an accusation against the Poles which struck Siła-Nowicki so painfully, escaped my notice when I read Błoński's article for the first time. Reading it then, I was moved and agitated. I was captured by its fundamental, beautiful and noble train of thought. I was reminded of my own sins. Not the sins cited by Ewa Berberyusz. These I was spared by accident. Yet I am well aware how I would have reacted in similar circumstances: looking at Jewish children in need of help, I would have certainly run away from them, as far as possible.

I have, however, on my conscience a much worse guilt, which was not, perhaps, a result of anti-semitism, but of insufficient religious upbringing, of which, at the time, neither I nor those close to me were fully aware. (We are insufficiently, only 'a little' Christian!) That guilt of mine, which bordered on cruelty, was my indifference to the Jewish fate. I was completely indifferent to the human beings who were perishing in the ghetto. They were 'them' and not 'us'. I saw the smoke from the burning ghetto, I listened to what was happening there, but – it concerned 'them'. Perhaps, this was 'self-defence', an escape from the horrors of the occupation. But it was not just that. Other girls of my age behaved in the same way, with indifference, having also received only a superficial religious education.

I believe that already at that time my conscience, without my being fully aware of it, was reproaching me for my feelings towards the perishing Jewish people, perishing human beings! Otherwise, I would not have remembered it so well. How could this have happened in a Christian society?

Yet, I would like to explain something. (Perhaps, to find justification in Jewish eyes?) I would like to repeat: my attitude, which I described above, towards the 'strangers' then perishing, terrible and unchristian as it was, was by no means an expression of anti-semitism. I reacted similarly in other cases when, in accordance with the division into 'us' and 'them', I placed in the 'them' category human groups other than Jews.

I also remember the behaviour of people when, in turn, I found myself among the hunted. After the Warsaw Uprising of 1944, I and my mother were thrown out of Warsaw and we heard the following exchange: 'Are they catching people?' 'No, only Varsovians'.

Błoński affirms the guilt Poles bear for their passive behaviour and their insufficient effort to resist, but not for participation in the crime of genocide. During the Week of Jewish Culture, Bartoszewski, in a lecture or in the course of a discussion, rightly said: 'Only he has done enough for another human being who sacrificed his life for him.' More could have been done. But are we, all of us, capable of the heroism described by Bartoszewski? Only such heroism would have constituted 'enough'.

Błoński maintains: this shared responsibility, through failure to act, is the less crucial part of the problem we are considering.' (He means, if I understand it rightly, the question of our responsibility in general.) He explains: 'More significant is the fact that if only in the past we had behaved more humanely, had been wiser, more generous [more Christian in spirit] . . . genocide would perhaps have been "less imaginable", would probably have been considerably more difficult to carry out, and almost certainly would have met with much greater resistance than it did.' In other words, the people who witnessed such events, would not have become infected with indifference and savagery.

These are saintly words. Siła-Nowicki is indignant about them and confronts them with indubitable facts, but he does it only on his own plane of reasoning. Of course the Poles could not have rendered more aid to Jews, because, in reality, they did only as much as they were capable of doing. Not everybody is capable of heroic acts. The results would have been the same, even if the Poles loved the Jews, even if the pre-war relations between the two peoples had been incomparably better.

After all, the Poles, despite the underground struggle, despite the solidarity of the whole nation, were not able to rescue the prisoners of Auschwitz, or save Warsaw from burning out during the uprising. And so, on the plane of facts, arguments could be exchanged interminably. Of course, on this plane Siła-Nowicki is right and he is entitled to voice his views as a person who lived through those times, who witnessed it all with his own eyes and fought.

However, when one enters the plane of Błoński's article, when one grasps its deepest sense and the issue which provided the impulse to what he wrote, then everything appears in a different light. Błoński will never be accepted, unless that plane is understood and accepted. This comprehension cannot be absorbed through the medium of words alone, it can only be arrived at in some supra-intellectual dimension. It has to be accepted or rejected, and no amount of discussion can bridge the gap between the two positions.

I know, I well know, what Błoński had in mind: we are responsible for the destruction of the Jewish people as we are responsible for the continuous wars, for moral depravity, for all the evils of the world. Because we are all (all mankind – this ceases to be a problem of anti-semitism or Polish–Jewish relations) interconnected vessels, collectively responsible for the sum of good and evil in the world. In the realm of facts, we are not responsible, or rather less responsible. (If I did my utmost, I could not save the blacks in South Africa, I could not stop the fighting in Lebanon, nor even reduce alcoholism in Poland.) I think that is what Mickiewicz had in mind writing in his *Księgi Narodu i Pielgrzymstwa Polskiego*:[5] 'To the degree that you will magnify and improve your souls, you will improve your rights and magnify your frontiers.' And these are not empty words.

NOTES

1 KIK – Klub Inteligencji Katolickiej (Club of Catholic Intelligentsia).
2 *Szmalcownictwo* – the practice, during the German occupation, of blackmailing Jews hiding among 'Aryans', robbing them of valuables under threat of denunciation to the Gestapo. *Szmalcownik* – a person perpetrating it.
3 AK – Armia Krajowa (Home Army), the Polish underground army during the German occupation.
4 *Ten jest z ojczyzny mojej* (*He Who Is from my Fatherland*) – a book giving a factual account of activities aiming to hide and save Jews, undertaken by Polish individuals and groups. Published in 1968.
5 Adam Mickiewicz, *The Books of the Polish Nation and of Pilgrimage*, published in 1832, reprinted in Adam Mickiewicz, *Powieści poetyckie*, ed. W. Floryan, Warsaw, 1983; vol. 2, pp. 209–262.

12

POLISH REASONS AND JEWISH REASONS*

JERZY TUROWICZ

No other subject we have dealt with in the columns of our paper has provoked such a strong reaction from our readers as the subject of Polish–Jewish relations and, in particular, the problem of Polish society's attitude to the Jewish Holocaust perpetrated on Polish soil during the Second World War. Following the publication of Jan Błońksi's article [chapter 2] and later the articles by Stanisław Salmonowicz, Ewa Berberyusz and Stanisław Siła-Nowicki [chapters 3, 4 and 5], we have received nearly 200 letters and articles. The majority of these expressed views critical of Błoński's argument; but there were among them also voices in support of it. Some people expressed surprise that our paper had agreed to publish Siła-Nowicki's article! Let me make it clear right from the beginning that – just as the voices of our readers have revealed such a wide diversity of opinion – we, who have always been committed to the idea of the plurality of viewpoints, deemed it right and proper to publish the work of someone whose views are diametrically opposite to those of Professor Błoński.

This does not mean that our newspaper (or the writer of these words) does not have our own opinions in this matter; we have opinions which we shall now attempt to express. But before I proceed to do so, let me add that among those many letters and articles which we have received there were many just and reasonable contributions well deserving publication. Lack of space allows us to publish only a small proportion of them. In our last issue, we printed a valuable study by Teresa Prekerowa

*This article was first published in *Tygodnik Powszechny*, 5 April 1987.

assessing the available data concerning the number of Jews whose lives were saved by Poles during the German occupation. In this current issue of *Tygodnik Powszechny*, the reader will find articles by Kazimierz Dziewanowski, Jerzy Jastrzębowski, Janina Walewska and also an interview by Ewa Berberyusz with Stanisław Krajewski. With this we are closing the discussion for the moment. It seems likely, however, that we shall be coming back to this subject many times in the future.

The arguments of those who disagree with Jan Błoński can be roughly summarized as follows: it was not only Jews, but Poles also who were killed during the German occupation; we had to save our own lives; in so far as it was possible, we did try to help and succeeded in saving some Jewish lives. Our conscience is, therefore, clear. After the Germans, the next to shoulder the blame should be the Western Allies who abandoned the Jews of Central and Eastern Europe. Some of our correspondents go so far as to claim that there was no anti-semitism in Poland; and, if it existed, it was justified. They are of the opinion that on the whole *Tygodnik Powszechny* is giving too much space to these problems which are no longer with us in Poland today. The matter should, therefore be considered closed, once and for all.

It is not my intention here to try to defend the case put forward by Jan Błoński, whose article I consider not only right but also very timely. Neither am I able, in the space of one article, to define precisely my position in relation to the whole of this vast, complicated and difficult subject of Polish–Jewish relations. I would like nevertheless to take a very clear and unambiguous stand on a few basic points.

As for the argument: 'We were also being killed.' We must not make an equation between the fate of Jews and the fate of Poles in the Second World War. Nobody is further than I am from the intention of denying or undervaluing the extent of Polish suffering during the years of the German occupation. Poles died by their thousands in concentration camps and in the Gestapo prisons; a great many were shot as hostages. The proportionate losses of the Polish population were, in relation to those of other countries occupied by Hitler, the highest. But the 3 million Poles who lost their lives during the war were not just victims of the Nazi terror. This figure includes also people who died in battle, in various theatres of war, as well as in the Warsaw Uprising, and those who died at non-German hands. These 3 million represent about 10 per cent of the then Polish population. In contrast, the 3 million Polish Jews who died as victims of the 'Final Solution' represent more than 95 per cent of the Jewish community of our country.

But it is not the numerical proportions which matter here most; the difference between the fates of Poles and Jews during the war years is also qualitative. If Poles were dying in great numbers as victims of the Nazi terror, it was because of the German desire to subjugate the Polish nation and to crush its resistance. In the case of Jews, it is the entire Jewish nation which was, by Hitler's decree, sentenced to death. Every Jew, whether old man or new-born baby, man or woman, was condemned to death solely because they were Jewish. This decision was systematically implemented: the Jews from the ghettos were gradually transported to the death camps; those who lived outside, in 'freedom', risked their lives every day.

Some say that Poles were to suffer the same fate, that they were 'next for the gas'. No, this is not completely true. Undoubtedly, in the event of Hitler's victory, our fate would have been more than grim. Everybody knows that it was Hitler's design to kill off the Polish intelligentsia, and that the rest of the population was to be deported to the territories annexed by Hitler or to be used as slave labour in the service of the *Herrenvolk*. But all this still does not amount to a decision to exterminate the entire nation. Jews are right when they look upon this attempt at the extermination of the whole Jewish nation (and insist that others should also do so) as something unique in the history of mankind. They are right when they divide their own history into the times before and after the Holocaust.

The next problem: the problem of Polish anti-semitism. We all know that Jews had been settled in Poland for centuries, having been brought there by our kings and given many privileges, or having fled there from persecution in Western Europe. We are rightly proud of our tolerance. But this does not alter the fact that in the nineteenth and especially in the twentieth century anti-semitism in Poland existed and was on the increase. Some of our correspondents complain that we have not given a definition of what we mean by anti-semitism. This seems a rather strange objection. I can understand that young people, born after 1945, may not be very clear what anti-semitism is. But older people, those who remember Poland before the war, surely have no difficulty in identifying it. In any case, it is not difficult to give a definition of anti-semitism. It is simply a dislike of a particular ethnic group, a dislike of varying degrees of intensity, in its extreme form manifesting itself as enmity and hatred. This feeling is directed towards *all* Jews, including those who have assimilated or are in the process of assimilation. Let us add that anti-semitism, as we understand it, is not merely the dislike itself but all the consequences resulting from it. These may take diverse forms, ranging from general attitudes to concrete legal discriminations which found practical expression in such acts as segregation, boycott, and so on.

Can one really claim that there was either none or hardly any anti-semitism in Poland, or deny as Mr Siła-Nowicki does – that it significantly increased in the 1930s? The main springboards of anti-semitism were the political programmes spearheaded by the right-wing associations such as the National Party (*Endecja*) and the Camp for a Greater Poland closely allied with it, as well as the All Polish Youth, the *Falanga* and the National Radical Camp. To some degree, the anti-semitism of these political groupings was incorporated into the programme of the *Sanacja*[1], after Piłsudski's death, in the last years before the outbreak of the war. The opposition to this anti-semitic programme came from the left wing and democratic political groupings as well as from some circles of the Catholic intelligentsia. It remains, however, a fact that anti-semitism as such had a wide social base in Poland. Evidence of this can be found in the sizeable literature and journalism of that time, including – regrettably – certain sections of the Catholic press, such publications as *Mały Dziennik*, published in Niepokalanów.

Without aspiring to a scholarly analysis of the subject, one can point to three main sources of anti-semitism in Poland. The first was the economic factor, namely the competition arising from the important role which the Jewish population played in industry and especially in trade. The second would appear to have been a specific form of xenophobia, a dislike of people who were perceived as 'aliens', people of different custom and dress, different culture and religion, partly also having a different

137

language. The third source was, of course, religious: attributing to Jews, all Jews, even contemporaries, responsibility for the death of Jesus. This was often bound up with the groundless accusations levelled against Jews of carrying out ritual murders.

While questioning Jan Błoński's contention that, as a result of anti-semitism in inter-war Poland, Jews were 'second-class citizens', our correspondents speak of the relative affluence of certain sections of the Jewish community and of the disproportionate representation of Jews in the professions, such as law or medicine. Well, nobody would claim that they made bad lawyers or doctors, and their 'high profile' in these professions may have something to do with the fact that they were barred from others. It may, however, be salutary to look at the problem through Jewish eyes. Here they were, having lived in this land for generations, looking upon Poland as their country – as they had no other to call theirs – and every day they met with resentment or even contempt, sometimes outright hatred. Their children were harassed at school by Polish children; they saw slogans such as 'Jews, go to Madagascar'; they witnessed the introduction of measures such as the *numerus clausus* and the 'ghetto bench' at universities; from time to time they were witnesses (and victims) of anti-Jewish demonstrations which ended fatally for some of them, even though – thank God! – these were not pogroms on the scale of those which took place in Tsarist Russia or in Romania. Can one be surprised that – given all this – Jews felt themselves to be 'second-class citizens'? Is it not only natural that these conditions weakened their loyalty towards the Polish state and society, but also strengthened their solidarity and loyalty towards their own community?

The strongest protests, even indignation, of our correspondents were directed at Błoński's contention that Poles ought to feel a sense of shared guilt for the Holocaust. One has to say outright that some of it may be due to a misunderstanding. Jan Błoński's arguments and those of his opponent, Władysław Siła-Nowicki, are conducted on totally different planes. Błoński states quite clearly that we Poles do not bear any responsibility for the genocide of Jews which took place on our soil. I suspect the misunderstanding has arisen because he does not formulate his thesis clearly enough. He certainly overstates his case when he asserts that if we did not take part in the genocide of Jews it was only because 'we were still Christians' and because 'God held back our hand'. This is a serious accusation, unjust and misguided. I strongly contend that – despite everything – the likelihood of our participation in the crime of genocide did not exist. But this is not to say that the problem of a shared guilt does not arise.

Firstly, I would like to make a few remarks about the problem of saving Jewish lives during the occupation. One must remember that in the specific conditions of the Nazi occupation of Poland, which were incomparably more difficult than those in any West European country occupied by Hitler, the scale of assistance offered to Jews was impressive. We have nothing to be ashamed of when we compare it with similar efforts mounted in the West. In the last issue of *Tygodnik Powszechny*, Teresa Prekerowa gave a very well documented account of just how widespread this action was;[2] personally, I have doubts whether, for the sake of scholarly accuracy, she does not minimize the numbers of those involved. If one counted all the nuns who hid Jewish children in convents; people who issued Jews with 'Aryan' papers; parish priests who produced false certificates of baptism; people who acted as guides for those in hiding when they had to move; would not the number of those involved – directly or indirectly – in the action of helping Jews be a lot higher? But as for the question whether we could do more: Władysław Bartoszewski, whom we all know as a man deeply and effectively involved in these activities, once said that only he who paid for what he did with his own life could claim that he was not able to do more. It remains beyond doubt that even if, in the most auspicious circumstances, it might perhaps have been possible to save twice as many Jewish lives as were saved, the overwhelming majority did not have a chance of survival and had to die. Let me add that during the German occupation the average Pole had neither an occasion nor an opportunity to assist Jews in their plight.

There is no need to repeat here the obvious and unquestioned truth that the whole responsibility for the Holocaust is to be borne by Nazi Germany. Not a small part of the blame for not helping Jews must be laid at the door of the Western Allies and one can even point to certain sections of the Jewish community in the West which did have some chance of resisting the 'Final Solution'. This problem is discussed in the current issue of

Tygodnik Powszechny by Kazimierz Dziewanowski (chapter 9). We shall deal here only with what concerns us Poles.

So what about this shared guilt which Poles – according to Professor Błoński – should be ready to accept? Our correspondents write : 'We do not feel guilty'; and, in principle, they are right. If there is need for an examination of the individual conscience, only those who committed an unjust deed or failed to do what was just should feel guilty. The question of collective guilt or collective responsibility is quite another matter.

Now, it may be appropriate to make a few comments of a theoretical nature in connection with this problem of the collective responsibility of Germans for Hitler's crimes, a problem so hotly debated in the first years after the war. (Please, do not assume that I am making a parallel between the responsibility of the Germans and that of the Poles!)

It is obvious that the *legal* responsibility for the Nazi crimes must rest with the direct perpetrators of them, the SS, the Gestapo, and the higher echelons of the Nazi Party. But the collective *moral* responsibility has to be, rightly, considered that of the whole German nation. It was, after all, German society which had given power to Hitler in free, democratic elections, in the full knowledge of what it might lead to, as Hitler's programme formulated in *Mein Kampf* was widely known and freely available. It is only those who actively opposed Hitler who can consider themselves free from the moral responsibility for the Nazi crimes.

Now I return to the Polish debate, by repeating emphatically that I am not making the slightest comparison between the responsibility that the Germans must bear and what Błoński calls our shared guilt. This guilt has to do almost exclusively with the fact of Polish anti-semitism. At this point, once again, there is need for a qualification: there is no *direct* connection between Polish anti-semitism and the Jewish Holocaust. It is not true – as we have pointed out many times before in *Tygodnik Powszechny* – that the Nazis located death camps in Poland because the Poles were anti-semites. They were placed there because this was where the greatest concentration of Jewish population happened to be; also, because Poland was separated by the Reich from the West from which Germans were hiding their plans for the extermination of Jews. Those who handed over Jews into

German hands (in Poland as elsewhere) need not have been necessarily anti-semitic; they were simple criminals. It is also well known that, on occasions, Polish anti-semites actively helped Jews.

Secondly, the Nazis directed their hatred not only to the Jews, but also to people known to be active Christians, as they were well aware of the link between Christianity and Judaism. Therefore, the anti-semitism of the Nazis, which was racist and pagan in inspiration, was very different from Polish anti-semitism.

All this, however, does not mean that there is no *indirect* connection between Polish anti-semitism and the Jewish Holocaust. Hitler's devilish plan for the physical extermination of the entire Jewish nation was a culmination, the final conclusion of the anti-semitism which had been established for centuries in Europe and elsewhere. This anti-semitism was propagated, we have to admit with regret, by Christian churches, including the Catholic Church. Church historians know all too well the long story of discrimination and persecution which Jews were subjected to on religious grounds; they know of the contempt with which Jews had to contend, of the unceasing attempts at their conversion. In fact, the attitude of the Catholic Church to the Jews has effectively changed only in our own century, owing to the efforts of recent Popes and the Second Vatican Council.

Our Polish guilt has, therefore, to do with anti-semitism. Karl Jaspers is reported to have said that, before the Holocaust, anti-semitism was merely a wrong political doctrine; after the Holocaust, it became a crime. Those among us who have never been anti-semites and who may even have fought against it, cannot nevertheless absolve ourselves totally from the collective moral responsibility for the anti-semitism which was so widespread in our country.

If we had not had such anti-semitism in Poland before the war, perhaps we would still have been unable to save many more Jewish lives, but our attitude to their extermination, which was taking place before our eyes, would have been different. We would not have had that sometimes very evident, indifference, or those inhuman and unchristian responses of the type: 'Hitler has solved the Jewish question for us!'

Pre-war Polish anti-semitism did not disappear during the

occupation, although the experience of it, which was to some extent shared by the two nations, brought forth also attitudes and deeds of solidarity. Tragically, this anti-semitism raised its head again, and quite violently, in the first months after the war, when those few Jews who managed to survive made an attempt to claim back what was theirs. It is horrifying to think that anti-Jewish violence was still possible after the experience of the Holocaust. This anti-semitism, albeit much reduced, is still with us, even though we have practically no Jews left. It is a great pity that a serious discussion on the subject of Polish–Jewish relations did not take place much earlier; it is good that it is taking place now. To talk about these things is not a form of masochism, as some seem to suggest. Several million innocent people, including women, children, and the old, people who were our neighbours, were murdered before our eyes, on our soil, and we were helpless witnesses, unable for the most part to do anything about it. This fact is so horrifying that we cannot ever forget it, nor can we fail to ask ourselves whether this does not still present a moral challenge to us.

And may I suggest that it is at least insensitive – to avoid a stronger term – to accuse the Jews of being passive, when we consider their fate.

Poles, in the overwhelming majority, are members of the Catholic Church. We are Christians, Catholics, or at least this is what we consider ourselves to be.

Therefore, we should know that the Church considers anti-semitism a social sin, that it has decisively turned its back on its own past in this respect. We should know the Church declaration as stated in *Nostra aetate*, which firmly rejects blaming Jews for the crime of deicide; it reaffirms that in the eyes of God Jews remain a chosen nation; that the New Testament has its roots in the Old. In short, anti-semitism cannot be reconciled with Christianity, as it cannot be reconciled with the commandment, 'Love thy neighbour', which is a commandment given to the whole of humankind.

If the present discussion brings about some collective examination of our national conscience; if it makes us reject the notion that, since we ourselves were victims, we are therefore blameless; if it contributes to the deepening of our moral sensitivity – this means it was necessary. The change in our consciousness and attitude, the new awareness of the problem thereby achieved, will allow us to develop further the Polish–Jewish dialogue. The aim is better mutual understanding, getting rid of resentments and misunderstandings, and the re-discovery of that which should bind the two peoples who, for centuries, shared the same country. That is why – despite protests from some of our readers – we shall continue to concern ourselves in these columns with the problems relating to Polish–Jewish and Christian–Jewish issues.

NOTES

1 *Sanacja* – the camp of Piłsudski's followers.
2 Teresa Prekerowa estimated that approximately 1–2.5 per cent of Poles (between 160,000 and 360,000) were actively engaged in helping Jews to survive. According to Prekerowa, the number of Jews saved, who survived the war hiding among the 'Aryan' population is variously estimated (because of incomplete records) at between 40,000 and 60,000. Of all the Jews who sought safety among the 'Aryans', only about half actually survived. Thus the number of Jews who were hiding was 80,000 to 120,000. Since an average of two to three people were usually involved in hiding one Jew, the total number of 'Aryans' active in rescue efforts was 160,000 to 360,000, against some 15 million who, Prekerowa estimates, *could* have offered help. She arrives at this 15 million as follows:

		millions	millions
Poland's 1939 population			35
less:			
Jewish losses		3	
Polish losses		3	
Poles deported to forced labour camps and who fled the country		4	
Poles living in the Western Territories of Poland which were incorporated into the Reich, from which Jews were resettled in the General-Government		4	
Children and young people under 18		6	
		20	20
Those who could have helped:			15

13

THE EIGHTY-FIRST BLOW*

KAZIMIERZ KĄKOL

In the course of preparing for Eichmann's trial, an Israeli policeman had occasion to describe his suffering at the hands of the Nazis. When he spoke of the eighty strokes with a rod that he had once received, he met with disbelief. He put the voice of doubt then expressed which claimed that he could not have survived such a beating as being on a par with the criminal action of the Nazi who administered a beating. 'I've just received the eighty-first blow', he declared.

I was told this at the hospitable home of Benjamin Anolik, in the Lohamei Hageteot kibbutz which is situated near the town of Nahariya, on the evening of 15 February. I was told that one of the films made to meet documentary needs, commemorating the time of struggle and destruction, was entitled precisely that: *The Eighty-first Blow*.

I am plagued by the vexing thought that we Poles, so tragically and bloodily lashed by the ravages of war, legitimately, one should have thought, taking pride in our struggle, our sacrifice, and our implacable posture, have now received our eighty-first blow.

The eighty-first blow is aimed by way of a throwaway remark, made stealthily but with determination; it comes in the guise of defamatory insinuations based on *a priori* views which assume knowledge of anything and everything, or in that of confessions of sins uncommitted and pleas for forgiveness by those concerned for the good name of the Polish nation, who speak and suffer for the nation and its name.

*This article was first published in Stolica, 22 March 1987.

The eighty-first blow is delivered in a variety of ways.

We are shown photographs of Demianiuk in all German papers with captions explaining that he is accused of crimes committed 'in the Polish death camp of Treblinka'. Only one publication was good enough to set the record straight by correcting it to *German* death camp.

We see how the traditional view of deeply-ingrained Polish anti-semitism is used to explain the reasons both for the location of the death camps on Polish territory and the fate of the Jews who were left without effective help. . . Such distortions as that the Poles, by and large, looked on with indifference at the destruction of their Jewish neighbours, or how the help that was offered was quite insufficient, or how very culpable they are of the sin of neglect, are heard repeatedly. . . It might in fairness be admitted that nowhere in Europe was there the death penalty for helping Jews except in Poland, where a whole family was subject to execution if one of its members committed such an offence; but the barriers go up when it is suggested that the severity of the punishment in Poland reflected the posture of the Poles as anticipated and observed by the Germans.[1]

Categorical opinions are formulated in ways reminiscent of the blind expatiating on colours. Conversely, one is tempted to draw inferences based on veiled insinuations, in full awareness of the fact that the hearers of these inflammatory views have no way of verifying them for themselves. . . How many viewers of Lanzmann's *Shoah* will note his deceit in presenting Warsaw of the 1980s as that of April 1943? A cheerful, carefree, well-off Warsaw instead of the terrorized, choking and impoverished city is what we are shown. Yet it is an undeniable fact that the rest of Warsaw, on the eve of the merciless destruction which befell the Warsaw ghetto was itself quite destitute.

The leading witness on the circumstance of Polish guilt 'by neglect or inadequate resistance' is supposed to be Czesław Miłosz and his poetic journalism. I am not aware of the details of the anti-Nazi activities of Miłosz under the occupation. It is probably better for mankind that he formulates his socio-poetic theses from the position of an observer. Had he died like K. K. Baczyński then. . . The moralizings of an observer are, of necessity, of a different calibre.

The 'insufficient resistance' thesis is undoubtedly justified if the actual state is measured by the wishes, aims and aspirations of us, the people of those times. However, and this is in no way 'haggling over mitigating circumstances', one must bear in mind the sea of real conditions separating aims and intentions from their implementation. These conditions remain unnoticed by the manipulators trying to distribute guilt in order to lighten the burden resting on German shoulders. So fascinated are they by leading a 'penitential auction', that they are prepared to place on the shoulders of their own nation responsibility for sins that have not been committed.

Resistance, help, rescue initiatives, were closely related to the ratio of populations – of the persecuted population's needs in relation to the needs of the entire population (which itself was earmarked as next in line for liquidation). The figures were of fundamental significance and we don't need divine assistance to judge how these numerical proportions determined the possibility of help. . . And they determined them adversely, as did the mass incidence of difference in posture, behaviour, dress, as well as language. . .

Those considerations which would affect the possibility of survival of the whole *nation* cannot be placed on an equal footing and compared with those which pertained to the salvation of *select individuals* or *groups*.

Salvation for the nation seemed and, indeed, continues to seem theoretically possible only through victory in the war against fascism. Maybe suitably announced retaliatory air raids linked with ultimatums aimed at halting the mechanism of destruction could have had some effect. The Polish state authorities, basing themselves on underground sources, did their utmost to ensure that the powerful Allies were fully informed about the crime perpetrated against the Jewish nation. The strenuous steps taken by the Allies to deny the ghoulish facts, and further, their holding back from initiatives designed to save the nation that was perishing, drove Shmul Zygielboim to suicide in the hope of breaching the wall of indifference put up by the mighty.

The relationship between the destruction of the Jewish nation and the war was direct. The extermination of the Jewish nation hinged on the Wehrmacht's military successes and on the territories held and occupied by the Nazis. The gas chambers brought death and the crematoria belched smoke for as long as the Wehrmacht stood fast on the Eastern Front.

Hence the divisions of Belgians, Dutchmen, Frenchmen and Spaniards, abetting the Germans in their conquest, were guilty of indirect participation in the crime. The Lanzmanns of this world won't throw that in anyone's face. . . Polish divisions, on the other hand, were locked in constant struggle with the Nazi hordes. Neither the opening campaign of 1939, nor the struggle on all fronts during the Second World War, can be treated as anything other than action in defence of the Jews as well.

Individuals and groups engaged in rescue initiatives to save their Jewish brothers from extermination have to be seen and assessed realistically, that is, with due regard for their complexity in their entirety.

The complexity consisted of the fact that the genocidal intent, though already peddled in Nazi publications from 1933 onwards, struck everybody as being so at odds with all human feelings, so improbable, so irreconcilable with the civilized condition, that, given that nation's high level of cultural achievement and its war economy's demands and needs, even facts went unheeded.

The genocidal noose was tightened gradually. Select stages of this operation did not justify final conclusions for a long time. The hapless victims of destruction were deluded with hopes of the survival of the majority: tearing people from their natural environments and placing them in ghettos accomplished the disintegration of local communities with the severance of ties of loyalty and solidarity, and promoted internal divisions within the community. Simultaneously, the general biological degradation engendered by starvation rations progressed apace. The remorseless upshot of this was the ebb of physical strength, a weakened will to survive and fight.

Ghetto communities were not of one mind when it came to conscious action to thwart the Nazis' exterminatory designs. Old and young, healthy and sick, weak and strong, all tied by some family link or other, differed in scores of ways: in terms of knowledge, qualification, practical skills, the opportunity to melt into society at large. . .

The philosophy of survival by passive submission to fate, grounded in the consciousness of defeat that befell Hitler's militarily organized opponents, was not insignificant. The fate of Poland, Belgium, France, Holland, Yugoslavia, Greece, the mighty Soviet Union, was most demoralizing. . .

In a situation where the Eastern Front was 2,000 kilometres from Warsaw, and the Second Front in the West was only in the minds of strategic planners, the decision to initiate the Warsaw Ghetto Uprising was, of necessity, a decision concerning choice in the form of death (in combat, going down with all guns blazing) and, unfortunately, not a decision opening the road to life and freedom. We acquainted ourselves precisely with the risk that was attached to insurrection a year later, when the Eastern Front was only a few kilometres from Warsaw.

Individual rescue initiatives could only benefit those who undertook the initial decision to seek a way out of the ghetto. Death stalked beyond the ghetto walls – unquestionably pouncing on those who were unmasked; such fatal certainty did not seem to come into it in the ghetto, at least to begin with. . . Only those could be saved who understood the situation, knew how to behave, who obeyed the rules of disguise and deception and made practical use of this knowledge. . . Only those could be saved who were in a different position to Janusz Korczak. . . not hamstrung by the imperative of remaining, in solidarity, until the end.

Those aiming the eighty-first blow write on the subject of help in such a way as to suggest that no doubt could exist about the possibility of providing such help. That is the basic lie. . .

The material possibilities of help measured by the supply of weapons and ammunition, financial means, shelters protecting against the cold and betrayal, medicines and medical and nursing personnel – were very limited. Those lashing the Polish nation seem to assume that the question of aid was merely a matter of good will, of readiness to offer it. They refuse to take cognizance of the fact that those whom they blame directly or otherwise for the lack of help could not support their own cause a year later in August 1944. 90 per cent of the Polish insurgents in 1944 went into battle with as little chance of success as a fly trying to stop a train.

It is not true that the necessary means were jealously guarded and sat upon. There were no means.

'Antek' Cukierman, a hero of the Warsaw Ghetto Uprising, and a founder-member of the Lohamei Hagetaot kibbutz, knew the truth. . . He was in the habit of saying 'One swine could

betray a hundred Jews to the Germans. But to save one Jew, you
needed the participation of a hundred Poles.'

It is believed that the Poles saved approximately 100,000 Jews.

ANNOUNCEMENT: Concerning the death penalty for aiding
Jews who have illegally left the Jewish district.

Recently, a larger number of Jews have illegally left the
district allocated to them. They remain in the Warsaw region
to date. I remind you that the third directive of the Governor-
General of 15 Oct. 1941 (VBI. GG.S.595) anticipates that not
only Jews leaving the Jewish district will be sentenced to death,
but also anyone helping them hide in whatever way. I
emphasize that it is not only the offer of board and lodgings
that is considered as the rendering of help to a Jew, but also
their transportation by whatever means, buying various goods
for them, etc. I turn to the population in the Warsaw area with
the appeal to report immediately at the nearest police or
gendarme post any Jew illegally remaining outside the Jewish
district. Whoever has helped a Jew, or is still helping, and
reports the matter at the nearest police or gendarme post by 4
p.m., 9 Sept. 1942, will not be held liable for punishment.
Equally, whoever sends articles bought from a Jew to the
address: Warsaw, Niska 20, or who notifies the nearest police
or gendarme post of this by 4 p.m., 9 Sept. 1942, will also not
be held liable for punishment.

Warsaw, 5 September 1942
Chief of SS and Police
for the Warsaw Region

NOTE

1 This sentence contained errors in the original which were corrected in
Stolica of 5 April 1987. The version printed here is the corrected
one.

149

14

PILATE'S GESTURE*

RYSZARD ŻELICHOWSKI

'They demand that with my own hands I kill children of my nation. I am left with no option but to die.' These words, from Adam Czerniaków, chairman of the Jewish Council in the Warsaw ghetto, in a brief suicide note to his wife, presaged the next stage in the tragedy of the Jews of Warsaw. In a note to the Council Executive he wrote: 'I have decided to go. Don't take it as an act of cowardice, or flight. I am powerless. Sorrow and pity are breaking my heart and I can no longer take it. My action will draw everyone's attention to the truth and maybe will lead into the appropriate course of action.' Did this act of despair of a man who learned the truth have any meaning at the time? Gustaw Alei-Borkowski, commander of the Peoples' Guard in the ghetto, wrote that Czerniaków's suicide was 'a shock and warning'. Dr Emanuel Ringelblum assessed Czerniaków harshly: 'His duty was to call upon the whole of Jewish society to offer the enemy active and passive resistance. This type of defiant call could have torn the Jewish masses out of their lethargy. Czerniaków's personal sacrifice proved useless and was lost in the stampede of events.' But could it? Could the Chairman of the Council count on the support of the outside world? Certainly he tried. On 15 November 1942, a report entitled 'Liquidation of Jewish Warsaw' was compiled by the united underground organizations in the ghetto for the Polish government in London. The tragic timbre of the dossier, supplemented with a tabulation of deaths, plans of the ghetto and Treblinka, ended in the pathetic plea:

*This article was first published in *Stolica*, 29 March 1987.

What is left of Polish Jewry demands of the Polish government and the governments of Allied states: (1) the immediate dispatch of a neutral international commission to Treblinka to verify the facts given in the report; (2) immediate reprisals against those guilty of the tragedy visited upon the Polish Jews; (3) immediate retributive action against Germans living in Allied countries.

This report was brought over to London by Jan Karski (Jan Kozielewski), Home Army courier and government delegate, as early as the first days of December 1942. The details of this mission were published in the USA in the book *Story of a Secret State* (London and Boston, 1944). The Bund leader who briefed Karski entreated him:

We want you to tell the Polish Government, the Allied Governments, and the great Allied leaders that we are helpless against the German criminals. We cannot defend ourselves alone, and no one in Poland can defend us. The Polish underground authorities can save some of us, but not the majority. The whole nation will succumb to annihilation. A handful might survive, but the fate of 3 million Polish Jews is sealed. No power is capable of averting it. . . Put the responsibility for this on Allied shoulders. Please ensure that no leader of the United Nations can later say that they did not know that we are being murdered and that we can only be helped from outside. . . You asked what course of action I would recommend to the Jewish leaders. Tell them to go to all the more important British and American offices and institutions. Tell them not to leave without assurances that a method for saving the Jews has been adopted. Let them refuse food and water, let them die slowly before the eyes of the world. Let them die. That might move the world's conscience.

Moved by the plight of the Jewish community, Karski reached British and American government representatives, notably Eden and Roosevelt. On 10 December 1942 the Polish emigré foreign ministry in London directed a note to the Allied governments which reported on the scale of oppression and extermination of the Jewish population. As a result, a declaration condemning the 'bestial policy of extermination conducted in cold blood' was issued, still in December, simultaneously in Moscow, London, and Washington. Numerous other declarations, notes, and words of condemnation were to prove meaningless as far as the Polish–Jewish population was concerned. In January 1943, the Nazis began the final liquidation of the Warsaw ghetto. The appeal of the Jewish National Council in Poland that went out that month, addressed to foreign Jewish organizations – The American World Congress of Jews, the Jewish Workers' Organization and the Joint in the USA, was tragic:

> Brothers! The remnants of the Jews in Poland live in the knowledge that in the darkest hour of our history you did not help us. Say something. This is our final appeal to you. . . In face of the danger of the extermination of the surviving 400,000 Jews, we demand of you: (1) revenge on Germany; (2) to force the Nazis to stop the murder; (3) weapons to fight for our lives and our dignity; (4) contact through a delegate in a neutral state; (5) the rescue, through exchange, of 10,000 children; (6) 500,000 dollars for the purpose of self-defence and help.

There continued to be nothing to stop the Nazi criminals in the realization in stages of the 'solution' for the 'Jewish problem'. The liquidation of the Warsaw ghetto prompted the defence by the weakly-armed units of the Jewish Combat Organization. The Home Army High Command and Government Delegate radio-transmitters reported the course of events day after day. Telegrams were addressed, among others, to Shmul Zygielboim and Ignacy Szwarcbart – members of the Polish National Council in London. The radio-telegram transmitted on 11 May 1943 concluded with the words: 'The world of freedom and justice remains silent and inactive. How astounding. This is the third telegram in the last fortnight. Send us a telegram immediately reporting on what you have achieved. We expect financial help for the remnants trying to save themselves.' In the carefully documented work *Poles–Jews 1939–1945* (Warsaw, 1971), S. Wroński and M. Zwolakowa write:

> The appeals to the Allies, the Pope, Jewish organizations, did not result in the help expected. Certain addressees remained silent, others pleaded for help but unavailingly. The most tragic protest against the Western world's passivity with regard

to the Nazi crimes in Poland was the suicide of Shmul Zygielboim in London, on 13 May 1943, on the thirteenth day after the Bermuda conference, when it became known that the expected aid from America and Great Britain was not to be.

The Secretary of the Treasury at the time, Henry Morgenthau, noted in his diaries which were published in 1947 that the US government had detailed information on the mass extermination of Jews in various European states as early as August 1942. He blamed the State Department for the suppression of these facts, which stemmed from the fear of the pressure of public opinion which would have forced the US government to do something. Morgenthau wrote:

On 17 December 1942 the State Department received a telegram from London quoting the note of the Ministry of War Economy to the Embassy. The Foreign Office, it emerged from the note, was anxious about the difficulty in accommodating a larger number of Jews should they be allowed to leave enemy territory. For this reason it opposed the initiating of financial agreements, despite the fact that such agreements could have been accepted by the Minister of War Economy. . . The note was an infernal mixture of British reserve and diplomatic insinuation, cold, prim, and in effect a death sentence.

The fate of the millions of Jews in the Nazi-occupied countries was now a foregone conclusion. The chance of survival was thus restricted to members of the plutocracy whose ransoms served to buttress the German economy. Those isolated 'acts of charity' neither impinged upon Reich interests nor affected the course of its genocidal policy; if anything, it misled representatives of Jewish organizations abroad. The Nazi diplomat Fritz Hesse, in his memoirs *Das Spiel um Deutschland* (Munich, 1953), confirmed the fact that the talks conducted in 1945 on the subject of 'concluding with America an agreement on the question of sparing the Jews were (still!) merely the opening gambit in the negotiations on German surrender with the Western Allies'.

Until the very end, efforts to halt the Nazi crime machine proved unavailing.

Recently it was the forty-fourth anniversary of the Warsaw Ghetto Uprising, the despairing act of those the world tried to forget. They themselves will not forget about it. As *Życie*

Warszawy reported on 6 March 1987:

'Poland has always offered every assistance in pursuing war criminals,' declared Efraim Zuroki, the head of the Jerusalem branch of the Simon Wiesenthal Centre at a press conference in London. . . 'Since October 1986 . . . the American branch of this Centre, with its headquarters in Los Angeles, has supplied eight Western governments with lists of suspected war criminals. In Australia the number of such suspects is 65, in Canada – 26, in West Germany – 44, in Great Britain – 17, in Sweden – 12, in Venezuela – 3, in Brazil – 1, whilst in the USA – 74.'

15

THE DISSEMINATOR OF ANTI-SEMITISM?
*A Rejoinder to Jan Błoński**

WITOLD RYMANOWSKI

Tygodnik Powszechny of 11 January 1987 carried an article by Professor Jan Błoński entitled 'The Poor Poles Look at the Ghetto'. The article contains statements of the type covered in article 178 of the penal code and is therefore guilty of the offence of slandering the Polish nation in accordance with article 270 of that code. It concerns the attitude of the Poles and the Polish nation to the Jews both in the course of centuries past as well as, and primarily so, in the period of the Nazi Holocaust.

Professor Błoński points to the alleged injustices suffered by the Jews in Poland, forgetting that pre-Partition Poland was a real haven for the Jews expelled from other European countries. The pyres of the Inquisition were burning in Spain at the time, the Inquisition was dealing with masses of converted Jews, while the so-called Marranos, despite being ostensibly baptized and church-going, remained true to the Mosaic faith. In the German states pogroms against Jews occurred constantly at the hands of fanaticized urban mobs, bent on looting.

In those times, apart from the Ottoman Empire, Poland was the only refuge for the Jews in Europe. There was even a saying in the West – given that proverbs are the wisdom of nations (as the Polish saying goes) – *Polonia paradisus Judeorum* (Poland is the Jews' paradise). Against the backdrop of the difficult situation for European Jewry, this was not far from the truth, because let us consider: Jews were not subject to military conscription; they paid no direct taxes, only lump sums which were annually negotiated by the self-governing Jewish councils as

*This article was first published in *Zycie literackie*, 12 April, 1987.

a whole; they enjoyed freedom of trade, and, first and foremost, they monopolized the economy, which was of immense importance; the right to practise usury, that is to charge interest on loans, was theirs alone.

Thus there was nothing odd in the fact that great wealth should have accumulated in their hands and thereby also political influence, because always and everywhere money talks. Frankly, it gave rise to an extraordinary privilege, without analogy elsewhere in Europe, according to which – by the Lithuanian Statute – a Jew assimilating with the Polish nation and converting to Roman Catholicism automatically become ennobled and received a coat of arms. By way of precedent this practice subsequently spread to the Crown as well.[1]

Thus in any objective assessment as opposed to that obtained through the gloomy glasses that Professor Błoński deliberately dons, it must be asserted that Jews, in contrast to the millions of serfs and the impoverished townspeople who were oppressed by the nobility, constituted a privileged group which, most importantly, effectively represented the only class in the Polish–Lithuanian Commonwealth to concentrate finance and liquid assets in its hands. To be sure it may be noted that there were after all magnates and peers who were *bene nati et possesionati*, (well-born and well-endowed) but it must be remembered that military service and the statutory obligation for them to provide military units during the interminable wars of the seventeenth and eighteenth centuries were frequently their ruin. With the possible exception of the Ukrainian *latifundia*, estates survived with the help of Jewish loans. Thus Professor Błoński's jeremiad on the theme of Jewish suffering in ancient Poland smacks of a deliberate juggling with facts, which is difficult to understand, because surely a professor of two universities – the Jagiellonian and the Sorbonne – cannot be suspected of ignorance?

In the post-Partition era, in consequence of the introduction of new laws, the Jews lost their precious monopoly on lending rights, the negotiated lump-sum tax from the Jewish community *en masse*, as well as the prestigious rule of ennoblement upon assimilation with the Poles. With few exceptions, they did not participate, however, in the uprisings of 1830–1, 1848, or 1863. Maybe it was due to this failure to participate in these uprisings, that throughout the nineteenth century, the decisive force of capital remained principally in Jewish hands. This was of no minor significance in a country deprived of financial means, with a population that, perhaps with the exception of the Prussian-ruled areas, was completely unprepared for engaging in trade and industry. Since the Jews dominated capital, the economic life of the country revolved round them, especially in the Congress Kingdom after the Drucki–Lubecki reforms. The privileged position of the Jews was even reflected in a characteristic class stratification. No Jew or Jewess, even the poorest, was ever a domestic servant, rarely were they factory workers – not even in Jewish-owned factories at that. Noteworthy friction or grievances did not exist here, and the relations between both nations were tolerable.

On the other hand, clashes did occur on purely capitalist grounds, in free market competition, which is the apple of the capitalist economy's eye. The resurgent Polish bourgeoisie, after centuries of decay, as well as the influx of small-holders and, indeed, landless peasants from the overcrowded countryside (who besides taking the most menial positions in factories – which were sometimes German but usually Jewish-owned) began to turn their hands to urban crafts, traditional small handicrafts, and to a minor extent trade. (Reymont's *The Promised Land* (1899) is clear proof and testimony in this regard.) A confrontation ensued between the Jews on the one hand, who were superbly organized, experienced in trade, and above all united in solidarity – a most important factor because of the Jewish traders' mutual aid in money and kind – and on the other hand, the large wave of peasants sweeping into the towns, commercially inept and disunited. Of course, neither backward townspeople who were advancing, nor the *petit-bourgeois* of peasant lineage, could ever dream of competing effectively against such a superb, indeed, masterly and world-class adversary. That the adversary was world-class can be seen in the fact, which is no secret, that the greatest trading houses in Paris, Frankfurt, Berlin, Vienna, London, New York, Los Angeles, Buenos Aires or Melbourne were in Jewish hands, hands which have proved themselves in competition with the indigenous and experienced commercial traders in those places.

In the professions, such as law and medicine, competition again reared its head, and here too the Jews had the upper hand.

This found expression in the fact that in such towns as Kraków and Lwów, 70 to 80 per cent of lawyers were Jewish, while in medicine, despite various obstacles, the figure approached 50 per cent.

The Jewish intelligentsia in the inter-war years was, for the most part, Zionist, with a separate and intense national consciousness, dreaming of rebuilding *Eretz Israel*, which surely brings them credit. But by the same token, they had no wish to be embraced by their younger brothers, that is the Poles, contrary to what Professor Błoński seems to imagine, basing himself on select quotes from Mickiewicz. By then, the Jews were already acutely aware of their national identity and were infused with messianic pride, regarding themselves as the nation called upon before all others by Providence to serve higher aims. This was, in any case, put in writing by the greatest Western politician of Jewish extraction, Disraeli (Lord Beaconsfield), architect of the British Empire in the Victorian era.

The sorrows of Professor Błoński that those 'poor Poles' did not treat the Jews (who looked down proudly at them – because of their messianic religion, history and their capital) as brothers and did not accept them into the 'brotherly community' look ridiculous. Professor Błoński would have those 'poor Poles' deny their own national pride and historical legacy, and submit to the hegemony of the 'elder brothers'. That is what the professorial gullibility or, let us hope, his inherent kindheartedness leads to.

But leaving aside the earlier pre- and post-Partition periods, let us consider the greatest crime of genocide by Hitler's Germany, the Holocaust, and the surprising conclusions of the kindhearted Professor. At the end of his long article, Professor Błoński confronts the 'poor Poles' with no more nor less than their complicity in the murder of Polish and other Jews by Hitler. This complicity is of a moral nature. Thus it could be assumed that it was these 'poor Poles' who induced, in some Machiavellian manner, the Führer and his Nazi henchmen of the SS to exterminate Polish Jews and to feed the Auschwitz incinerators with Greek, French, and German Jews. But, for Błoński, this moral guilt is insufficient; he is surprised that words (which, as far as can be made out, relate to the competitive struggle between Polish and Jewish shopkeepers and the invective that was hurled, including the frenzied diatribes of Neuwerth-Nowaczyński or

Loewe-Stroński) were not followed by deeds, that is the physical participation of the Poles in the Holocaust. According to the Professor, God alone saved the 'poor Poles' from committing this crime, staying their hand, already raised eagerly in the urge to participate in the Nazi genocide. A feeling of horror and speechlessness must overcome every Polish patriot. Błoński seemingly believes (if logic and argument is pushed to its natural conclusion) that non-Christians of various descriptions – freethinkers, socialists, Muslims – were to a certain degree desperate to participate in the Holocaust, and only those who were still a little Christian obeyed this call of God which prevented the 'poor Poles' from participation in *Shoah*.

In all that has been written to date, a voice more demeaning of the Polish nation, consciously casting aspersion and cruel insult, could not be found. Błoński issues these accusations despite the knowledge that the Jews who survived (apart from those who took part in the heroic uprisings in Białystok and Warsaw), did so thanks to the heroism of the Poles who daily exposed themselves and their families to the threat of death for sheltering Jews. He must also know perfectly well, since he cannot not know, that the Home Army condemned to death the *szmalcownicy*, that is those on the peripheries of society who blackmailed and betrayed Jews in hiding to the Nazis.

Professor Błoński avers that Polish soil was contaminated by virtue of the fact that the Nazi murderers chose it as the scene of the Holocaust. It should be asked all the same of the learned scholar and Professor: since when has the blood of martyrs befouled the soil it fell on? What urged him towards such a diabolically perverse conclusion? Polish opinion – as, indeed, that of the entire civilized world – holds that the ground at the sites of execution of innocent victims is sanctified, not sullied.

Błoński's perverse idea of Polish soil, drenched in the blood of martyrs regardless of their nationality, race, or creed, as being ostensibly contaminated for us, betrays a lack of courage because Jan Błoński knows full well that mass exterminations of Jewish populations were also carried out in the Ukraine (Babi Yar near Kiev, Rawa Ruska and Bełżec near Lwów) and in many other places in Byelorussia, Lithuania, Latvia and the western parts of the Russian Soviet Republic. A far greater number of Jews – the millions of Jewish inhabitants of Lwów, Tarnopol, Stanisławów,

Brody, Berdychev, Grodno, Wilno, Minsk, Vitebsk, Homel, Smolensk, Kiev, Odessa, Jassy, Kishinev, Chernovits – were murdered by the Nazis aided and abetted in those areas by the Russian Vlassov troops and the so-called (Ukrainian) 'SS Division Galizien', than the number that perished on ethnic Polish territory. It would be interesting to have Professor Błoński's comments on the subject. Has Ukrainian, Byelorussian, Lithuanian and Russian soil been contaminated by the Holocaust for centuries to come, and do the Ukrainians, Byelorussians, Lithuanians and Russians also share in the moral responsibility for the extermination of the Jews? It can be safely assumed in advance that neither Professor Błoński nor those sharing his views will express themselves on this issue. It is easy to brush aside the little man with impunity, and in the case of the great man to keep one's mouth firmly shut, for the latter could slam the table with his fist. He who is not convinced by the remarks in this article should study Karl Marx's 'Zur Judenfrage' ('On the Jewish Question'). . . and to suspect Marx of anti-semitism would, of course, be nonsensical.

NOTE

1 The ancient Polish Commonwealth consisted of Poland proper, known as the Crown (*Korona*), and the Grand Duchy of Lithuania.

16

THE HIDDEN COMPLEX OF THE POLISH MIND:
*Polish–Jewish Relations during the Holocaust**

ANDRZEJ BRYK

The recent Polish search for the lost history of Polish–Jewish relations is not an abstract intellectual exercise. It is morally legitimate and necessary, and long overdue. At stake is the Polish people's choice between freedom, which requires as full a recognition as possible of history, and imprisonment as a people desperately committed to nationalistic myths.

In those fortunate countries where history is not political, not an arena for battle, historical controversies are usually conducted on the margins – however noisy – of society. In those unfortunate countries where history is intimately and painfully interwoven with the present, controversies are usually substitutes for deeply hidden fears, political preferences or insecurities.

Many contemporary Poles need a glorious yesterday as a dependable justification for a grey today. Modern Polish history has been a story of nearly consistent defeat and internal failure. A defeated people lives by myths, clings to myths. Apologetic and martyrological versions of national history only mirror an incurable romantic despair. Poles thus look at their history in terms of 'honour' versus 'shame' because categories of victory or national success are largely beyond the modern Polish consciousness and any of the institutions which shape it. Honour seems to Poles the only reliable justification of their national existence.

The history of Polish Jews in the twentieth century forms only a part of Polish history. Yet because of the Holocaust and its effect on contemporary consciousness this history has acquired a paramount historical and moral importance. The Poles, reduced

---

*This article was delivered as a paper at the International Conference on the History and Culture of Polish Jewry, held in Jerusalem, February 1988.

to slavery and decimated, were forced to observe the destruction of Polish and European Jewry by the Germans. Although they did not choose for themselves the role of witnesses, they have the duty to bear witness.

The historical facts – actually – provide scant help on the subject of Polish–Jewish relations during the war, or less than some would expect.[1] Although we have little choice but to be preoccupied with historical investigation the questions at issue are basically moral. Yet how we articulate them conditions the particular type of answer we receive.

Neither the question of complicity nor of Polish collaboration with the Germans is at stake. Nor can there be a question of a practical possibility of the Poles saving the Jewish people. There was no complicity and not the slightest possibility of saving the Jewish nation.[2] The fundamental question concerns the attitude of the Polish population, the Polish underground state and its armed wing – the Home Army (*Armia Krajowa*). Did they include Polish Jews[3] in what Helen Fein calls 'the universe of obligation' – that circle of persons 'towards whom obligations are owed, to whom rules apply and whose injuries call for expiation by the community'?[4]

The concept of 'the universe of obligation' enables us to connect both pre-war Polish attitudes and immediate post-war Polish attitudes towards the Jews. In every state, that nation which dominates decides what the rules of mutual obligations are, to whom they apply and what their limitations are, if any. 'Injuries or violations of rights of persons within the universe of obligations,' writes Fein, 'are offenses against the collective consciousness which provoke the need for sanctions against the perpetrators in order to maintain the group's solidarity. Those outside the boundaries do not provoke such a need.'[5]

The independent Polish state, which was created after the First World War, had a most ambiguous relationship with Polish Jews. They were the only minority within the boundaries of the new state who did not have any innate, national interest in opposing the 'new' Poland. Poland after 1918 faced tasks which were, in practice, beyond ready or rapid solution. It achieved much. It also had its failures and lost opportunities. The Polish–Jewish chapter was such a lost chance.[6]

The central drama of interwar Polish history was the new

state's strategy of political development. Crucial to Polish pre-war political thought was the basic problem of whether to construct the state around the 'nation' or around 'society'. The majority of the political parties accepted the nation–state concept by the end of the Second Republic, thus establishing the predominant political tone. This concept also, and most important for our considerations, constituted the core of the whole educational system, with support and justification from the dominant Polish elites, including the Catholic Church.[7]

The nation–state concept enforced a particular address – in attitude and ultimately in politics – to the so-called 'national minorities'. The structural, economic and cultural separation of the Yiddish-speaking Jewish civilization was an issue for the Polish state to solve. That issue could be perceived as an insoluble one, which was the case in the late 1930s, or as one that could be solved. Each of those choices demanded a different set of policies and strategies. Each was based on a different value system. Good politics require deflecting or neutralizing, not exacerbating problems which resist any legislative solution. For such recalcitrant issues as the acceptance by one ethnic religious group of another, education is required.

The Polish state as the stronger partner of the Polish–Jewish equation had the duty to pursue disarming and delaying tactics towards the problems of the mutual co-existence of Poles and Jews. Moreover, it had a duty to interpret the difficulties inherent in that co-existence, not in terms of its final irreconcilability but in terms of its ultimate conciliation. The choices were not purely theoretical because from them stemmed a totally different set of political tactics and educational options. After 1935 Polish–Jewish relations were portrayed by nearly all the consciousness-forming Polish elites as being insoluble within the context of the Polish state. The mass emigration of the Polish Jews or containment of them within strictly prescribed spheres of society was at the core of the policy which resulted from this position.

Post-1935 political and social education worked along the path of the traditional, Western standpoint towards the Jews as formulated by St Augustine. In such a scheme the Jews were envisaged as locked into an antithetical, antagonistic position *vis-a-vis* the rest of the society.[8] After 1935 Jews were portrayed as 'rootless cosmopolitans spreading pornography', or as the

'Judaeo-communist mafia', as an 'alien element' – all that in the context of the nationalistic and exclusivist ideology of which the Catholic Church was one of the most important exponents. A particular outgrowth of that antithetical position was the allegedly more sophisticated notion of the insoluble nature of Polish–Jewish relations in the context of 'the place in the conflict',[9] with the corollary of economic boycott, ghetto benches at the universities, and so on. That line of reasoning was based on the conviction that the Jews were irrevocably hostile to Polish independence, were alien in the Polish state, and should be weakened so that their pernicious influence could be contained, especially in the economic sphere.[10]

The Polish economy was, of course, not healthy and the state had a duty to work towards its improvement, which it did.[11] The internal occupational structure of the Jewish population (its concentration in certain fields like commerce or some professions) was the outcome of the sorry state of the economy. Yet, irrational attitudes, derived from anti-semitic prejudice, which Poland unhappily shared with other European countries, saw Polish Jews in the troubled economic structure as the cause of those troubles, when in fact the Jews, together with others, for instance Polish peasants, were its victims. The economic troubles were portrayed and explained by the Polish nationalists as the consequence of an innate conflict between two peoples and their cultures. This Polish exploitation of anti-semitism to justify particular economic policies was not only logically ridiculous, but was, more significantly, only a manifestation of a deeper prejudice made to appear respectable or justified through an apparent difference in economic interests. Anti-semitic policy in this case was not the outcome of the real situation in the 'place of conflict'. The 'place of conflict' was perceived and translated into the political, social, and cultural language in terms of anti-semitic prejudices.

Such a policy quickly disrupted and unravelled the tenuous fabric of Polish–Jewish co-existence, cooperation, and trust instead of strengthening it. Finally, even fully assimilated Jews who felt themselves Polish, belonging to Polish culture, were reminded that they were not accepted as part of the 'Polish interest'. Polish elites have thus to be charged not only with the failure to recognize the true nature of the nation's economic and social problems. They also, by exercising their anti-semitism, contributed to the destruction of the social fabric, thus acting ultimately against the interest of the Polish state.[12]

Even if one concedes the view that the Jewish economic and demographic problems were insoluble within the context of the impoverished Polish state,[13] the exacerbation of these problems, the subversion of the old pluralistic ethos and the dissemination of hatred constituted a betrayal of moral decency and of the most admirable traditions among the Polish elites.

Although state institutions tried to fulfil their legal obligations towards Polish Jews,[14] the government retreated more and more under the pressure of the anti-semitic parties and their programmes. At the same time the prevailing educational stance within the society (the press, the pulpit, the school) was pushing the Jews outside the pale of equal moral obligation into the anthitetical position.[15]

The German occupation, as far as Polish–Jewish relations are concerned, can be roughly divided into two periods: 1939–42 and 1942–4. In the first period both populations found themselves terrorized, though in neither could anyone yet have imagined the Nazis conceiving the Holocaust. The most significant development was the gradual but definite separation of Polish society into two peoples: Jews were herded into ghettos, which presented no logistical difficulties since they were mainly unassimilated and the Germans had a monopoly of the means of terror. Yet what is important is whether a psychological separation followed and whether it was taken for granted. The ruthless segregation imposed by the Germans, although it elicited a kind of sympathy based mainly on similar experiences of suffering, caught the Poles at large, who had been brought up in an anti-semitic cultural climate,[16] morally and psychologically unprepared. There was a real mental confusion, an initial moral inability quickly and unequivocally to recognize the intentions and consequences of the Nazi policy. The separation between the two groups was reinforced by neither having any tangible, institutional means to co-operate which predated the terror. Each could turn culturally and morally to nationalistic or ethnic traditions which underlined their differences. Exclusivist, egoistic tendencies were natural consequences of a drastic situation in which the first goal was survival.[17] In this sense, the Nazi occupation in Poland can not even remotely be compared to the Nazi occupation in the West.

One can argue that such a separation, given the separation of the Jewish population from the Polish before the war, was unavoidable. Yet the question of the boundary between separation by the Germans and abandonment in the psychological sense is still an important issue. The problem of climate, of mood, is accessible to us only indirectly; nevertheless the psychological indifference to the ghettos – even before contacts were punishable by death – seems to have been widespread. And here the question of the 'universe of moral obligation' cannot be avoided. Poland was of course not an exception in this regard, yet such an attitude was crucial in Poland, just because the Germans murdered the Jews there.[18]

It is my conviction that the struggle for moral clarity, for the unequivocal moral recognition of the Polish Jews as part of the Polish universe of obligation, became after 1942 the most complex, delicate and overwhelmingly educational problem facing the Polish underground state and its democratic elites. I would formulate the problem as follows: this educational effort has to be recognized not as the manifestation of a silent nation under genocidal terror itself, which wanted, but could not, or was afraid to help the Jews, but the other way round. The Polish underground state's elites represented the cream of Poland and did decide to go against the stream of indifference. The moral problem is not diminished by the additional explanation that even if there had been widespread moral compassion it could not have translated itself into practical, really significant help, which since 1941 had been severely punishable, with a death sentence for anyone who helped the Jews.

One instance of the attempt to 'go against the stream' is the extremely complex, morally ambiguous, manifesto written in August 1942 by Zofia Kossak-Szczucka. She was a head of the small Catholic underground organization the Front for the Rebirth of Poland. Protesting against the possible and assumed silence of the Poles in the face of the murder committed by the Germans, she went on:

> Our feelings towards the Jews have not changed. We still consider them to be political, economic, and ideological enemies of Poland. What is more, we are aware that they

166

consider us to be responsible for their misfortune. Why, on what grounds – that is a mystery of the Jewish soul, but it is a fact that is being confirmed again and again. The awareness of these feelings, however, does not relieve us of our duty to condemn the crime.[19]

Zofia Kossak-Szczucka later became one of the organizers of the Żegota, the special section of the Home Army (AK) created to help the Jews in an organized way. Yet, the question remains why she wrote as she did. She apparently tried to draw a fine line between those basic values which Christians – even when anti-semitic – could never abandon and what she perceived as a legitimate clash of Polish and Jewish interests.

There has recently been another interpretation, apparently confirmed by Zofia Kossak's post-war statements, that the wording of the manifesto was the only way through which the education of the Polish general public could begin.[20] Such a supposition, which can actually be legitimately derived from the text of the manifesto, confirms that large sections of Polish society had enormous difficulties even in making the distinction which Zofia Kossak did.

It also confirms that such was the prevailing general mood that excluding Polish Jews from the universe of moral obligation had become morally debasing. If one looks at the press outside of the major Home Army publications, exclusivist feeling is clearly visible.[21] It has also to be stated that the Home Army did not really take decisive steps to try to stop the criminals blackmailing the Jews and those Poles who hid them. The death sentences on blackmailers began only at the end of 1943, by which time most Polish Jews had already been murdered.[22] Of course, the Polish underground state was very rigorous in using due process of law, which in the infernal conditions of the German occupation was an extremely lengthy and dangerous procedure. Nevertheless, the members of Żegota had difficulties convincing the leadership of the Home Army even to publish some fictitious death sentences as a form of education and deterrence.[23]

Only with the Holocaust of the Polish Jews and the decimation of ethnic Poles themselves did the slow, painful, hesitant process begin, set in motion by the Polish underground state elites, of forming a community of feeling, of including the Polish Jews in the universe of moral obligation, a community which in the words of Stanisław Vincenz 'never awakened, never matured into full awareness'.[24] From this perspective, it becomes easier to understand the role played by the underground elites with regard to anti-semitism within the community at large. We can, and should, say, as has Henryk Grynberg, that 'accusing the Poles of co-operating in crucifying the Jews is as inconsistent with the truth . . . as accusing the Jews of crucifying the Messiah.'[25] But one should also recognize the dilemma of a Polish community raised in a largely anti-semitic culture and subconsciously accepting Jews as aliens suddenly in a situation where its culture offered no moral means to resist an easy acceptance of the fact of the annihilation of the Jews by the Germans. It is precisely this legacy of the Holocaust that post-war Polish culture has been very reluctant to face.

The Home Army elites, as part of the Polish underground state, which attempted to educate the community, the contradictions of the process notwithstanding, and which created Żegota, a unique and heroic body, deserve acknowledgement for struggling to lead a substantial section of the nation into a different moral consciousness.[26] The murder of the Polish Jews by the Germans could not have been in the slightest prevented by the Polish population, itself under genocidal terror. Yet it should have been morally much more difficult to bear, and it was not. So it is that Jerzy Andrzejewski could write:

> For all honest Poles the fate of the perishing Jews must have been exceedingly painful, for the dying . . . were people whom our people could not look straight in the face, with a clear conscience. The Polish nation could look straight in the face of Polish men and women who were dying for freedom. Not in the face of the Jews dying in the burning ghettos.[27]

At this point we need to look more closely at the Polish military underground, the Home Army (AK). It is not easy on the Polish side to talk about this question, because the Home Army is one of the most sacred legends of the Polish heritage. I am not going to deal with all the aspects of the policies and attitudes of the AK towards the Jews.[28] But some points have to be clarified. Until 1942, that is until the great deportations, the issue was practically non-existent. The AK was weak, capable only of acquiring intelligence, and building up its network. As with other underground structures, it 'was not the Home Army's task to provide social welfare or to save people. If it had been, the AK would have tried to rescue Poles from Auschwitz, from Pawiak. . .'[29] This argument is acceptable as an explanation until 1942. After 1942 the aims of the Polish underground and of the Jewish people, including their respective military units, diverged totally. The AK undertook a merciless struggle with the Germans but there was a grain of rational calculation in it, planning based on a different time sequence. For the Jews the time for decision, for rational action had passed. Theirs was a totally different existential situation. The Polish underground could buy time, employ delaying tactics in preparation for the final uprising. The Poles could operate on the basis of a calculus of cost which, of course, implied choice. The Jews had no choice. They had been reduced to the most basic existential situation, the total abandonment of hope.[30] That process took place in conditions of debasement to the most inhuman level in the ghettos. Such conditions affected the Poles too, but not to such a great extent, and they had a much wider range of means to counterbalance them.

The Poles could still think after 1942 about responsible and irresponsible action; for the Jews such a choice was irrelevant, or if taken proved to be futile.[31] So, the Home Army as an organization and its leadership could avoid suicidal choices. Yet the question still remains whether the AK could, in fact, avoid suicidal choices for the Polish population after 1942. The validity of the theory of the suicidal choice can only be tenable as the explanation of the AK behaviour towards the Jews if it applies both to the Polish and to the Jewish side. Only then we can say that desperate, suicidal military choices lay outside the concern of the AK, even if there was moral sensitivity, responsibility and deep enough compassion.[32]

Yet, one can point to suicidal, even if spontaneous, choices made by the Home Army on behalf of the Polish population. There was a desperate defence of the people of the Zamość region, where desperate acts of revenge were taken for the massacre of the inhabitants of entire Polish villages.[33] In other words there was a boundary of bestiality beyond which the calculus of costs did not apply, because moral responsibility outweighed any rational calculation. That was visible not only at the individual unit level but also at the level of the command of the AK. It was aware that the time could come when suicidal choices might have to be made. The commander of the AK stated on 10 November 1942:

As to the operation of annihilation of the Jews carried out by the occupier, there are signs of disquiet among the Polish public lest after the operation is completed the Germans will begin the liquidation of the Poles in the same manner . . . If the Germans do indeed make an attempt of this sort, they will meet with active resistance on our part. Without consideration for the fact that the time for our uprising has not yet come, the units under my command will enter armed battle to defend the life of our people. In this battle we will move over from defence to offence by cutting all the enemy's arteries of transport to the Eastern Front.[34]

There was thus a moral responsibility, strong enough, where the Polish underground was prepared to act irrespective of the cost. The AK did not accept equal moral responsibility for the Jewish citizens of the Polish state. Therefore the incorporation of the Jewish fight into the story of the heroic struggle of the Home Army, or even Polish history, can be made only with very strong qualifications and with an awareness of moral problems, which should never be ruled out of order on account of historical, military, or other factors.[35] It should stand as a moral problem at the core of Polish history simply because we can never be sure that if the history of Polish–Jewish relations before the war had been shaped differently, more Poles would have felt and acted in moral outrage.

In this context it is dishonest to enlarge the Home Army's legend and its deeds by portraying it as not doing enough because the Jewish side failed to respond to its military initiatives – the view unfortunately incorporated into Polish school textbooks.[36] The moral and existential dimension of the Jewish fight and suffering was beyond Polish organizational concern and reach. It would be better if it were otherwise, but it was not. The Jews travelled their path alone and the Poles were able only sporadically and symbolically to join it – the more glory to those Home Army soldiers who died at the walls of the Warsaw ghetto and to the members of Żegota, who suffered such heavy losses.

Such distortions – evident in our school textbooks – show that the Poles subconsciously need to incorporate the Jewish resistance and fate into their history, that the Jewish struggle elevates the Polish fight, that this incorporation is in fact a precondition to establishing a moral position in relation to the events of the war. This constitutes, in a certain sense, a tacit admission by Poles of some form of moral guilt. I think that such an incorporation is for the Polish side necessary and possible, but with humility, not arrogance. It is permissible because it was in fact already invited by the Warsaw ghetto fighters in their farewell address to the Polish nation.[37] The symbolic and humble answer from the Polish side came only during the Solidarity union congress in 1981, although it was only barely noticed and hardly incorporated into Polish consciousness.[38]

Having said that one may add, and one should add, that there was no way that the different Polish and Jewish nations living in a new state could develop a sense of mutual moral responsibility in a period as short as twenty-one years. There was not enough time on the Polish side. Polish nationalism after 1918 had, arguably, to pass through an initial stage of exclusiveness, but this does not excuse the opinion-forming Polish elites or their failure to recognize this phenomenon as a problem. Even if the results – in hindsight – of the German occupation had been the same, consciences would have been sharper and the healing role of politics and public education could have been felt during the war.

It was extremely difficult for the Poles to shake off the mental legacy of cultural anti-semitism. There was a total confusion or silence in the underground press. To admit that the Jews, if only morally and symbolically, were part of the Polish universe of obligation required the revision of anti-semitic convictions, and it required an admission that the struggle was for a culture in which Jews were equal.[39]

So, what is the hidden complex of the Polish mind? There is a tendency to look at Polish–Jewish relations during the war through the lens of Polish relations with the Germans. In such a view there is a clear-cut dichotomy – a merciless struggle. It is difficult for the Poles to enter the shadowy triangle of Polish–Jewish–German relations. The Poles would like to incorporate the entire war experience into the Polish–German dichotomy. The fear is that if Polish–Jewish relations cannot be incorporated into this dichotomy, there exists only another dichotomy – Poles and Germans collaborating.[40]

The refusal to get outside this myth of dichotomy and the inability to recognize the shadowy sphere of Polish–Jewish relations next to the deadly Polish–German fight causes the Poles to fall into the intellectual and emotional trap they have set for themselves. Because most Poles have difficulty in recognizing any other model of Polish–Jewish relations, they are unable to confront the issue of the anti-semitic cultural tradition in Poland in its entirety. Thus they tend to overlook that tradition or to relegate its influence during the war into the margin, as confined to a criminal element. But what is crucial is not the marginal actions, whether heroic or vile, but attitudes and their impact in the context of a terrorized, demoralized society unprepared and forced to witness the total murder of its neighbours.

The trap is that, since the magnitude and pervasiveness of pre-war anti-semitism in Poland cannot be hidden or diminished, on the basis of their own criteria of a clear-cut dichotomy, the Poles stand condemned, and find themselves in the dock together with the Germans. This in turn causes their justified protests and arouses their indignation which is perceived by outsiders as a defensive attitude of trying to hide something. The Polish discussion about the film *Shoah* is, in large part, a classic example of such behaviour.[41]

The clear-cut dichotomous model is of course a distorted myth derived from the heroic version of national history, a by-product of the unfree and unnatural national developments of the last few decades. Yet the anachronism of that model for explaining Polish–Jewish relations is especially clear. That model – which was for a long time also the standard model of explanation of American, French or Jewish reactions to the Holocaust – has elsewhere been reluctantly, albeit decisively, rejected.[42] Polish anachronistic thinking and defensiveness is on this point especially irritating, not because anti-semitism in Poland was exceptional (on the contrary it was like any other traditional form of this ideology), but for the sheer and simple reason that the Germans decided to murder the Jewish nation and millions of other Gentiles on Polish soil. The fact that the Poles were forced to be witnesses does not really change the moral duty of confronting the issue.[43]

Feelings of moral sensitivity, let alone moral responsibility, did not, for the Poles, come out of the war. Anti-semitism in Poland should have evaporated after the war, should have been put irrevocably beyond the pale of civilized politics. This did not occur. There are many reasons why anti-semitism retained legitimacy as a political weapon after the war.[44] Yet one cannot escape the conclusion that the last chapter of Polish–Jewish co-existence on Polish soil could have been closed differently, if again the Polish elites, especially the Catholic Church, had perceived the political situation properly. This was still some-times possible until 1946. After that date the political momentum reached a level beyond which any rational, let alone moral, arguments in the sphere of Polish–Jewish relations could not work. I do not claim that the disarming of Polish anti-semitism was bound to succeed. It is quite probable that the onslaught of Stalinism would have prevented the luxury of sustained edu-cational effort. But it was never tried. And there was nothing until very recently to start with.[45]

Apart from some Polish intellectuals, the Polish elites, in particular the hierarchy of the Catholic Church, did not take up the moral challenge of the Holocaust.[46] The Jewish question after the Holocaust became for the Church hierarchy a political question in the confrontation with the communist government. The Jews were perceived as again taking the wrong side in this political conflict. In this sense, Polish post-war relations with the Jews were, as Abel Kainer has written, a misconstrued encounter with communism.[47] The drama of post-war Polish–Jewish relations is that the problem of anti-semitism in Poland was not disarmed by any strong moral condemnation by the Catholic Church, which had behind it the support of the overwhelming majority of the Polish nation. The issue was left totally in the hands of the government side, in the hands of the communists, who did not have that support. The Jews, threatened and having no choice, went to those who could guarantee them security. The tragedy is that the communist side then, and later during the Stalinist terror, used the fight with anti-semitism for its own political aims and one of the weapons in that fight was the murder and persecution of Polish patriots, members of the AK, as well as former members of Żegota.[48] Both the Polish elites and those

Jews employed in the communist apparatus fell into this trap.

In the official fight against anti-semitism the facts about the AK were falsified and the lies made a part of the official currency of intellectual propaganda. The AK was equated with the extreme right NSZ. The soldiers of the AK were silenced, as were members of Żegota. They were unable to give the true picture, and the AK was officially declared 'fascist' and persecuted. The assistance provided by the Communist underground to the Jews was unrealistically inflated[49]. Real anti-semitic outbursts, such as the Kielce pogrom, were exploited in the political game. In other words, a real moral change, a fight for the soul of the nation, was never attempted. The Church failed to recognize the true interests of the nation. Its policies cannot be justified on the grounds that the Church, under attack itself, had different priorities. This is because, on this particular point, the national interest was identical with the precepts of the Ten Commandments.

To make a strong statement against anti-semitism required from the Church hierarchy a substantial dose of far-sightedness and political wisdom in conditions of bitter political conflict when the survival of the Church was at stake. We may regret that the Church did not have such a far-sighted view, that a chance to close the history of the Polish–Jewish relations after the Holocaust was lost. Yet, one may argue that intellectual and political wisdom is usually something which is perceived with hindsight and is rarely accessible to the actors taking part in current events. Nevertheless the Church lacked moral sensitivity. That there was no attempt to repudiate the evil heritage of anti-semitism – the more honour to people like Bishop Kubina who prevented a pogrom in Częstochowa – is in itself a moral reproach. That lack of sensitivity was the legacy of anti-semitism on the part of the Church.

There was not enough moral sensitivity to include Jews as part of the traumatic Polish experience. The Jews did not become a part of the Polish universe of symbolic obligation and there was not enough courage and clear recognition of what was important and what was not. That would have required a look beyond immediate politics and the recognition of certain moral imponderabilia.

It is thus necessary to look at anti-semitism in Poland in the period 1944–6 not only as a reaction which stemmed from the primitive identification of the Jews with communism, which was not supported by the majority of the Poles, but as an inability to overcome anti-semitism despite the Holocaust and so as an integral part of the moral guilt of the war *vis-à-vis* the Jews. This inability and moral insensitivity, especially in the context of the total lack of free public life, which prevented any education of society at large, permitted anti-semitism to become legitimate in the Polish consciousness. If only to a mild and limited degree in public, as distinct from private discourse, anti-semitism became a matter of opinion, not a moral crime. And that is why in the drama of 1968 anti-semitism, in however small a part of society – and however odiously stimulated, manipulated and used by the competing factions of the communist apparatus – played perhaps on an empty stage, but with a full world audience.

It might be argued that this was merely primitive, traditional anti-semitism. But after the Holocaust such qualifications are meaningless and empty. As Emil Fackenheim has written: 'Not all anti-semites are murderers. A Jew wants to say that, but he cannot say that . . . [This is because] the Holocaust ruptured Jewish–Gentile relations once. If unmended that constitutes a barrier beyond repair.'[50]

In this context, it seems to me that Polish culture in its entirety after the Holocaust has not made an effort to understand, let alone to integrate, Jewish sensitivity.[51] In the Talmud, *Pardes* is a mystical orchard where the suffering of the innocent is contemplated. One must not too lightly enter that orchard, for one runs the risk of madness, loss of innocence, and even death. Yet, only if one enters and identifies with the pain of the victims, can one earn the right to question.[52] Polish culture, Polish education need to enter the Jewish *Pardes* of the Holocaust to recognize its tragic emptiness and insanity, because the Holocaust is in fact a universal phenomenon and cannot be reduced to the issue of the relationship between the Poles and the Jews. If we enter that Jewish *Pardes*, perhaps it will be easier for us to understand 'how little despair was there in us, how much there was in need of salvation.'[53]

Poles sometimes interpret this problem wrongly. Many think it only a Polish–Jewish dispute, merely a disagreement which, of course debases the Holocaust into a trivial bickering between two nations. In fact this is not an argument between Poles and Jews – at least it is only marginally so. The problem in fact involves fundamental issues of contemporary culture, of Christianity, and of the anti-semitic climate of the modern civilization which contributed, however unintentionally, to the Nazi leap into evil (itself fundamentally both anti-Jewish and anti-Christian). Both psychologically and culturally the Holocaust constituted a decisive rupture between the Christian world and the Jews.[54] If so, then *Tikkun*, the final mending, becomes a moral duty exclusively of the Gentiles.

In such a perspective the silence of Polish culture after the Holocaust, Polish bargaining, the fallacious idea that there can be some equality of partners in a discussion, the often subconscious attempt to relativize the Holocaust, can only be perceived as trivializing and offensive. The factual arguments between Jews and Poles, which have been going on, often nastily, for decades, do not finally in themselves constitute the issue. The Polish side has had difficulty in grasping that Jews have been struggling for the acceptance of the uniqueness of the Holocaust very often by indirect means, even through libellous accusations, bordering on the irrational. Yet it has to be added that faced with moral insensitivity towards one's suffering, one fights with anything at hand, very often with shock. This shock aims to elicit the moral minimum which is the precondition of any dialogue.

This moral minimum has never, until very recently,[55] been unequivocally recognized within post-war Polish culture, whether by the Polish Church, government or the intellectual elites. The educational system has reflected this blindness.[56] From outside Poland these refusals or suppressions have been seen as arrogance, an arrogance bordering on a tacit admission of hidden moral guilt. The arrogance has been especially painful for Jews because the Jewish nation was murdered on the Polish soil. Those who were present, who after the Jews suffered the most, should, it would seem, readily understand the devastation and the moral issues.

If such a moral transformation did not occur, if anti-semitism surfaced after the war, then the conclusion seems inescapable that what happened to the Jews was considered 'not our business'. If this conclusion is correct, then Poles stand indicted for a moral insensitivity which undermines the bases on which

Poles defend their national honour. Is this not one of the tragic posthumous victories of those who annihilated the Jews and decimated the Poles?

So, where do we stand right now? I think that the so-called Polish–Jewish dialogue is a misleading term. There is only, or still, an internal Polish dialogue caused by the freeing of public life during recent years in Poland, and also by something which Ruth Wisse calls 'the inadvertent effect of the Jewish historical consciousness and the pressure it exerts on those European nations who contributed to or [as in Poland (author's note)] bore witness to the genocide of European Jewry.'[57]

The Jewish chapter in Poland as an ongoing presence and contribution to Polish history is closed forever. It has been brought to an end by the evil deeds of others. And that is why that Polish–Jewish dialogue cannot be truly reciprocal. The Jewish people are making their future and their history elsewhere. But for the Poles the issues remain fundamental. By an honest reappraisal of Polish–Jewish history Poles may gain not only a healthier culture and polity, but – I hope – perhaps also something else.

It is said that there are still Moroccan Jews who have kept the keys to their ancestral homes in fifteenth-century Spain and Portugal. Perhaps there are still Polish Jews, or those who have inherited their legacy, who keep their keys to Polish culture, not only the keys to the Jewish cemeteries of their murdered brothers and sisters. If this is possible, then we must ask what part of that culture, what part of the Polish heritage, can be part of their heritage too.

That opening to a Polish heritage cannot yet – if ever – happen without, as Jan Błoński said, 'expiation' on the Polish side. The lack of that expiation would be perceived as the continuation of arrogance and would degrade our culture to a provincial status. Polish culture has the luxury of choosing from a wide variety of different streams. One of those most powerful and appealing, albeit a little forgotten, is the tradition of tolerance and pluralism. The rebuilding of that tradition, whose lack is the greatest loss of the modern Polish educational system, will be an enormous enrichment of the present dominant interpretation of the Polish national past. This would constitute the final ending of the historical road of those 'two saddest nations in history', and the beginning of the moral one about which Ksawery Pruszyński wrote:

> As mankind's nationalistic insanities cool . . . Polish thought will then reach out . . . will seek guidance from the distant past . . . It will try to uncover from the rubble the knowledge of how such a great (multinational and multidenominational) building which gave centuries of peace and liberty to so many generations was erected . . . Sooner or later Polish thought, heedful and concentrated, will march towards those trails and those eras. It will walk on the great routes of the black trail which today are being swept by history's blizzards. It will walk in this blizzard, over the potholes, with a faint oil lamp, stumbling and getting stuck – and searching . . . until it arrives at its destination.[58]

When in the Book of Genesis Jacob ended his quarrel with Laban they built a cairn of stones and called it *Gal Ed*, the cairn of remembrance. It ended the argument and set the course for the future. Sooner or later that *Gal Ed* of the Polish–Jewish search for moral equilibrium, which is also one of the chapters of Poland's search for its lost history, will finally be behind us.

NOTES

1 See T. G. Ash, 'The life of death', *New York Review of Books*, 19 December 1985.
2 Professor Yisrael Gutman, Director of the Centre of Holocaust Studies at Yad Vashem in Jerusalem stated in a recent discussion: 'This feeling of identification of Poles from all social spheres and their anti-German solidarity is a previously unheard of historical achievement and one of Europe's greatest under Nazi occupation . . . all accusations against the Poles that they were responsible for what is referred to as the 'Final Solution' are not even worth mentioning . . . There is [also] no validity at all in the contention that Polish anti-semitism or other Polish attitudes were the reason for the siting of the death camps in Poland'. See 'Polish–Jewish relations during the Second World War: a discussion', *Polin*, 1987, vol. 2 p. 341. The question of complicity can and must be a problem of collective national culture today for the Austrians, Latvians, French, or Slovaks. In Poland, the problem of complicity was a marginal phenomenon, important as a topic for research, but not a problem for a collective Polish culture today.
3 The discussion centres mainly on the Polish Jews, citizens of the

Polish state. As far as the European Jews were concerned they were transported from their respective countries much later during the occupation and usually straight to the gas chambers.

4 Helen Fein, *Accounting for Genocide National Responses and Jewish Victimization during the Holocaust*, Chicago, 1984, p. 33.

5 ibid.

6 Of course one must look at the position of the Polish Jewry in the inter-war period within the context of the social and economic structure of the Polish state and other groups and classes beset with insurmountable problems. See on this point Jerzy Tomaszewski, 'Some methological problems of the study of Jewish history in Poland between the two world wars,' *Polin*, 1986, vol. 1 pp. 163–75. Yet, what concerns me here is the policy towards the Jews which went beyond that interdependence, which singled them out in the negative sense as being exceptional.

7 See Czesław Miłosz, *Native Realm*, New York, 1981, p. 106.

8 See on this point N. Rotenstreich, 'Postscript', in Y. Bauer and N. Rotenstreich, (eds), *The Holocaust as Historical Experience*, New York, 1981, pp. 275, 277.

9 Such an interpretation is still today represented by some of the commentators on Polish–Jewish relations in the historical context. See an article in an independent, quasi-*Endek* journal: W. W., 'Żydzi, Polacy, Antysemityzm', *Polityka Polska*, 1984, vol. 6, pp. 36–40.

10 Edward Wynot, 'An unnecessary cruelty: the emergence of official antisemitism in Poland, 1936–1939', *American Historical Review*, 1971, vol. 76.

11 Jerzy Tomaszewski, *Rzeczpospolita wielu narodów*, Warsaw, 1985, pp. 151–66.

12 The Polish elites also caused propaganda and world-image problems, but we should also bear in mind from the often unwise political activities of the Jewish political parties.

13 See the interview with the Editor of the Paris-based monthly *Kultura*, Jerzy Giedrojc, in *ANEKS*, 1986, no.44, pp. 40–2.

14 The acceptance of the Polish Jews who had resided in Germany for years and who were ejected to Poland in 1938 was such a case in point. See Jerzy Tomaszewski, *op. cit.*, pp. 197–207.

15 That traditional European Christian anti-semitism where Jews were assigned an antithethical yet firmly historical position was totally contradicted by Nazi Germany. Nazism took the Jews from their legitimate historical, however inferior position, and threw them outside of history. That antithetical extra-historical position was not only never contemplated by traditional Christian anti-semites but they were never psychologically capable of doing that. In that sense Nazism made a leap into another dimension, which was facilitated and made possible by the primitive absorption of scientific changes in the nineteenth century, of which racism was the most sinister offshoot. See Czesław Miłosz, 'Poland and the Jews: and Interview,'

Tikkun, vol. 2, no. 2, pp. 36–42.

16 Władysław Bartoszewski, a member of 'Żegota', the special group created by AK to help the Jews, writes: 'I must state honestly: if I had assimilated everything I heard at school and at Church on the subject of the Jews, I would have become an anti-semite. Only an inner resistance to stupidity and compulsion of thought led to my being able to defend Jews during the war,' in 'Jesień Nadziei – Warto być-przyzwoitym', *Spotkania*, 1986, p. 49.

17 As one of the Home Army (AK) soldiers said: 'Jews are rather perceived as ballast.' Quoted in Stanisław Vincenz *Tematy Żydowskie*, London, 1977, p. 69.

'No one seemed to provide the Jewish side with any organized, not so much material, concrete help – that was usually not very feasible, but even spiritual. Why were the telephones silent?' Interview by the author with Yisrael Gutman, to be published.

See also an interesting observation of Barbara Toporska, 'It is interesting that anti-semitism under the German occupation increased and influenced the circles which before the war were not anti-semitic . . . It was said: "The German propaganda caught on this point". That was not true . . . every Pole considered it his duty to reject everything that the German propaganda said . . . Anti-semitism was increasing despite anti-semitic propaganda . . . And the only reasonable explanation of this unusual phenomenon was, perhaps, the upsurge of Polish nationalism . . . under the pressure of German nationalism . . . This shows that nationalism . . . when it crosses the boundary of national consciousness turns against everyone who is alien, thus also the Jews. Of course the peasants' anti-semitism was more cruel than that of the intelligentsia, which did not soil its hands . . . yet what is the moral difference between one who gave away Jews and one who was saying that "the solution of the Jewish problem is after all advantageous for the nation"?' Barbara Toporska, 'Wybieram wątek najmniej popularny', in Józef Mackiewicz and Barbara Toporska, *Droga Pani*, London, 1984, p. 117.

18 For instance in the USA during the war the Jews were constantly portrayed in surveys as constituting the greater menace to America's security than the Germans or Japanese. See D. Lipstaedt, *Beyond Belief: The American Press and the Coming of the Holocaust 1933–1945*, New York, 1986, p. 126.

19 Quoted in Aleksander Smolar, 'Jews as a Polish problem', *Daedelus* spring 1987, p. 36.

20 See the interview of Ewa Berberyusz with Stanisław Krajewski in *Tygodnik Powszechny* 5 April 1987 (chapter 8).

21 See J. T. Gross, 'Polish–Jewish relations during the war: an interpretation', *Dissent*, winter 1987, pp. 77–8. Also Smolar, 'Jews as a Polish problem', *op. cit.*, p. 37; and J. Majchrowski, 'Geneza politycznych ugrupowań Katolickich', *Libella*, Paris, 1984, p. 68.

22 Teresa Prekerowa, 'The "just" and the "passive"', *Tygodnik*

Powszechny, 29 March 1987, (chapter 6).

23 The memoirs and official reports of the former members of Żegota contain many such complaints. See my interview with Y. Gutman, *op. cit.*

24 S. Vincenz, *Tematy Żydowskie*, *op. cit.*, p. 88.

25 H. Grynberg, *Prawda Nieartystyczna*, West Berlin, 1984, p. 48.

26 Germans were responsible for the breaking up of morality within the Polish and Jewish communities under terror. That education of the nation *vis-à-vis* the Jews has to be understood as part of the wider effort by the Polish underground state to prevent demoralization of the community under the most severe occupation in Europe.

27 J. Andrzejewski, '*Zagadnienia polskiego antysemityzmu*', in *Martwa Fala*, Warsaw, 1947 p. 108.

28 It was comprehensively, although a little one-sidedly, discussed recently by R. Lukas, *The Forgotten Holocaust – The Poles Under German Occupation 1939–1944*, Lexington, Kentucky, 1986.

29 W. Bartoszewski, 'Polish–Jewish relations during the Second World War – a discussion', *Spotkania*, 1986, pp. 34–6.

30 To all resistance fighters inside and outside Nazi-occupied Europe resistance was a doing. For Jews . . . resistance was a way of being,' Emil Fackenheim, *To Mend the World* (New York) 223–4.

31 The most agonizing discussion in the Jewish community today is whether the *Judenräte* had the right, were doing the right thing, to try to pretend that they were taking rational action. The discussion started with Hannah Arendt in her *Eichmann in Jerusalem* (London, 1961) and has continued till today. See 'The Judenrat and the Jewish response' in Bauer and Rotenstreich, *The Holocaust*, *op. cit.*, pp. 155–282.

32 That is very often the most standard justification of the position of the AK on the Polish side. As the most classic example see A. Szczypiorski, 'Polacy i Żydzi', *Kultura*, Paris, 1979, no. 5, pp. 7–8.

33 For instance the activities of an AK unit headed by 'Ponury' in the Świętokrzyski region.

34 Y. Gutman, 'Polish responses to the liquidation of Warsaw Jewry', *Jerusalem Quarterly*, Autumn 1980, 17, p. 49.

35 The classic example of the dismissal of the problem is seen in an article by an outstanding Catholic intellectual Jerzy Micewski: 'when all is said and done, we as a society and as a nation have no reason to suffer from complexes on account of our attitude towards the Jews.' In 'Tradycje historyczne katolicyzmu polskiego', *Znaki Czasu*, 1986, 1, p. 82.

36 In a school textbook by A. Szczęśniak for the last year of elementary school we read: 'The overwhelming mass of the Jewish people during the occupation was passive . . . When in 1942 [the Germans] began the liquidation of the ghettos, the terrified and deceived Jewish people allowed themselves to be taken without any resistance to the concentration camps. When the Home Army headquarters gave orders to rescue the deportees, and the fighting units – with heavy

casualties – liquidated the German guards of the transports, the Jews transported to death did not want to escape. In that situation the AK stopped attacking the transports', *History, Eighth Grade*, Warsaw, 1984, p. 76.

37 We send you our fraternal greetings . . . The struggle raging here is for your freedom and ours . . . Long live the brotherhood of arms and the blood of fighting Poland', quoted from the statement by Karski, J. Lerski, J. Nowak, S. Wiesenthal, M. Borwicz. J. Lichten, published in *Kultura*, Paris, no. 9, September 1983.

38 During the Solidarity union congress in Gdańsk in September 1981 one veteran of the Home Army stopped the congress celebrations of his exploits during the war and pointed out that the convention had among its members a hero of considerably greater stature, Dr Marek Edelman from the Łódź delegation, the last surviving leader of the Warsaw Ghetto Uprising. The Congress rose for a standing ovation. See H. Krall, *Shielding the Flame: An Intimate Conversation with Dr Marek Edelman, the Last Surviving Leader of the Warsaw Ghetto Uprising*, New York, 1986, Translator's Afterword, p. 121. The Ghetto uprising and the Jewish fight had become a Polish fight with the recognition of its lonely distinction.

39 Of course the Polish attitude is here neither exceptional nor unique. That was a common stance of the whole Western world, which put the Jew outside the universe of moral obligation, both in the countries which collaborated with the Nazis – like France or Slovakia – and also the Allies. See Michael R. Marrus and Robert O. Paxton, *Vichy, France and the Jews*, New York, 1981; also David S. Wyman, *The Abandonment of the Jews: America and the Holocaust 1941–45* New York, 1984.

40 This assumption is commonly made in Jewish historiography and journalism, especially in the USA.

41 As an example see W. Siła-Nowicki, 'A reply to Jan Błoński', *Tygodnik Powszechny* 22 February 1987, (chapter 4). It is striking that Lanzmann himself, having directed a very honest and profound film about the annihilation of the Jews, has been unable not to fall into that trap of the false dichotomy – this time against the Poles – in many of his interviews.

42 As for the stance of the Jewish world community towards the Holocaust, see Haskell Lookstein, *Were We Our Brothers' Keepers? The Public Response of American Jews to the Holocaust 1938–1944*, New York, 1988. Also Randolph Braham (ed.), *Jewish Leadership During the Nazi Era: Patterns of Behavior in the Free World*, New York, 1985.

43 That was Jan Błoński's appeal in his article 'The poor Poles look at the ghetto', *Tygodnik Powszechny*, 11 January 1987 (chapter 2).

44 For a lucid explanation of this, see A. Smolar, 'Jews as a Polish problem', *op. cit.*, pp. 45–64.

45 In that sense Kazimierz Brandys wrote: 'The Poles did not mourn their Jews. After 700 years of common life on Polish soil the Poles

did not shed even one tear over the Jews turned into ashes. For their surviving brothers and sisters the greatest pain was just that silence. The Church and the nation were silent. They decided to forget. To pretend that there were never Jews in Poland . . . There were no flowers in the small towns and settlements, no services in the churches. People moved into empty houses. The cemeteries were covered with grass. It was decided to forget. That was a treason to a common heritage, a treason to a very old, very intimate attachment. One feels cold in heart and in mind upon this thought. Arguments? Please find the arguments against the pain of heart.' In 'Miesiące 1982–84', *Kultura*, Paris, 1984, pp. 54–5.

46 The common people could not be expected to do that. The Poles were decimated, neurotic, wanted to forget everything connected with the war. But the elites should have done that. People also had their personal interest – property left by the Jews.
47 Abel Kainer, 'Stosunki Polsko-Żydowskie', *Spotkania*, nos. 29–30, p. 57.
48 See T. Woźniak, *Zapłuty Karzeł Reakcji*, Warsaw, 1983, and T. Toranska, Oni: *Stalin's Polish Puppets*, New York, 1987, interview with Berman.
49 See Adam Ciołkosz. 'Broń dla Getta Warszawy', *Kultura*, Paris, 1969, vol. 170, pp. 15–45.
50 Fackenheim, *op. cit.*, p. 305.
51 That lack of sensitivity is visible for instance in the Oświęcim (Auschwitz) Museum.
52 See M. Berenbaum, *The Vision of the Void*, Middleton, Conn., 1987, p. 192.
53 Wiktor Woroszylski, 'Mechanizm', *Więz*, 1986, no. 4, p. 160.
54 Fackenheim, *op. cit.*, p. 278: 'Christianity is ruptured by the Holocaust and stands in need of a *Tikkun*.'
55 See J. Błoński (chapter 2) and Jerzy Turowicz (chapter 13).
56 See the review of Polish school textbooks by M. M. Drozdowski in *Tygodnik Powszechny*, 13 September, 1986.
57 Ruth Wisse in *Commentary*, May 1987, p. 5.
58 Quoted by A. Michnik in 'Shadows of the forgotten ancestors' in his *Letters from Prison and Other Essays*, Berkeley, 1985, p. 216.

17

ETHICAL PROBLEMS OF THE HOLOCAUST IN POLAND

Discussion held at the International Conference on the History and Culture of Polish Jewry in Jerusalem on Monday 1 February 1988

Professor Józef Gierowski (Chairman): This discussion has its origins in the article published not long ago by Professor Błoński in *Tygodnik Powszechny*, which evoked a very lively response both in Poland and abroad. This article dealt with a very important problem of the Holocaust period, a problem which we intend to discuss again today. In advance, I should like to stress that we will not discuss the causes of the Holocaust, nor the situation which prevailed in those years on Polish lands. These basic facts are, we assume, known to everyone here. In 1939, Poland found itself under German occupation and partly too under Soviet occupation. The German zone of occupation was divided into two areas. One of these was directly incorporated into the Reich and was an integral part of that state. The other, the General-Government, was also ruled by the Germans; here they did not share the most important functions of government, and had at their disposal a sufficiently strong army and police force to carry out their policies of terror in relation to both Poles and Jews. These facts will not be part of tonight's discussion. I refer to them only to remind you of the conditions our society found itself in from the moment the country was conquered by the Germans. Nor will we discuss tonight the question of how the policy of the 'Final Solution' of the Jewish problem came to be adopted. This is a matter which is also fairly well known. It is clear that the responsibility for the planning, organizing, and implementation of this 'final solution' lies with the Germans, even if there were people who opposed it in Nazi Germany and also even if there were collaborationist groups of various other nationalities who aided them. These facts do not, however, change the basic character of the process and basically in our deliberations this whole question has a secondary significance. What is most important, what we are most concerned with here is the problem of how to react to murder carried out before our eyes. Can one be indifferent to it, should one not have taken some steps, even if these would not have stopped or limited this genocidal action? In other words, even if our possibilities of action are restricted, is there not some kind of moral, ethical rule which compels us to act on each and every matter and in each and every situation?

There are two fundamental questions for us here which I hope this discussion will answer. The first of these, which anyone who experienced the occupation and had some possibilities of action almost certainly asks himself, is whether he, as an individual, did all he could, within his power, to save others and whether all those in his situation, that is the nation, also did everything in their power to save fellow citizens whose lives were in danger. That is a fundamental question, dealing with ethical attitudes. The second question, arising from the first, concerns the more general influence of the Holocaust, the destruction of the principles of inter-national and inter-ethnic coexistence, which occurred as a result of it and caused a certain weakening of ethical feelings, an undermining of moral values, amongst both individuals and nations, and above all amongst those who were connected in some way with the 'solution' of the Jewish question. I have in mind here countries from the European cultural sphere. But I am also thinking about the effect which the Holocaust has had generally on people right up to the present. I hope that we will also find an answer to this question today, the question of the negative influence of the Holocaust on human attitudes and on the behaviour of nations – or at least we shall get some suggestions for answers in this area.

I will request the members of our panel to speak in turn. As our first speaker, I invite the person who in a certain sense has been the originator of this discussion, Professor Jan Błoński.

Jan Błoński: Professor Gierowski has been kind enough to recall my article and therefore I would like firstly to say why I wrote it and what its general aim was. Several years ago, I spent some time, a year, abroad, outside of Poland, and then I read many articles and books on the Holocaust and particularly on the behaviour of the Poles during the war. I read what Poles in Poland and Poles who had emigrated had written; I also read what foreigners, other historians, had written. I came to the conclusion at the time that perhaps I should condense it all, to familiarize the Polish reader with foreign views on the subject, with which they have the chance to acquaint themselves, relatively rarely in Poland. This was a slightly odd decision, because I am not an historian but a student of literature. Yet, because the subject concerned me in a personal way, I believed I was capable of writing an informative article. When I started to work, I became aware that it was very difficult to write what I wanted and, in practice, impossible. It was not a question of facts which might not have been known to Polish or foreign authors and readers. It was clearly not a question of the facts. There may have been differences over the facts, but this divergence was too great to be explained on this basis. It was rather in the understanding of the facts that the differences lay, and the differences were so great that I needed a dozen odd pages to explain each one. And naturally I could not afford so much space and came to the conclusion that I had to approach the matter in a more fundamental manner. I am thus not going to speak now about how these issues are presented by specialist historians, but about our ordinary knowledge of the Holocaust and of Polish Jews generally. In everything that has been written in Poland on the subject, and I have in mind here to a large degree literature, journalistic publications, school textbooks, memoirs, and so on, a fear is palpable, a hidden or suppressed fear that we Poles should not give a bad impression, that we should, as you might say, appear at our best, a fear that we might be regarded as being heartless, that as a nation we should not be made to bear the responsibility for those terrible catastrophes which took place on our territory, which somehow fouled and disgraced that earth. This fear, even dread, is the main reason why almost every Pole who writes or speaks about these events takes up a defensive position. At the outset, this attitude seems justified, as the world knows very little about Poland, does not understand Polish history and does not know what our country went through during the occupation. Yet this attitude totally distorts the picture of the past, and often, especially in official statements, its identification of anti-semitism with Nazism naturally leads to the conclusion that there was no anti-semitism in Poland. Reflection on the Polish defensive attitude quickly leads in turn to the conclusion that before one starts to think about the issues, before one starts to weigh up these events and the arguments of the Poles about them, one has to prepare oneself morally, ethically. It is not enough to look at facts, as facts are bad witnesses for people, who look at them from the point of view of their own emotional and intellectual interests. Although intellectually it is not always productive, it is better that historians and even people as a whole should not be primarily concerned with finding a morally comfortable stance. Taking this statement as our starting point, we must (this is more or less how I understood my aim) look more deeply into why this resistance, why this defensive attitude, is so often to be found in Poland, and particularly into why it is so full of panic, so vociferous. In my opinion it is born of a deep and hidden feeling of guilt.

But why is this feeling of guilt so strong in Poland? Because it is immediately associated with the responsibility for genocide, a responsibility no one even wants to consider. After all, we claim, were not Poles also doomed to destruction? I am not comparing the Holocaust, which is something totally different, in any way with Polish suffering. Yet the fact is that the Polish nation was also being condemned to slavery and conceivably to destruction. It is an awful paradox, particularly in the first period of the occupation, which I still remember, that precisely when the Jews were being separated from the Poles, made to wear armbands, and shut up in ghettos, less was heard of the killings of Jews, attention was concentrated rather on the awful terror which reigned in the western territories of Poland. All of Poland's attention was fundamentally concentrated on this, at the time when the systematic destruction of the Jews began. Thus Poles did have a feeling that they were the next in line to the gas chambers; not entirely so, but the feeling of danger was naturally very strong. Thus it is very difficult for us to live with the idea that the Poles were in some way jointly responsible for the Holocaust.

It was, however, my strong belief that such an idea had to be considered, so that Poland's past and wartime experience could be fully examined, examined to the end. Only then could we

Poles, who would like to be entirely pure, better understand our own behaviour and release ourselves from the burden it places on us. Does all this mean that I think that the Poles, as a nation, aided the Nazis in killing the Jews? I was sorry when I heard that a few journalists, even abroad, had so understood my argument. I was sorry, not only because it was untrue, sorry that they had attributed such nonsense to me, but because they had shown themselves incapable of understanding what moral responsibility is. They only understand criminal responsibility: whoever is caught is guilty. Poles were not guilty of aiding the killings. In Poland, perhaps, the Germans has fewer direct helpers than anywhere else, to a large degree perhaps because the Poles in Poland had no social organization, since there was no state. In other countries, in Hungary, in Romania, and elsewhere there were puppet states of various kinds and many collaborators. But the question is not one of accounting, it is not important whether in Łódź there were 20 per cent more informers than in Strasbourg or 20 per cent fewer. This is not the issue. The issue is that one can be co-responsible without co-operating – this was the idea of my article. To put it most generally, Polish responsibility is, in my opinion, centred on indifference, indifference at the time of the Holocaust. Naturally not the indifference of everyone. There were those who were not indifferent and we pay tribute to them. The result of this indifference was that Jews died with a feeling of solitude, with a feeling of having been abandoned. This indifference was explicit, one could somehow feel it when one was a child. Naturally, there were those who helped whether from humanitarian or mercenary motives, although every historian agrees that even the most intensive help in Poland could not have saved many, such was the enormous disproportion in the forces and means at the disposal of the Poles and the German occupiers. Polish responsibility is also related to the fact, and I place great importance on this, that indifference often developed into enmity. Imagine Poland, or anywhere in Europe, where the religious coexistence of nations of different religious persuasions had developed in a good, or at least an acceptable, manner. The Nazi Holocaust would then have been more difficult to imagine and to carry out, and would have had to take a different form. Responsibility, understood in this manner, the Poles share naturally with their neighbours, with the whole of

Europe, with Christianity. They even, perhaps, share it with American Jews. I know what a tragedy it is for the Jews in the Diaspora, in America, who did not see what happened. I know, I well understand, that tragedy. Yet it is more important to stress that we, unlike them, are not absolved by the fact that we did not know what was happening, firstly because we were on the spot and secondly because the Polish responsibility is greater by virtue of the fact that Jews lived on Polish lands, and we Poles should have known better, understood better than to make them a scapegoat for our own political and social difficulties. In short, I believe that the Holocaust is a call for us Poles to take a new look at ourselves as people who, albeit in a small, in a very small degree, allowed it to take place. The Holocaust compels us to look at ourselves differently, in other words at our past, at our identity as human beings and as a nation, made up of individuals. It is precisely this self-analysis and a change in our way of seeing ourselves which a considerable part of the Polish people shy away from. The understanding of co-responsibility means in this case an acknowledgement of blame for the past and signifies a new assessment of that past. Such an acknowledgement and assessment is needed by ourselves more than the Jews and, personally, I am very glad that the younger generation in Poland understands this in an increasingly explicit manner. This will certainly find its expression in future historiography and has even already started to find expression. Thank you very much.
[*Applause*]

Józef Gierowski: Thank you very much Professor and now I ask Mr Scharf to take the floor.

Rafael Scharf: I am limited by time, by the Chairman's tolerance and what is more important, the audience's patience – those are narrow boundaries. I have, therefore, prepared only loose pages, which can easily be shuffled and, if necessary, omitted. I shall raise, at random, a few problems which I consider to be fundamental. Perhaps these fragments will join up, in some way, to form a more coherent account.

When I was thinking what title to give to my talk, various ideas came to mind. At one time, I thought to call it: 'To My Polish Friends', but this echo of Mickiewicz ('Do Przyjaciół-Moskali') could have sounded, in my mouth, a bit pretentious. I played with the title, 'At the Crossroads', imitating the famous 'Al Parashat Derakhim' of Ahad-Ha'am an excellent heading, universally applicable; are we not eternally at some sort of crossroads – I discarded it as too general. I thought of calling it, 'Very Difficult Accounts' – but that would give the impression of a contest and it is my intention to get away from 'settling' of accounts. I tried to call it 'Not all is Black and White', which does define my approach, but in the end I brought it down to the simple, 'Talking – With Whom and About What'?

With whom, then? If there is to be a dialogue, one must have a clear profile of one's interlocutor. I take here a model which one might define as 'elitist'. I want to sit down to the table with the best and not the worst. Not with those who hated the Jews before the war, who were betraying them to the Germans during the war and who drove them out of Poland after the war. Not with the Poland of 'Grunwald', the Poland of the Moczars, not with those who sell copies of the Protocols of the Elders of Zion, nor with those who at every opportunity spout virulent rubbish about Israel or write that Korczak ill-treated Christian children, and not with those who, like that journalist in the paper *Ład* in Warsaw, declare that 'if the Jews don't change their ways time will come when we shall have to hide them again in cellars' (it is easy to guess how many he would hide). Nor yet with those whom I often overhear in London, declaring 'No matter what we say, the Jews they shout us down anyway'. There is no shortage of dimwits, cranks and bigots anywhere, sadly also amongst us, the Jews. I quite understand that a Pole cannot enter into a dialogue with those who hold that every Pole is an anti-semite; who have seen and continue to see in Poland nothing but anti-semitism; who maintain that the extermination camps were located in Poland because the Germans could count on the passivity of the Poles and that there is no point in discussing these things any further.

I want to speak with Poles about a Poland which gave birth to Kochanowski, Mickiewicz, and Norwid, Konopnicka, Prus, Orzeszkowa, Gomulicki, Dąbrowska, Nałkowska, and also Turowicz, Błoński, Bartoszewski, Kołakowski, Anna Kamieńska, Wiesława Szymborska, Miłosz, Ficowski. About a Poland where there flourished, and died, a Jewish civilization, unique and unrepeatable.

In one of my earlier addresses I remarked that the culture which existed cheek by jowl, nay, right in the middle of the Polish community, remained totally unknown and uninteresting to the Poles, indeed, they would have been staggered to be told that something was taking place here which deserved to be called culture.

It is worth considering here how the Poles, generally, saw their Jewish fellow citizens, as that view, after all would have formed their opinions and attitudes. In the first place, then, they saw the dark, motley crowd, Jews in their traditional garb, with beards and side-locks, in 'kaftans', in skull-caps, in black hats; in the small towns, in market places, jabbering, noisy, uncouth, poor, though their poverty was somehow different from the Polish poverty. They saw the petty merchants, the small shopkeepers with whom they traded and from whom they bought, often on credit, in spite of the slogans 'Buy from Your Own' and the officially sponsored boycott. The Jewish shopkeepers were competitive, the more so as Poles very often regarded trade as being below their dignity. The Poles saw the artisans, watch-makers, cobblers, tailors, unsurpassed in their skills. They saw the middle classes in the larger towns, who in their dress and behaviour differed little from the Poles, although their lifestyle was somewhat different. They saw 'landlords' owners of tenement-houses – bricks-and-mortar being the preferred Jewish investment – of which the proportion of Jewish owners was substantial. They saw, at school, fellow students who, if they differed at all, differed by their diligence and ability. They saw colleagues at university who often (let it be said – not always and not everywhere) were forced to sit on separate benches. They saw the Jewish professional classes, the doctors and lawyers, amongst them doubtless some of the best. They saw a few (and even those seemed too many) Jews in high positions, probably converts. (We Cracovians remember the following vignette from the 1930s: at ceremonial processions during state celebrations, Archbishop Sapieha walked at the head with the then Mayor of the city, Kaplicki-Kapellner on his right, and General Benio Mond on his left). On the literary scene they saw great luminaries of contemporary literature – Leśmian, Tuwim, Słonimski, Wittlin, writing often for that excellent paper *Wiadomści Literackie*, owned and edited by Grycendler-Grydzewski (and Borman). This illustrated a process of osmosis at the boundaries between the two communities, and it comprised that part of the Jewish community which identified with the Polish national aspirations to a degree only possible under the regime of Piłsudski. The process of assimilation became increasingly difficult and un-rewarding, and this it so happens was in keeping with the instinctive stance of the overwhelming majority of the Jewish community. That majority was separated from the Polish community and all the more effectively as both sides favoured separation. To give you a small example: at the time when I lived in Poland in the inter-war years, not once did I go into a Polish house or flat, unless you count a peasant's cottage rented for the holidays in Zakopane or Zawoj. What is more, I did not look upon this as a deprivation, I took it to be the most natural thing in the world. I had many non-Jewish friends at university, we also had many such clients in our legal practice, but as a rule there were no social contacts.

The reasons for this were many, but the main one was that the Poles did not consider the Jews to be their equals as human beings. They looked down on us from a position of natural superiority. Regardless of their social position, Poles, as a rule, considered themselves to be better and superior to Jews, any Poles to any Jew; superior, as it were, by definition. This lack of a feeling of any common bond, the result of existing conditions, comes closest to explaining the fact that the greater part of the Polish community was insensitive to the fate of the Jews under the occupation. Quite apart from 'the scum on the periphery of society' (the term commonly used in Poland); apart, also, from that section of the political and moral spectrum which openly welcomed the destruction of the Jews by foreign hands; granting also that there must have been vast numbers of good, ordinary people who were deeply shocked by the monstrous spectacle re-enacted in front of their own eyes and who had genuine compassion for its victims, it is an undeniable fact that the majority of the Poles remained indifferent.

We know that active help was risky and demanded courage and altruism. It was simply not to be expected that general attitudes, developed over the generations would change overnight. Teresa Prekierowa, on the data available to her, estimated that 1–2½ per cent of the population actively participated in helping the Jews. (This includes a considerable number who did this for money, but that is a mere detail.)

One can argue the accuracy of statistics and round off a percentage here and there (I do not decry the value of work done in this field, I value it highly), but the Jews have no need of statistics, *they know how it was*. Poles, generally, do not know, they cannot know, perhaps they do not want to know. The Jews are bitterly resentful, but no one would claim that they were expecting it to be different – and that alone provides a tragic commentary. The rancour, which they are not slow to express, sometimes noisily, is not only against the Poles, but against the world in which such things were possible and tolerated. And in the last instance, against the Almighty who has also not covered Himself in glory (but this is a separate theme).

A question occurs: are we to judge human behaviour by the absolute standards of ethics and morality, or are we to deem these concepts utopian and unattainable and resign ourselves soberly, not to say cynically, to the fact that dark and primitive instincts effectively dominate human nature and cause humans to be base and cruel?

And further: if in our weakness or understandable concern for our own lives and the lives of those close to us, we are unable to behave morally and measure up to those high principles which we know from religion and philosophy and which we approve in theory, do we in such a situation consider our behaviour blameless and justified by rational requirements; or rather, are we left with a sense of shame that we did not live up to the call of conscience, shame increased by the knowledge that someone else – true, not many, but somebody, somewhere – did live up to it? I am putting these thoughts for consideration to those who sleep peacefully since, as they say, 'nothing could be done'.

Błoński's example, the moral tone of his utterance, prompts me to raise the discussion above a mere settling of scores, recrimination, verbal squabbles and rhetorical victories. That sort of contest might have been in order in the past, nay, it has been unavoidable; blunt speaking helped to clear the air of accumulated poison. At that stage I was myself an active participant in that debate. Dealing with this most painful and touchy theme, I expressed the view that when the cattle-trucks were rolling towards Auschwitz, Treblinka, Majdanek, Sobibor, Chelmno and Bełżec and when day and night the smoke belched out of the chimneys, carrying over the fields the stench of burning bodies; if it had been known then, that it was not Jews who were burning, but native Polish husbands, mothers, wives and children, the nation's outburst of wrath and fury would have been uncontrollable, 'even if they had to tear up the rails with their bare teeth' was the phrase I used. That phrase has often been thrown back at me and its crops up in discussion again and again. I have not been moved to change my view, but I believe today the temperature of the discussion has cooled down and one can use a different language. We are nearing a time when there will not be a single eye-witness, no one who themselves went through that inferno, there will no longer be survivors from the camps and from the bunkers, those who owe their life to 'Aryan papers', those whose salvation proved to be the exile in Siberia. There will be no one from Gomułka's Fifth Column, no Jews from the security apparatus and none from the expellees of 1968; gone will be those who have never recovered from their love of Poland, those who on the banks of the River Thames dream of their Vistula, and those, who like myself – and forgive me if it sounds precious – after 50 years away from Poland put themselves to sleep with lines from the 'Crimean Sonnets' or the 'Grave of Agamemnon'. I believe that then the historical perspective and the parameters of these issues will change. With the passage of time it will become clear that the agenda is not about us alone; that our debate and controversy is merely incidental to something bigger and more comprehensive. What is at issue here is a great, common cause of universal significance. The extermination of the Jews on Polish territory was a crucial event in history, marking the crisis of Christianity and the crisis of our civilization (some people regard those concepts as synonymous, but fortunately that is not so). Those events cannot be forgotten or ignored, they will weigh upon the future generations for all time.

What lessons will human beings draw from this, how will they face up to it, conscious of the enormity of evil which they are capable of perpetrating; how will they renew their faith in the basic moral values in a world of which, in Adorno's words, 'we cannot be too much afraid' and where there exist instruments of destruction which put even the gas chambers in shadow? On answers to these questions hang all our tomorrows.

I revert to my title: what shall we talk about? Someone might say that there is nothing to be added to what has already been said in the context of Polish–Jewish discourse. Let me answer with the sentence from the Hagada which begins: '*Af im kulanu hahamim*' (Even if we were all wise . . .) which in free translation might be taken to mean that although we have learned from many sources and have absorbed a great deal of wisdom, nonetheless it is incumbent upon us to tell this story . . .

I know not everybody will agree with me that there is plenty to talk about. Many of my friends both in Israel and in England say, 'Why bother yourself, and us, with these matters, what good will it do? Everything connected with that time is so sad and painful, why rub salt into open wounds?' I take the point but am not persuaded by it. To turn one's mind away from these topics would be, in my view, an impoverishment, and I suspect that those who want to distance themselves from them would distance themselves from other serious topics as well.

I believe that the more things concerns us the better. Surely there is plenty to talk about; our history – the part which is common and the part which is separate; about how things really went between us, at close quarters and at a distance; about the climate that nurtured us, the conditions which formed us; about mutual influences, good and bad; about the wrongs endured and the benefits received, about that which united and that which divided us, about all of that, as long as it is not superficial but serious and with concern for truth. This does not mean that we shall see the truth in the same way, because the truth is complicated and has many dimensions; we are sensitive to some of its aspects, blind to others; only some segments of it are accessible to each of us. The sheer awareness that this is so seems to be a step in the right direction.

We, who form a link in the chain of the 1000 years of Jewish presence on Polish soil, does it not behove us to remember that part of our heritage is to cultivate it and pass it on. Every brick, every stone, every graveyard, every footprint, each document, each scrap of paper, each trace in whatever form, is valuable beyond measure for a nation whose roots give sense to its history and whose memory of the past vouchsafe the continuity of its existence. The history of the Jews did not begin in 1948 with the creation of the State of Israel. A large part of the history was enacted on Polish lands. Should one, could one, turn one's back on it, bury it, forget it? Surely not, surely the very opposite must be the case.

I learn from the papers and friends in Poland that there is, mainly among the young, a growing and lively interest in things Jewish; history, literature, monuments, and relics. One of them wrote to me thus: 'Are we, the Poles, not a strange nation? For forty years all these matters were hidden under a shroud of forgetfulness, a shamefaced silence, a programmatic taboo – as if the Jews never existed. And now, suddenly, this seemingly spontaneous outburst of interest, curiosity, desire to know. Is this salutary? Where will this lead to?' What shall I answer him? Better late than never? If such interest has been awakened and if it is genuine and not merely morbid or psychopathic, then I applaud it and I think that there is a helpful role for us to play in this pursuit. I am not afraid, as my correspondent seems to be, of the possible undesirable consequences, that the pendulum will once again swing in the opposite direction – we are by now beyond reach of any malevolence threatening from that side.

I think that when this new generation, this 'late grandson' as Norwid put it, becomes acquainted with that part of their history and discovers how it was with the Jews in Poland and what sort of community it was, this will not only open its members eyes but will be good for their souls. They will need to ponder about the past and face up to it squarely. I want to believe that a generation of Poles is coming into its own, which is not poisoned by the virus of anti-semitism and anti-Judaism. That is, however, not our problem but theirs, because we shall never again, as a community, find ourselves, physically in close proximity.

I read Błoński's article, for the first time, with growing excitement and quickened pulse. At one point he makes reference to one of the speakers at the conference in Oxford in 1984, whose words, he said, inspired him to ponder these matters. From the words quoted by him it was clear that he was referring to me. I was startled and also moved to see how one word, a sentence, a thought can strike another man's mind, can germinate there and bear fruit beyond expectation. I was talking then, at least that is how Błoński understood it, to the effect that we Jews no longer expected anything from the Poles but the admission that they have been, in some way, at fault. For many years we listened, waited for a sign – but we heard no voices. In the end, I had thought we would be straining our ears in vain. But now, at last – we hear the voice of Błoński.

Many people in Poland say that Błoński is fouling his own nest and that even if what he has to say is true, he should not be saying it in public as this brings succour to Poland's enemies. That is an old argument – 'Do not rock the boat'. We know it particularly well in Israel where there is a widespread tendency to merciless self-criticism, but also great concern that this should remain in the family – a slippery path.

More than a year has passed since Błoński's voice sounded. I would like to assure all those who feared that it would have a harmful effect on Poland, that quite the opposite has occurred. His article is seen, in itself, as a certain rehabilitation of sorts. When, paradoxically and undeservedly, I am put in the role of an *advocatus Poloniae* I myself, in many instances, recall this article and those which followed. I maintain that one can no longer speak loosely about the Poles' opinion on the subject without taking into consideration these new voices, which save the reputation of Poland.

That reputation is a source of considerable difficulty. It rebounds on every Pole abroad, particularly in America, where in a foreign forum he has continually to explain – and not always knowing the facts – that not every Pole is and was an anti-semite. That 'foreign forum' is very often not well informed in the matter, but always knows one thing and that is enough: that in Poland life for the Jews was bad.

Poles often complain that it is the Jews who influence this unflattering opinion, by spreading falsehoods, greatly exaggerating their past misfortunes and generally blackening the good name of the country of their birth.

If that were true, the question arises why should these Jews (I am talking of those at whom the reproaches are directed) want to do such things? Is it pure malice, is it because they are naturally nasty people? Does this ring true? Or is it perhaps, if such is their perception, that it is the result of their experience, their ordeals, their feelings of injury? I am putting it thus in order to illustrate how quickly, if we are not careful, we can find ourselves back to square one: seeing one's own side of the picture alone.

All the more, it seems to me, that the public reckoning of Błoński offers a different model and calls for a new climate of relationship. It deserves an adequate response. It behoves us to remember that anti-semitism is not a peculiarly Polish invention. It is an age-old sociological, theological, and political phenomenon which, to a greater or lesser degree, is always with us, which defines us and in the absence of which (but there is no danger of that) we would feel strange. We would certainly be a different nation, a different community, different people – it is doubtful that we would be better. That does not mean that one should accept anti-semitism complacently and turn the other cheek. Quite the opposite, one must fight it by all possible means – I think that our meeting here in Jerusalem, the capital of the Jewish state, is a significant act of that struggle.

At the source of Błoński's discourse are poems of Czesław Miłosz. This is understandable. Poetry touches the essence of our being, our thoughts and feelings and brings forth resources which we ourselves are often not aware of. Yosif Brodzky, in his Nobel Prize acceptance-speech, said: 'It is more difficult to break a man who reads poetry than one who does not.' I am thinking at this moment of Max Boruchowicz – Michał Borwicz, who, sadly, is no longer with us, missed as none other. In his book *Literaturze w obozie (Literature in the Camp*, Kraków, 1946) he describes how fragments of poetry known by heart were a kind of life-belt, which in the most atrocious conditions of human degradation helped him, and others, to survive. I am thinking of that scene in the Janowski camp when a 'selection' was taking place, when his comrade, on the point of collapse, begged him with his eyes for a word of solace, and how Borwicz then spoke aloud a couple of lines of poetry (some banal verses of his own, he says) and how these words, somehow, renewed his friend's failing strength and will to live.

My Polish of 50 years ago is no match for Błoński. But in order to remain in stylistic harmony with him I seek recourse to someone else's words and want to end these remarks with an excerpt from a poem by my friend Jerzy Ficowski, entitled fittingly 'The Way to Yerushalaim':

through woodlands rivers
through an autumn of bowed candlesticks

through gas chambers
graveyards of air
they went to Yerushalaim
both the dead and the living
into their returning olden time
and that far they smuggled
a handful of willow pears
and for a keepsake
a herring bone
that sticks to this day

Józef Gierowski: Ladies and Gentlemen, I haven't got the heart
to break in, but I would appeal to my colleagues to make their
remarks shorter as otherwise we will be here for a long time. I
call on Professor Erlich.

Victor Erlich: Much of what I was going to say has already been
said, either a year or a few minutes ago. I am afraid I may be
redundant. In any case, I promise to be brief.

I shall limit myself to several statements and a few quotes. I
start by citing two characteristic remarks in the discussion, which
took place a year ago in the columns of *Tygodnik Powszechny*.
Ewa Berberyusz writes: 'Possibly even if more of us had turned
out to be more Christian, it would have made no difference to
the statistics of the extermination, but maybe it would not have
been such a lonely death'. Jerzy Turowicz said: 'If we had not
had such anti-semitism in Poland before the war, perhaps we
would still not have been able to save more Jewish lives, but our
attitude to their extermination taking place before our very eyes
would have been different.' This is in my opinion the crux of the
matter. The point is not that only a relatively small number of
Poles saved Jews, because helping Jews carried the penalty of
death during the Nazi occupation. I would rather pay tribute and
express gratitude to those who at the risk of their own lives saved
their fellow Jewish citizens rather than dwell on the rarity of such
heroic acts. For me the most painful fact concerning the attitude
of the Poles to the extermination of the Jews is something else,
notably: the widespread indifference and even enmity for the
victims, a breakdown on a wide scale of a feeling of human
solidarity with the murdered Jews. It is obvious that such an

attitude is not an exclusively Polish phenomenon, nor was it a homogenous one. This is a very complicated problem. Helplessness in the face of horrendous events taking place in front of our very eyes, horrors which we are not able to oppose effectively, sometimes result in the psychological need to turn the other way and give us a residual feeling of complicity. Such a feeling, difficult to sustain, can in turn produce enmity not only towards the perpetrators but also paradoxically towards the victims. In other words the attitude which I am talking about cannot be reduced to anti-semitism. But there is no way in which this factor can be overlooked, especially since we are in possession of the often quoted report of the AK Commander, General Grot-Rowecki, who wrote to the Polish government in London in September 1941 that the overwhelming majority of the Polish population was 'of an anti-semitic disposition'. There have been some unfortunate attempts to account for this stance by referring to the alleged behaviour of Jews in the eastern areas in September 1939 when the Soviet army entered there. (Incidentally, the fact that some, I repeat, some Jews from Białystok, Pińsk or Wilno greeted the Red Army, can be explained not by enthusiasm for the Soviet Union, but by an awareness that for the Jews it was, when compared to the Nazi regime, the lesser of the two evils.) More important to attaching decisive weight to the negative effect of such actions is scarcely possible for those like myself, who remember the growth in anti-semitic moods in Poland in the 1930s, the galloping 'Endecification' (that is, becoming more nationalistic and right wing) of the regime of Józef Piłsudski's successors and Polish society in general, where the treatment of minorities is concerned. Parenthetically, the history of reborn Poland is not the only proof of the fact that a nation once suppressed does not always on gaining sovereignty show tolerance for other ethnic groups.

Going back to the Polish situation, I recall that after the Przyłk pogrom, Premier Sławoj-Składkowski stated 'that economic boycott of Jews is OK, but beating up people is wrong'. Moreover for many Polish parties, judging by their programmes then, the presence of the Jewish community in Poland was a 'problem' which required a drastic solution – notably mass emigration.

It is the task of history to reconstruct the processes as a result of which a country which in the sixteenth century had been an example of religious tolerance and cultural pluralism came to be in the nineteenth and particularly in the twentieth century one of the centres, and to quote Jan Błoński, of a particularly severe and virulent anti-semitism. I am not a historian and must restrict myself to a statement of this obvious fact.

One more thing. Today, in the twentieth century, Polish–Jewish relations have taken on the character of a vicious circle. Amongst many Jews, a feeling of distrust was born in relation to the Poles as a result of official or popular Polish anti-semitism, and this contributed behaviour which could be construed as anti-Polish, in conditions of a national catastrophe. Those acts, in turn, added oil to the fire, and fanned a deeply rooted and 'virulent' prejudice. The historical significance of the discussion which was initiated by Jan Błoński's article, a discussion which we are continuing today, rests on the fact that remarks such as those made by Jan Błoński, Ewa Berberyusz and Jerzy Turowicz help us find a way out of that vicious circle. They help us create the conditions for a Polish–Jewish dialogue devoid of prejudice and misunderstandings, of irresponsible generalizations and self-protective denials, for a dialogue marked by mutual respect and, perhaps more important, respect for what are at times painful facts. We have started that dialogue late, and the path is a long one. Perhaps, however, by a joint effort we will succeed in fulfilling our common duty – and to once again quote Jan Błoński – to confront our past in truth.

[*Applause*]

Józef Gierowski: Thank you very much. I now ask Professor Gutman to take the floor.

Yisrael Gutman: I think it is difficult to accommodate the terms Holocaust and ethics. When I was a child, one spoke of the days of contempt, and when I grew up the days of contempt became the days of bestiality. At that time, moral norms and ethical principles were totally driven out of our world, which was never, as is well known, a paradise. Morality and humanity were condemned, they were to be found in the underground and in the camps, and death meted out to man by man became an everyday occurrence. I do not share the opinion that the whole of Poland was contaminated by the venom of anti-semitism, that Pole and anti-semite are synonyms. What is more, remarks of that kind are not exclusively to be found in certain Jewish circles, but were in their time a widely propagated view by serious *Endek* politicians and by the extreme right in Poland (the ONR). I also do not agree with the thesis, which one often hears, that the Nazi authorities set up the death camps on Polish soil because of the anti-Jewish attitude of the Poles. No one asked the Poles if they wanted Treblinka and Birkenau in their country, and the occupation regime in Poland was one of the most brutal and arbitrary forms of oppression in Nazi-occupied Europe. And not only that. Polish anti-semitism, like every variant of that phenomenon, had its detestable and cruel characteristics. It did, however, differ from ideological anti-semitism which was based on a racist philosophy. The Polish anti-semite ridiculed and humiliated the Jew, he saw in the Jew a foreign and unnecessary ballast, and in extreme situations attacked him, but in my opinion, he was not capable of planned and systematic genocide. We often ask ourselves the question whether and to what extent the murder, which we call the Holocaust, a crime having no equivalent in human history, is the outcome of anti-semitism. Sartre maintained that anti-semitism was a step in the direction of the chasm which Auschwitz symbolizes. But I think a more correct assessment is that anti-semitism in the form of racism was the most degenerate personification of an obsessive and consistent anti-Jewish campaign which had been prevalent in Europe for ages. Both the Church and Christianity had a hand in the growth of that nightmare, and the Church engraved on the forehead of every Jewish child the stigma of Cain. The great luminaries of European culture, figures of the calibre of Shakespeare, Voltaire, Wagner, and Dostoyevsky, contributed to and perpetuated the negative Jewish stereotype in the mind, in literature, and in the arts. Modern nationalistic currents and political parties have their part in this, as they not only used the Jew as a scapegoat for their own purposes but also accused Jews of every possible and impossible baseness and intrigue, their aim supposedly being to take over the world. Our Israeli historian, Jakob Talmon, was certainly right when he argued that anti-semitism was a Trojan horse which enabled racism to invade the heart of Europe. It is most probable that after the Jews the Poles, Russians, and others, whose noses or language were not to the preferred taste, were next in line. Thus it happened that the ghost of hatred, which had been tolerated and nurtured through many an age, grew to be a monster, which not only destroyed the Jews but threatened Christianity, European civilization, and human existence as a whole. In an atmosphere which resulted in the isolation and elimination of the Jews from the ranks of the human community, indifference, the turning of one's back, and silence in the face of tragedy – even callous acquiescence, or here and there active cooperation in the stealing of property and crimes – came to be possible.

Jan Błoński in his wise and courageous article writes: 'We feel after all that not everything was in order, and how could it have been? The coexistence of communities, like that of individuals, is never untarnished, and, in this case, we have to do with a stormy and unhappy coexistence'. I shall return to certain fragments of that coexistence, or lack of it during the war and occupation, later.

Sometimes I hear Jews accusing the Poles of deliberately not helping them even though they could have done so. Such observations are expressions of pain, which eclipse a sensible attitude. More could certainly have been done to save Jews, but the Poles in the conditions of the occupation could not have fundamentally changed the fate of the Jews. The Allies perhaps could have done so, but even that is not certain in the final phases of the murderers' insanity. I shall permit myself to say more – there is no moral imperative which demands that a normal mortal should risk his life and that of his family to save his neighbour. Are we capable of imagining the agony of fear of an individual, a family, which selflessly and voluntarily, only due to an inner human impulse, bring into their home someone threatened with death? Are we capable of understanding the pressure of those fears when a fugitive had to be kept out of sight of neighbours and relations, when a neighbour or friend dare not hear the cough of a sick person nearby, and those hiding the fugitive lived in an unending fear, when all that was needed was one house search for both the hider and the hidden to have an end put to their lives? The Poles should be proud that they had so many just lights, of whom Ringelblum spoke, who are the real heroes of the deluge. And we can never do enough to thank these rare people. But by force of events, such willingness to sacrifice could have been only a marginal phenomenon. We Jews do not have a body of saints in our faith. I will surely be an undesirable intruder when I say that before the beatification of a baptized Jewess, who died a Jewish death, a Christian who shared the fate of the Jews should perhaps have been beatified.

And from this, to the agonizing questions and insinuations. In the course of my work, I have looked at the entire Żegota [Council for Aid to Jews] archives. Professor Bartoszewski, who is sitting next to me, knows these details from his own personal experience. For a historian it is a fascinating exercise. There are some documents which not only explain, but shout. Żegota people were devoted to the cause of the Jews. But it is striking that they saw themselves as spokesmen of a difficult and unpopular issue, that the Delegatura Rządu [Representation of the Polish Government in London] and often the underground authorities had a harsh attitude towards them. And as I have already spoken about the inappropriate questions posed by Jews, I shall refer to similar questions on the part of Poles.

It is often asked why did Jews not escape from the ghettos and cross to the Aryan side? There is a ready answer – they were frightened, they were cowards. It is true they were frightened, but was that only due to the fact that they were cowards? Several months ago, the Hebrew poet Abba Kovner died in a kibbutz. As a young man, not much older than twenty, Kovner was the first to state unequivocally, at the end of 1941, that Nazi Germany aimed at the total extermination of the European Jews and he called on the Jews to fight in self-defence. He was a partisan leader and the organizer of the remnants of Jews after the war, and in our country a poet of great stature. Shortly before his death, Kovner wrote words of thanks for a woman, whom he called *Imma*, mother in Hebrew. He regarded her as his second mother. That woman was Anna Bortkowska, the Prioress of the Benedictine Sisters' Nunnery near Wilno. She hid a group of Jewish youths for a certain time in the nunnery and when she bade them farewell, said that she would like to go with them to the ghettos, as God surely at that time was to be found there. The watchful eyes of that Mother, of that small Mother, of that small lady with the enormous soul, spoke to Kovner and accompanied him throughout the long years of martyrdom and fighting. But that very same Kovner when he was asked why he did not cross to the other side replied: 'Those who put the question either do not understand or pretend they don't, that if we had done so, the very paving-stones of the Wilno streets would have called out – "There go Jews".'

The goodwill of an individual cannot whitewash reality, cannot change the fact that the Jews were generally regarded as something foreign. They were something which did not belong to the Poles and it was not worth putting oneself out for them to any great degree. Nor did one feel an obligation to do so. Nothing can change the fact that until the autumn of 1942 the Polish underground authorities did absolutely nothing to help those starving and suffering in the ghettos. Could they have relieved their lot? I think so. In this case quite a lot could have been done and without any great effort and risk. In the Warsaw ghetto alone, by the autumn of 1942, more than 80,000 human beings had died from starvation and disease.

Ringelblum wrote in his memoirs that even after a difficult day's work, it was impossible to fall asleep as the begging and whining of the child skeletons wrapped in rags on the stone pavements of the ghetto streets could be heard constantly. I also do not share the opinion of many Polish researchers that during the war in occupied Poland a diminution in anti-semitism occurred, because human misery united people and anti-German attitudes strengthened the links of joint solidarity. Unfortunately, the fact is that suffering people are not more sensitive to the torture and pain of others. The Poles correctly emphasize that Poles were exemplary in their decisively anti-Nazi attitude, but it would appear that this attitude did not entail support for the Jews. In other words, the anti-Jewish policies of the Nazis found a resonance, and sometimes were even popular, amongst many Poles. The call which went out from government circles in Poland was not to say too much about the Jews, as this was not regarded favourably in Poland. As proof of this, I would like to quote here a small fragment from an article by Stanisław Ossowski, 'After the Kielce slaughter'.

A more far-sighted, more cynical or more wilful person, or someone with greater historical knowledge might have recalled that sympathy is not the only reaction to the misfortune of others; that those whom the gods have singled out for extinction easily become repugnant to others and are even removed from inter-human relations. He might also recall that if one person's tragedy gives someone else an advantage, it often happens that people want to convince themselves and others that the tragedy was morally justified. Such people as owners of former Jewish shops or those who harass their Jewish competitors can be included in this group. And perhaps by citing a whole array of historical examples, I could express my doubt as to whether the reaction against the Nazi achievements will, in the short run, root out the influences of the Nazi spirit, which, within the course of a few years, attained so much, and which led awareness to become inured to certain offensive slogans because of their frequent repetition.

I am not saying all this so as to be able to bargain, as Błoński would put it, and have the upper hand in the bidding. I believe it is our task, indeed our sacred duty, to tell the truth even if it is unpleasant and unpopular for us. Our two nations, the Poles and the Jews, are sensitive to patriotism and that often leads to a situation where that patriotism is either wrongly or incorrectly understood.

Critics of Błoński's article accuse him of having added fuel to the Jewish fire against the Poles. I would like to tell those critics that, unfortunately, we never lacked that kind of fire. Once, as a young Zionist, I believed that we Jews would never harm another nation, others who lived amongst us, that the lesson of history which the Diaspora taught us would suffice. Today I know I was naïve and that explains and teaches us much.

And my last point: thanks to one of my colleagues at our university, I have recently read an article on literary criticism in Poland entitled 'Why we Love Błoński'. I want to tell you why Błoński is dear to us. Błoński, Turowicz, Bartoszewski, Gierowsk, these are people who are perpetuating the most splendid of Polish traditions. Let me quote what Mickiewicz said, perhaps somewhat pompously, of the upholder of Polish ideals: 'The person, who during the revolution inscribed on the banners "For your and for our freedom" had within him a Polish spirit. And he put the word "your" before "our" in spite of past diplomatic logic.' If Błoński's article and Turowicz's summing up and other similar voices appear in Poland, I tell myself and others that there is mutual hope.

[*Applause*]

Józef Gierowski: Please could Professor Bartoszewski now take the floor.

Władysław Bartoszewski: Ladies and Gentlemen I have not got a prepared text. Today I decided I was going to come and listen, to think and formulate on the spot a few observations, as the subjects which are being discussed at today's meeting are ones upon which I reflect constantly.

Although the subject is broader than Jan Błoński's statement, it was his article, nevertheless, that provided the incentive for our discussion. And to make everything clear, I would like to say that I belong to those Poles and even non-Poles who are totally in solidarity with his text, although each one of us is a little different and perhaps if we had written it, we might have used other words or formulated our views in a different manner. Błoński's creed and the exegesis of Turowicz are what I consider generally to be the way I see the matter, although I am not as talented as Jan Błoński and cannot write an article so beautifully and in a literary fashion. I also support the call of our Chairman today, Rector Gierowski, who formulated several ideas to be raised during our discussion today. But I must in advance say that there are two elements which condition in a certain manner what I have to say and in no way facilitate it. One of the elements is the generally known fact, that at this table I am the only one of the so-called Righteous, although there are many people in this auditorium without diplomas, who are just as Righteous and probably more so. This means that I feel bound to put forward the point of view or arguments of those (I don't know whether it is 1,500 or 2,000 Poles) with diplomas and this happens to be that very group who acted without thought of material gain. This is very inhibiting, as I am obliged to speak on behalf of others, of many people who are no longer alive today. On the other hand, the other complicating element, which changes my perspective a little, is that for the last ten years I have been working and for four and a half of them living amongst Germans, amongst young German people at German universities and all the time I am asked, as they trust me, why the Polish nation is anti-semitic. I have mixed feelings when I hear this question in the city of Munich, but it is a fact that this is what I am asked. I have mixed feelings when I read, as I did a few weeks ago, in an article by a German Professor that 200,000 Jews were slaughtered in the Świętokrzyskie Mountains by Poles from the Home Army (AK) after the war. The writer of the article was a person with the title of Professor. Of course he had to get it from somewhere. Naturally one shouldn't waste time on such matters, but such situations are my daily lot. Sometimes I am quite confused when I ponder the incompatibility of experiences and the non-transmittability of knowledge; the difficulties of getting through to common sense; the problems of discriminating issues and facts; and personal sensitivities about morality, about general rules, and the individual's ability to behave within the rules. There are so many issues here which overlap that I shall perhaps try to restrict myself to just a very few.

The first question is whether I, as an individual, did everything I could to save the life of others. No, as an individual I did not do everything I could to save others, be it Jews or other persecuted people, as that also was my obligation. Due to the specific situation of the Jews and naturally the dangers which were associated with helping them, only someone who died saving someone could have done everything. They could have justly said they had done everything they could. Those who survived must ask themselves if they could not have done more, if they did not neglect something, as they surely did. The crux of the matter is that those who have somewhat less reason for doing so are the ones who incline us to beat our breasts and undergo a moral reckoning. Those on the other hand who have real cause to do so are rarely inclined to beat their breasts.

The question as to whether the nation, a collection of individuals, did a lot is a much easier one to answer. No, the nation to which I belong did not do a lot, and I believe the same is true of other nations, although I am not qualified today to consider others, as we are talking about the problem of the Holocaust in Poland and not in France or Holland. So I am not going to talk about those countries. Did our nation do everything? No, the nation certainly did not do everything that was possible, nor can we be sure that it did all that was possible within the existing conditions, in which very little was possible, many things were impossible, partly even for economic reasons. The Germans tell me that 2,000 Jews survived in Berlin. And I ask the Germans, saying that that is marvellous, whether there were house searches in the homes of Germans who were not on Gestapo files in Berlin. No, never; it was possible to live thirteen years under Nazi rule and never be subjected to a house search. There was no street in Warsaw or Kraków where house searches did not take place every so often. These are things which are not comparable. However, the Polish nation did not do all that was possible even within the limits of that which was possible in this, and in other areas. I am not a member of the ranks of combatants who are self-satisfied. I have four or five qualifications which I consider allow me to regard myself as a combatant of the Second World War. And of all that service, the most difficult task, the most complicated for me, the one which I feared the most was the one which dealt with co-operation with the Jews. That was the most difficult task. It was far more difficult than any other I knew. And after the terrorized Jews, who knew how difficult it was to find help, those who knew how difficult it was to help are paradoxically those Poles who wanted to help them.

Loneliness is a terrible feeling. Having spent eight years in camps and prisons in my life, I know what isolation means. I know there is a difference between lonely isolation and isolation which is not completely lonely. An enormous difference. When I was in Auschwitz in 1940 and 1941, I was totally alone. I was there at a time when there were no parcels, no other external signs of solidarity from the surrounding world, and no discernible activities for the inmates. When I was held in other prisons or camps, I did not feel such loneliness. The Jews experienced a terrible and extreme loneliness in their suffering, both those in the ghettos and some of those who were in hiding, although they sometimes came across such good souls as Ringelblum described, without which many of those who survived would not have survived.

The Chairman of the discussion has asked whether restricted possibilities justify inaction. No they do not. A restriction in possibilities does not justify abstention from action. That was the common ethos of the best Poles, and perhaps not the best, but certainly the bravest Poles, and of the bravest Jews. Because, after all, it was not the poor, suffering, miserable, and vegetating masses in the ghettos, but the bravest and the most resilient, the young, who accepted this common ethos, the ethos of heroes, the ethos of battle. Some of them today would not do it again, some of them are not even doing it again, but then they considered that it was worth going down fighting, whereas suffering was something unworthy. This judgement was not correct. Suffering is not wrong, it can be beautiful, albeit painful. But the ethos of battle was prevalent amongst certain groups of Poles and Jews. Poles regarded the fact that the Jews did not fight as something inferior; some Jews thought likewise. This is an over-simplification in the understanding of youth, as the suffering of those who did not fight is no less important nor valuable, but that was how it was.

Each one of us is responsible for himself. I also tell my Germans that. But each one is also responsible for the historical record of their nation. As one takes pride in one's literature, art, or architecture, things to which we ourselves have not contributed, we must also feel jointly responsible for those things for which we are not ourselves to blame in history. I say that because, for understandable reasons and with great emphasis in Germany, in that splendid country, recently an attempt has been made within the framework of the so-called *Historikerstreit* [historians' argument], to argue that everything is relative because people have always slaughtered people. Napoleon was a cruel man, in the Soviet Union there was the Gulag Archipelago, so why are we bothering to discuss the Holocaust? The uniqueness of the planned system for destroying a whole nation is not a concept which is deeply rooted any longer in many minds, even of European intellectuals. But Poles cannot escape from understanding the uniqueness of the Holocaust. There were no people in Poland with doctors' titles who did not know what was going on 5 kilometres away. That was not how it was in Poland. The Poles knew. One can debate as to what extent they sympathized with the victims. It is my conviction that a cheap sympathy was general, one that did not imply any responsibili-ties. That is: 'Isn't it terrible, unpleasant, painful.' An expensive sympathy was quite rare. I am not going to argue here today with my friend Mrs Prekerowa, who is not present, as to whether deeds can be measured by 1 or 2 per cent. In this country, the principle of the 'Ten Righteous Men' originated. In Poland, there were thousands of Righteous and hundreds of thousands too few, because as always in such cases as also in every other country, only on our territory and not that of Holland or Belgium was the extermination carried out, and that fact places us in a special position.

Jan Błoński recalled in a beautiful and pertinent way today that there is a moral responsibility and that people too often confuse it with criminal responsibility. I do not know what the people who polemicized with him were thinking, but I must say that many of the remarks made in the debate with Błoński caused me great embarrassment and enormous sadness. I reflect that 40 years have passed since the end of the war – during which tens of thousands of young people have grown up amongst whom thousands are undoubtedly genuinely interested in various facts about the past, which they are not encumbered by, but simply want to know the truth. But there are also in Poland many people of one kind or another who react at such a level and in such a way as to be able to say, to know, that moral imperfection is a human trait, but that the facts were different. There were facts. Indifference is also responsibility. The Catholic believer knows that apart from the sins of commission, there are the sins of omission. The sin of omission can sometimes be very serious and Poland is after all a country which to a great extent has been moulded by Catholic customs and morality. A feeling for the sin of omission ought to be one that is deeply rooted amongst Poles, particularly amongst Poles.

Would amicable coexistence of the Polish and Jewish nations in this part of Europe have influenced anything? I am in agreement with Professor Erlich and other speakers that there would certainly not have been major differences in the implementation of the Holocaust as a process of biological extermination. This was because, overall, in each European country where the Germans carried out the Holocaust, the same percentage of people more or less died, although this in no way absolves those who committed the sins of omission.

During my life I have often followed the custom of quoting positive examples. That is not because I do not know any negative ones. It might even be that I am better acquainted with negative actions than many of my compatriots. I only had once to abandon my flat during the occupation, after being released from Auschwitz; that was when a letter denouncing me for helping the Jews was intercepted at the Post Office and brought to my home. I was not denounced for hawking secret newspapers, for being in the Home Army, for doing this or that, only because I was helping the Jews. And that was the only time when in order to save my skin I had to change my abode. Thus I know it all. If I have tried in a consistent manner, since my first visit to Israel 25 years ago (in 1963 I planted a tree in the Avenue of the Righteous), to collect documents containing information on positive actions, that is because I believe, maybe naïvely, but it is not my idea alone, that people should be educated on the basis of examples. It should be on the basis of difficult but possible models and not impossible ones, and not on instances which show that mankind is merely a band of hooligans. When educating people one should always say that so-and-so could act in a noble way, and so could another. It was very difficult, he died for his actions and someone else endured great suffering, but it was possible. I believe that in this way people of good will can be moved to a certain extent and we have many examples of the efficacy of such examples. But I am with Błoński, with my whole heart, in the problem which he has raised. With the problem that every nation is jointly responsible for everything that happens, even without its consent (that is the German problem), but by its insufficient counteraction, by its smallness, or by its fear. Every nation bears responsibility to the degree that each one of us in our own conscience knows what we do. There are no kinds of global historical guilt and there are no such things as good and bad nations. If I were to admit that the Poles during the war were a worse nation than others, firstly I would be speaking out of line with that which I believe; and secondly, I would accept the same assumption which many European nations regarded as correct, namely that the Jews are a worse nation than others. There are no nations worse than others and no nations better than others. We must beware, and the Slavs and Jews also, of evaluating the categories of a better or worse nation. But let us raise the value of the human being. We believe in man, in the Ten Righteous, we believe in honest and righteous people, we call them just. And I believe this is the only path into the future and it is a good

thing that this argument of Polish and other historians, and Polish moralists and the Polish youth has got off the ground. Let us hope it does not become bent in another direction because it is incredibly easy to beat someone else's breast, but to beat one's own is more difficult. Let us hope the discussion will continue. Thank you.
[*Applause*]

Józef Gierowski: Thank you very much Professor, particularly for the reply to some of the problems which were raised at the beginning. I now ask Professor Gross to take the floor.

Jan Tomasz Gross: Thank you. I am going to speak very briefly. And after me there is still Mr Turowicz. I am going to speak briefly, also, because I have the feeling that my presence on the platform with those sitting here is, in a way, unjustified. Unjustified, that is, in the sense that everything I could say on the subject, in contrast to the words which they utter here, is rather abstract. It is not rooted in any personal experience and memory, it is not linked to any situation, to any moments of decision, to people's faces. For myself, born after the war, and for all those generations which will follow later, that nightmare which happened in Poland, on Polish territory, about which we are talking today, is a problem which they must understand and come to terms with through the help of the techniques of detached scholarly investigation. In this sense the point of departure of Błoński's article is significant, namely his inability, which he mentioned, to summarize what has been written on the subject, what has come to pass between the Poles and Jews. There is an incredible amount on this subject and really there is no way of putting it all in order. This is due, above all, to the defensive attitude of the Poles about which he spoke, that every account invariably creates the possibility of making a charge of participation in genocide. And that was what I was thinking when I wrote, in a small text on the subject of Polish–Jewish relations and on what happened between Poles and Jews, that really in order to be able to sort out these matters, one has to be able to ascertain what happened. If we are not able to gain that knowledge in its entirety, then we should try to find enclaves of mutual relations where what one can call the 'third factor' is missing, where we can examine how the Poles behaved in relation to the Jews without the continuous context of the German presence. One may doubt whether there are such areas in the occupation experience, in the experience of the relationships between Poles and Jews, from which to a certain degree the German element can be removed. Well, I believe there are and I should like to name a few of them. I think that if we manage to put together a complete documentation on these separate enclaves we will achieve a considerable amount of knowledge, perhaps inconclusive, but in any case very important knowledge on the subject of what Polish–Jewish relations were based on, and how they developed. The first such enclave, and I wrote about this in my article, is that of the underground press. Naturally these papers reflected what the intelligentsia thought and the conscience of the authors. Press freedom was unrestricted and is comparable to that which only now is taking place in Poland as a result of the evolution of the independent press. A full spectrum of political opinion from the radical right to the left found expression in underground publications. I think it is imperative to collect together, without exception, everything that was written in the underground press on the Jews. We must collect and analyse everything according to the ideological categories which were associated with particular publications, and in this way we will obtain a full and, in a certain sense, irrefutable source of information on the views about relations between the Poles and the Jews. Not on their behaviour, but on what the Poles thought of the Jews. And, in a certain sense, it can be said that this is a moment in the relationship between Poles and Jews where the intermediary element of the horrendous repression, to which everyone was subjected by the Germans, is removed.

The second area is that of how attitudes affected behaviour. This is very important. We want to know about behaviour. It is a considerably more complicated matter and ideally one would need to have a full list of all the cases where Poles and Jews encountered each other and what happened. One should certainly be able to gather ethnographic material, but that would be a very difficult task and methodologically complicated. Yet I think, on consideration, one might be able also to find such an enclave, a situation where the Jewish–Polish relationship was not encumbered by the element of Nazi repression. This was during

214

the Warsaw Uprising of 1944. It would be necessary to draw up a full catalogue of meetings and situations, and of what happened between the Poles and Jews during the Warsaw Uprising. That is a moment when the German presence was as if in abeyance. There were not many episodes of encounter between Poles and Jews during the Uprising which began in August 1944 and the number of Jews who were hiding and had survived till then can certainly be estimated. Thus we can draw up such a catalogue. Again I am not talking here about any random knowledge, of using only part of these episodes and including them in some kind of narration on another subject, but about a total study.

And finally the third moment, which I think can be studied in its entirety, is the relationship of Jews to Poles in a period when the German presence was no longer there, but in a situation which is still closely related to the Holocaust, that is the period directly after the war, the years 1945–7. Naturally by then there was no longer the danger of Nazi repression, although the relationship between the Jews and the Poles then was a function of what happened during the Holocaust, and, without putting it into the context of the Holocaust, one cannot understand it. In a certain sense, it will also permit us to understand a bit better what happened during the occupation itself. Thank you very much.

[*Applause*]

Józef Gierowski: I now ask Mr Turowicz to speak.

Jerzy Turowicz: I have little to add to what the other speakers before me have said today, and in any case, whatever I say, repetitions are unavoidable. Thus perhaps I shall make just a few remarks from the point of view of the editor of the paper in whose columns Jan Błoński's article appeared and in which the whole debate ensued. When we printed the article, I was, as were my colleagues, aware that it would be an event to which there would certainly be a strong reaction. The reaction was greater than anything known in the course of the 42 years during which I have edited that paper. I cannot remember any article which provoked such a strong reaction on the part of the readers. We received nearly 200 letters and articles on the subject. We were able, as you know to publish only a very small part. There were amongst these, texts and letters which were explicitly anti-semitic, often anonymous. There was also no shortage of positive texts which were in solidarity with what Błoński had written. There were further statements of the kind, 'I'm not an anti-semite, but . . .' Finally there was often a reaction of consternation, the consternation of people who could not really understand how one could, as they understood from Błoński's article, accuse the Poles of complicity in mass-murder.

I think that no conclusions should be drawn from these letters, published or otherwise. One cannot generalize about them. This was not any sort of academic public opinion research nor a poll. If there were a whole array of voices which did not agree with Błoński, there is nothing strange in that, as after all people write to the editor if they do not agree with something, whereas if they are in agreement they don't usually feel the need to write. None the less, that whole debate disclosed the existence of anti-semitism still in Poland, today more than 40 years after the war. It has shown that it is an attitude which cannot easily be uprooted nor overcome, and one that even at times regenerates itself. However, I do not believe that one should exaggerate the size of this phenomenon. For myself and my colleagues on the paper, the decision to print the article by Błoński was something quite natural. We considered it to be our duty, that it was necessary to break through the taboo of silence on the matter, in spite of the anticipated reaction both in Poland and amongst Poles abroad, and also even of world opinion. And it is clear that the reaction was very strong and there was also a resonance in the West, in the United States, and here in Israel.

I should also like to stress the significance of the fact that Błoński's article appeared in *Tygodnik Powszechny*. This journal is probably correctly regarded as the leading Catholic journal in Poland, forming and expressing the opinions of Catholics, who constitute 90–95 per cent of the population in Poland. This paper has never published an article with an anti-semitic tendency. Even at the time of the Six Day War between Israel and the Arabs and the 'anti-zionist' campaign in Poland which led to the emigration of a substantial part of the remnants of the Jewish intelligentsia still in Poland, our journal resisted the organized anti-Israeli campaign and even opposed it. The paper has also written frequently about Christian–Jewish dialogue, from the

moment when the decree *Nostra Aetate* was published by Vatican
II. It has often written about Polish–Jewish problems and
decidedly condemned anti-semitism. I do not say this in order to
stress the virtues of the paper I edit; that has no significance here.
I only wish to underline the great significance of the fact that
Błoński's article appeared in the leading Catholic paper,
particularly if we compare the position adopted on this question
by the Catholic press before the war. I do not want to generalize
here, as there were many Catholic papers before the war which
were opposed to anti-semitism but there were also, as we know,
others. I think that this fact is proof of the change in social
awareness of the Poles, of Catholics, changes which, if one is
talking about Catholics, have two sources: one precisely due to
the fact that during the war, during the occupation, we were
witnesses of the tragic fate of the Jews, witnesses of the
extermination, and secondly, however, the evolution of the
Church's attitude to this matter.

Jan Błoński's contribution and that of the whole discussion
lies, firstly, in the fact that for the first time the view that the fate
of Jews and Poles in the years of the occupation cannot be placed
on the same level was so strongly stated. These were matters
which qualitatively were totally different. Arguments of the type,
'They also murdered us' or 'We were next in line for the gas
chambers' thus totally lack conviction. The main value of
Błoński's article was, however, that it raised the question of the
behaviour of Polish society in the face of the 'Holocaust' in the
way that it did. The article has enormous weight. I – who totally
sympathize with its aim – can only not agree with one
formulation, perhaps with one word. Błoński writes – perhaps he
does not mean his words to be taken literally: 'God held back our
hand . . . because if we did not participate in that crime [mass-
murder] it was because we were still Christians and at the last
moment came to realize what a satanic exercise it was.'

I am older than Błoński. I experienced the war and occupation
years as an adult and can – and not I alone, Bartoszewski will
confirm it – categorically state there were no possibilities for the
Poles to co-operate with the Nazis in their extermination policy. I
am saying that there was none, and could say so for two reasons:
the first one was due to the relationship between the Poles and
the German occupant, and the second was the fact that we were

after all Christians. Perhaps not very good Christians but Christians.

I shall leave on one side such matters as Bartoszewski was discussing a moment ago. One could argue with Mrs Prekerowa over figures, although I do believe that the Polish role in saving the Jews was quantitatively greater than she suggests. Naturally there were people who betrayed Jews for money and people who took advantage of the situation of the Jews, but they represented a marginal group of a kind which is to be found in any country. I am putting on one side the question as to whether in even more favourable conditions there were possibilities to save a larger number of Jews than those saved in Poland – they were not great. And finally, the question raised a moment ago by Professor Gutman, that there are no grounds on which to state that the camps were situated in Poland because the Poles were anti-semites. It results from this, which is surely obvious, that the Poles should not be made responsible or jointly responsible for the extermination of the Jews.

Błoński, on the other hand, is right and that is his contribution, when he refers to the relative indifference of a considerable part of the Polish people to the extermination, in spite of the fact that many Poles were stirred by the crime. But the masses were undoubtedly characterized by an indifference coupled with a helplessness, which to some degree was the result of pre-war anti-semitism in Poland and the conviction that it was not our problem. And if we are not able to recognize the collective guilt of the community or nation, because one is only guilty if one bears a penal responsibility, be it by action or by neglect, a collective moral responsibility, or even collective moral guilt, still exists. This was sometimes questioned by people after Błoński's article, but one can say that if I were a German living at the time of Hitler, an anti-fascist or even a child, or a German born after the war, I would feel my role in the joint moral guilt of the whole German nation, in spite of the fact that direct responsibility was only borne in the case of the German nation by individuals, although in this case very many.

Błoński's contribution has been to give rise to an awareness of that moral responsibility, responsibility for the sin of Polish anti-semitism of the past, which has perhaps not yet been finally overcome. This is of great significance for the Polish people and the Church in Poland. It is a fundamental contribution in the process of changing a way of thinking, of removing the remnants of anti-semitism. In any case, the dispute about Polish anti-semitism, the discussion on the subject of Polish–Jewish relations, is a matter which is much larger. It is a dispute, as Adam Michnik wrote in a recent article, over the choice of a model for Polish culture, what kind of culture it is, changing, as does any culture over the ages, and what form it ought to have.

It has been mentioned here that Błoński's article and the whole discussion had a great resonance in world opinion. In the West, there were reactions of a primitive type, of the kind that the Poles have finally admitted to joint responsibility. Fortunately, however, there were also reactions which were far deeper, stating that such an attitude brought recognition for Poland. I think I may express gratitude that we can talk about this in Jerusalem. In Israel these problems are much better, more objectively and rightly understood than for instance by part of the Jewish community in the United States, where an emotional reaction sometimes replaces a familiarity with the factual state of things and character of the Nazi occupation in Poland.

I was in Auschwitz two weeks ago, on Sunday, at the Birkenau and Auschwitz camps, together with Lech Wałęsa and his advisers. Lech Wałęsa, as a winner of the Nobel Peace Prize, travelled to Auschwitz to meet a group of Nobel prize winners who had gone there from Paris. Their group was headed by another Nobel prize winner, Elie Wiesel, the great writer and philosopher, who perhaps understands in a deeper manner than anyone else the meaning of the Holocaust, not only for the Jews but for the whole of humanity. I can say that I was happy when I heard from Elie Wiesel himself that he knew and had read Jan Błoński's article and also the whole discussion which ensued. He considered it to be a very valuable and important event, which will facilitate the rapprochement of our nations, following the misunderstanding that has evolved for centuries. Thank you. [*Applause*]

Józef Gierowski: Ladies and Gentlemen, in this manner we have completed the first round of statements. Mr Turowicz, thank you very much for your deep observations. I cannot, however, escape the thought, as it happens that we represent here more or less people with converging views, that the point of view of the left in all this, whose attitude to the Jewish problem was not always the same as that which we accept to be the norm in Poland, has not been reflected in our discussion. And even if those matters were subject to varying evolution, and if, as I admit, it was a good thing that Błoński's article appeared precisely in a Catholic paper, the issue of the left's attitude to these matters should not be totally forgotten. This is, however, just a supplementary observation. And now in accordance with what I said, we are ready to take a break and I would ask you to give questions to me in writing.

[Break of thirty minutes]

Questions (These were submitted in writing.)

Rafael Scharf: The first question addressed to me is 'What lessons for the situation in Israel today can we draw from the Holocaust.' Why does the person who wrote this question think I can answer it, in connection with that which I said? It takes us into a completely different sphere and I feel neither competent nor certainly authorized in Jerusalem, having come from London the day before yesterday and leaving in a week's time, to say something on the subject. I am very sorry.
[Applause]

Whereas the writer of the next question said I could respond in Polish, it so happens that English is more comfortable for me. I cannot, however answer it either. I read it: 'In your very eloquent analysis of anti-semitism in Poland and the subsequent indifference, to say the least, during the *Shoah*, you underlined an all-important conclusion. The Holocaust is Christianity's and Western civilization's great tragedy. In view of that, would you assume that anti-semitism is the exclusive responsibility of the Poles?' My answer is no. Another question. 'Would the Poles have been as anti-Jewish if Poland had not been Catholic, and if not why don't we call for dialogues and symposia with the representative bodies of Christianity and Western civilization instead of debating with a multitude of nationalities?' This again is a question directed to me, but by what jump of the imagination is it assumed that I, Felek Scharf, could answer a question like this? Moreover, it seems to me that the dialogues and symposia with representative bodies of Christianity and Western civilization take place every day of the week and we should welcome them, but they are not what we are talking about here.

Józef Gierowski: Thank you very much. Apart from that you don't have any additional points to make? Would Professor Erlich like to say something? Not in connection with the questions only but also in relation to the discussion, as I understand that there were no direct questions to you.

Victor Erlich: What Rafael Scharf said made a very strong impression on me but in one instance I differ from him. It is not that I disagree, but perhaps my experiences have been a little different from his. Mr Scharf said, as far as I remember, that he had no social relationship with the Poles. . .

Rafael Scharf: That is, I didn't go to Polish homes. Yes, yes.

Victor Erlich: My experiences were a little bit different. I had Polish friends; naturally most of the homes which I was in were Jewish but there were also Polish ones. It is true that the social contacts between the two communities were restricted and, I might say, sociologically lopsided, in that they occurred mainly in the milieu of the socialist, communist, and generally radical intelligentsia. There were also contacts amongst university students, but usually amongst people with leftish sympathies. In other words – Mr Scharf's remarks do not conform with my own personal experience.

Józef Gierowski: Thank you very much. Perhaps Professor Gutman. . .

Yisrael Gutman: Yes, I have some questions here, not questions but general statements and hence it is a bit difficult to answer them, but I will try.

The first question, the first idea is that the Poles' responsibility does not lie in their indifference but in the prevalence of religious, national, and popular hate. Many people considered the Nazi policies to be an opportunity to remove a national minority which was very embarrassing. Is this true? I think certainly in part. There is no doubt that there were Poles who said openly or to themselves that it was a good thing that the Jews were disappearing from Poland and the Poles would not have their blood on their hands. I think that was certainly the case. How many such people there were, whether it was general or not it is difficult to say today. That something of the kind existed is, I believe, virtually unquestionable and we can draw the conclusion from documents which we have, that such views were also expressed at the time. But I would like to say now that it was a period of barbarity, as Professor Błoński has said here, that it was easier to hear the voices of evil spirits, that the evil spirits had greater possibilities to flourish and that when we think about the atmosphere, it was one of a certain specific world. I believe that this truth should be stated, but it would not be correct to say, as long as we draw the lessons from it, that the nation always was and always will be like this.

Next, the second question. Most of the concentration camps were in Poland. Why? I think I have tried to say something about this but now I will attempt to explain what we know and do not know. Above all, we do not have any German document which states that the Germans set up and situated the camps in Poland because the Poles were anti-semites, or because the Poles wanted this to be done. It is also a fact, and this must be taken into consideration, that the first two camps which were set up, the Chelmno camp at the end of 1941 and Auschwitz, were not on what was then Polish territory; they were part of the lands which were incorporated into the German Reich. I do not know why. I can only surmise. I think there were certain reasons for siting them here, above all the fact that in Poland there were 3 million Jews. That is, half of those who were murdered were from this country. In addition, and this should be taken into consideration, Poland lies relatively far from the heart of Europe and it was easier to keep it a secret there than, let us say, in France or Belgium. Thirdly, Poland was a country where there was not an iota of autonomy, nor any possibility for the society to have any influence on what was happening. I do not want to be misunderstood but I do not believe that there is any serious and scientific basis for claiming that the reason that the camps were in

Poland was because of Polish attitudes.

The third question is that too much is said about the heroic saving of the Jews by Poles. The questioner argues rather that one should remember the joy that the Jews were being killed, a joy demonstrated by most Poles. Maybe a majority or maybe not. I have already talked about this and I am not going to go over this ground again.

The next question is as follows: suffering in Christianity has its value: it purifies the spirit, something like the path to the Cross by Christ. The Jews do not have the same attitude to suffering. To Christians, suffering is holy, as it serves a great purpose. That purpose exists. There is no purpose in the extermination of the Jews. Extermination is extermination, and the suffering of the Jews had no value. I do not think it is true that in Jewish tradition there is no sanctification of suffering and death. There is something. There is in the Jewish tradition a very important concept in relation to development of thought and theology which also sees in death, in heroic death, values and meanings for the future. I do not think it is some sort of misunderstanding to talk about values at all when the curse of extinction in the twentieth century is commonplace.

Józef Gierowski: Thank you very much, Professor. I shall now call again on Professor Bartoszewski.

Władysław Bartoszewski: I will try to speak quickly. Ladies and Gentlemen, I must add something necessary here to that which my friend Professor Gutman said. Because I agree with him, but understand a little better one of the questions which were put to him, and I would like to state clearly here that it was not a coincidence that Auschwitz was situated where it was, as there are documents on the subject. They have nothing to do with the Holocaust but with the decision on the creation of Auschwitz. The decision to set up Auschwitz was taken in April 1940 as a place to destroy the Polish intelligentsia. That was the first function of Auschwitz. . .

[*Another voice*] But not Birkenau. . .

We talked about the camps in general. Auschwitz naturally became the symbol of the whole idea of the Holocaust, perhaps incorrectly. Let me express my views more precisely. The decision was taken to set up Auschwitz because it was most practical to carry out the destruction of the Poles close to where they lived, but on territory, as Professor Gutman correctly said, which had been incorporated into the Reich and on which the setting up of the camp was started with the mass resettlement of the population of whole districts of Auschwitz, or Oświęcim as it is called in Polish. The whole of Zasole was emptied of Poles and the buildings (I dismantled them later) were left empty. I know that with certainty. And the camp was opened and for the first twenty months there was not a single transport of Jews in it. Naturally there were no gas chambers then, but masses of people died. Only on 26 March 1942 did the first of the Jews arrive, 999 Jewesses from Slovakia. Thus Auschwitz was set up for a clear purpose.

However in the memoirs of Höss, the Commandant of Auschwitz, and in Eichmann's testimonies the impression is given, the memoirs confirm it precisely, that at a certain moment a decision was taken in the Main Security Office of the Reich, which controlled the existing camp, that it was to be enlarged and used for new tasks. All this has been described and is known exactly from scholarly literature. The building of Birkenau then commenced. Birkenau started to be built many months before the Wannsee Conference and many months before the camp in Chemno was set up Birkenau had already been built. Poles, prisoners, built Birkenau. They went to the Command of the Birkenau Construction. That is well known from the history of the camp, from the camp's annals.

But if one is talking about the camps generally of course Dachau, Mauthausen, Gusen, Sachsenhausen and Ravensbrück were not in Poland and Westerbork was not in Poland. Not all the camps were in Poland. However, if one is talking about the centres of extermination, apart from these places, there was the activity of the *Einsatzgruppen* which killed about 500,000 Jews, the *Einsatzgruppen* A, B, C, D, even more, those four groups. And the rest were murdered in the camps at Sobibór, Bełżec, Chemno, Treblinka, and so on, not only in Auschwitz, which continues to be the symbol, but is not the place where the overwhelming majority were killed, only a considerable number. It is often forgotten that people were murdered systematically in many places and not only in Auschwitz. But this is a peripheral matter.

I have some questions here which I shall answer jointly as they really deal with one and a half problems. I quote one question: What was the attitude of the fighting Polish underground to the Jewish fighting underground and what is the significance of it for the problem being discussed here? Another: Poles often maintain that the Home Army attacked trains taking Jews to be exterminated to release them, that it took part in the Jewish uprisings in Treblinka and Sobibór. The Home Army not only did not do anything like that nor once did it destroy the railway line to Treblinka, which would have been possible. Is this proof of a bad conscience? My answer is as follows: firstly, the Home Army did not attack trains of Jews destined for extermination to release them, as likewise the Home Army never attacked any train going to Auschwitz or to any other camp with priests, officers and other people, whom they most probably liked, in order to release them.

Dr Krakowski: Those were not going to the gas chambers.

Professor Bartoszewski: At the beginning it was not known who was going where.

Dr Krakowski and others: It was known, it was known, Professor Bartoszewski.

Professor Bartoszewski: This is really a matter for another discussion. I myself was in Auschwitz and no one helped me.

A voice from the audience: You lie!

Professor Bartoszewski: Excuse me, but if you are going to talk to me in that way I will not reply to you. If the questions are yours I will not answer them.

A voice from the audience: They are not.

Professor Bartoszewski: In that case I will carry on.

Thus, Ladies and Gentlemen, the Home Army did not attack

trains, it did not attack any trains, and also did not take part in the Jewish uprisings in Treblinka and Sobibór. I do not know why people say that it did these things. I cannot feel responsible for statements which I know to be untrue. Thus I am not going to discuss them. It is a fact that some people who escaped were helped by Poles and some were harmed by Poles. On the other hand, whether it was done specially by the Home Army – I know nothing on this subject from the sources. I do not consider the failure to blow up railway lines to be cause for a bad conscience, because it is my deep conviction as a Second World War historian that if the lines to Treblinka had been blown up, those lines would have been repaired within three hours with the help of Poles or Jews who had been rounded up, and it would have had no influence on the further course of events. However it would have had a moral or symbolic meaning, as did the fact that several Poles died at the ghetto walls bringing help. That is always important, but that is all. If fifty and not two had died, the fate of the ghetto would not have been altered; if a hundred had died, it would not have changed. But, of course, it has a significance. I am very proud as a Pole that there were some Poles who helped, but only a limited number, which is both a great deal and also very little.

I turn to the question of the Polish fighting underground and its attitude to the Jewish underground. Down to 1942, more or less until the autumn of that year, the attitude was, above all, one of general distrust. That is, there were no well armed groups of the Polish underground at all, apart from small socialist and communist groups, who were prepared to assist the Jewish underground in Warsaw with occasional acts of help before the autumn of 1942. The attempts in Białystok also led to no great success. Arms were bought earlier, although the question of the supply of arms for the Warsaw ghetto is a lengthy subject and not one for tonight's meeting. The supplies of arms started after the first self-defence of the ghetto in January and continued between January and March. All that was delivered was literally supplied within the course of two and a half months. It was a lot and a little, as tens of pieces of arms is very little, but the same amount when you do not have any arms is also a lot. Of course, the Jews in the Warsaw ghetto, as Professor Gutman, and other Jewish researchers, know very well, did not fight only with these

226

weapons, but also with ones which were bought and collected, and with home-made arms and explosives, because if they had only had a dozen odd pistols they could never have fought. This is of course, a general reply. Why the situation was like this, regardless of the possibilities of the underground, is a complex issue. I would like to stress that there were not only anti-semitic motives, but there was undoubtedly also a feeling of alienation [*obcość*] and a failure in many cases to recognize the common aims and interests of the two groups. For many people, this feeling played a role. Alienation does not always have to be synonymous with enmity, as a lot of people in New York consider the Puerto Ricans to be foreign, but do not kill them. Many people do not like blacks but do not kill them. A large number of people can be antagonistic towards another national group but it does not mean there has to be some ultimate reckoning. But it is bad. It is always bad, because dislike and alienation are the beginning of a far-reaching dislike, perhaps prejudice, perhaps hate. That is bad, but it does not have to all be thrown into the same pot, as it is not the same.

There is a further question, asking me to comment on the text of the Appeal by Zofia Kossak-Szczucka. I would say the following. This appeal, which appeared in the form of a leaflet entitled 'Protest' in Warsaw in August 1942, concerned the mass action, just begun, of deporting Jews to the centres of extermination.

The author calls the crime by its name: 'the most terrible crime history has ever witnessed' and declares that 'one cannot remain passive in the face of such a crime. He also is silent in the face of murder becomes the murderer's accomplice, he who does not condemn, condones.'

However Zofia Kossak belonged to the older generation of Catholics who at that time, long before the Second Vatican Council, were hampered by a certain schematic way of thinking as far as Jews were concerned. For this reason, in the same appeal protesting against the crime, she states rather generally that 'Polish Catholics . . . consider Jews to be political, economic and ideological enemies of Poland'. Regardless of how we evaluate this way of thinking today, it should nevertheless be noted that Zofia Kossak was on the whole very severe in her judgements of people's actions or of the mistakes she ascribed to them. From 1943–4 she was herself a prisoner in Auschwitz-Birkenau, a witness of the suffering and humiliation of many women, including Polish Catholics like herself. In her diary, published after the war under the title *Z otchłani* (*From the abyss*, Rome, 1946), she states quite clearly that the martyrdom of these Polish women was God's punishment for enjoying themselves before the war, for wearing lipstick or silk stockings. Here she represents a view held by orthodox religious people of various creeds who see suffering quite simply as God's punishment for sins committed. A similar way of thinking did not prevent Zofia Kossak from being actively involved in helping to hide Jews both in and beyond Warsaw. She hid children in her own home and voluntarily took great risks in the name of that same love of one's neighbour of which she writes in the appeal mentioned above: 'he who dares to link the free future of Poland with a despicable joy at the misery of one's neighbour is neither a Catholic nor a Pole'. That is all I have to say at the moment. Thank you.

[*Applause*]

Józef Gierowski: Ladies and Gentlemen, I still have three matters which I should like to discuss. The first concerns 1968, namely with question as to whether a 'black list' was maintained. Even in relation to a relatively small number of people, is this not, the questioner asks, a certain indication of political or anti-semitic discrimination by the authorities? There is no doubt that it was certainly discriminatory, and the next question is what can be done about it. I think, and this kind of meeting is not without its influence, a certain change has taken place in relation to the majority of people who were forced to emigrate in 1968, and this type of action should be continued. I for my part undertake to bring these matters up with the relevant authorities if a letter by the interested party is sent to me.

The second question asks whether Polish youth is not learning the truth about the years when the murder of the Jews was going on and whether it would not be desirable to establish a joint Polish–Jewish Commission to investigate what is written in school textbooks. I do not think that at the present the question of a commission is the most pressing one facing us, but undoubtedly it could be suggested to the education authorities. Of course, I am in agreement with the view that information concerning the Holocaust and also political events, particularly the Kielce pogrom, should be given a fuller reflection in school textbooks. Disgraceful activities of this kind should be better known. Ladies and Gentlemen, there is another question to me, 'What do I mean by the left?' I meant that the Poles on this panel seem to be a team representing a certain part of Poland, mostly people connected in some way with the Catholic Church and its ideology. Perhaps I should go further. That is, I consider myself to be a liberal but, as is known in Poland, liberals, even when encouraged by such good-natured editors as Mr Turowicz, do not have serious clubs. However, in some form or another there was a left wing in Poland which had a specific attitude to the whole Jewish question and to the position of Jews under the occupation.

Returning to the thesis of Professor Błoński, it did not have a general character and does not refer to categories which are basically undefined, as for example the nation. A questioner asks whether we can speak here on behalf of that nation or can evaluate the behaviour of an individual nation, when in reality those things are far more complicated and in virtually every group of Poles they were diverse. In this way, the questioner asks, do not judgements over-simplify certain situations or exaggerate in the other direction? I think the subjects of our deliberations here were deeper and dealt with certain matters of an ethical nature, matters of a general character. Historians ought to try to establish the attitudes and behavioural patterns of specific groups and regions, but we are dealing rather with the issue of how to help people to understand themselves. It is a question of understanding ourselves, that is why all of us felt the need to speak on this subject. I read Professor Błoński's article with real recognition and with great satisfaction since he is a Professor of the Jagiellonian University, which is very close to me. He had the courage to raise a question of fundamental significance for our moral standpoint. I think, however, that much of what was said there, if not all, is in accord with reality, conforms to certain moral postulates, which should be put forward for individuals, groups, and the whole nation. And the results which deal with attitudes towards Jews and also in a certain sense to other nations ought to motivate everyone and should make them take a critical look at what happened during the war and draw conclusions for the future. I am very pleased by the phenomenon which can be observed in Poland at the moment that it is precisely the young people who are delving the furthest and demanding the most. Indeed it should not be Professor Błoński, but someone from my generation, since I am a little older, who should have said what he said. We are the people who had the opportunity to act. I look at myself critically. There is no justification for the fact that, during the war, I would have said I was working in such and such a Home Army department and thus am not going to concern myself with that. Today I know I should not have spoken in this manner. It is a delayed admission, but I would like young people to accept my admission. I am pleased they criticize me and others, as that is what their attitude should be, with a belief that the future, if it is a question of maintaining certain moral principles, will be better than the past which we went through. This is based on faith in a better younger generation. That generation is starting to understand very belatedly how much our country has lost by virtue of the fact that an incredibly important part of the nation was murdered or emigrated from the Polish lands. What we are undertaking at the moment is an attempt to save what can still be saved. This is also how I understand today's discussion and you have had the chance here to observe certain opinions which are quite convergent, as amongst ourselves here there was no serious disagreement up until now, unless Professor Gutman is going to want to say something in a moment. And because there was no real debate here, perhaps this has resulted in our not really dealing with the questions put at the beginning. One thing is unquestionable, and I repeat once again that which was probably best stated by Professor Bartoszewski: more could have been done and the sin of omission weighs on us. I am finishing, but Professor Gutman would like to add something.

Yisrael Gutman: I do not know if I should add what I wanted to say after your words. I generally agree with what Professor Bartoszewski said. We bicker a bit, but we like each other, although we always have something on which we differ, especially on the subject of help or the lack of help from the Home Army. I think that the Home Army had many officers in its ranks, including such people as, for example, Aleksander

Kamieński, whose attitude is worthy of admiration. The majority of its officers, however, did not trust the Jews, were not very interested in the fate of the Jews and were more indifferent than the average Pole or the Polish nation. The Jews who wanted to fight in Białystok or Wilno received no reply at all to their requests to the Home Army. In the case of Warsaw, after the autumn of 1942, following attempts which did not achieve any results, certain contacts were made which then received an official character. There was never total help, there was never identification with the fight of the Jews, and it is also true, and this should be said in an unequivocal manner, as has been often confirmed by Yitshak Cukierman (*Antek*), that the Home Army in the period prior to the uprising tried to convince the Jewish fighters not to start an uprising but to leave the ghetto. The uprising was thus undertaken without the approval of the Home Army. These things are difficult, particularly as we know that the Home Army partisans virtually did not accept any Jews and there were not many Jews in their ranks. There is still the People's Army (AL) in assessing the views of the military underground to the Jews, and I think its attitude was quite different. I do not have time to talk about this and unfortunately we have not got a paper on the subject, which is a painful one that gives much cause for thought. But I agree with everything else that Professor Bartoszewski has said.
[*Applause*]

Józef Gierowski: Does Professor Bartoszewski still want to say something?

Voices in the background: What about the Home Army's attitude to Żegota?

Władysław Bartoszewski:I can only add to that voice from the floor that it is a complicated problem. Żegota contained representatives from many parties and many of them were also in the Home Army, or had some connection with the Home Army, and the majority of those party military organizations linked to the Home Army, as was Żegota, whose original name was the Relief Council for Jews attached to the Government Delegatura. It is another matter that the Council's members strove persist-

ently for greater help and, as Professor Gutman has said, had great difficulties. We were not the darling child of the Polish underground. Our work in Żegota was necessary and tolerated, and, after a certain time, the advantages of this activity were recognized, but they were certainly seen differently from the standpoint of the Polish Socialist Party (PPS), the Democratic Party (SD) and the Peasant Party (SD) and by the other parties, which did not participate in it, although they also had their people in the Home Army. I want to finish in the following manner, as I have probably been to Jerusalem more often than any of the other Polish guests here at this table. I want to say that I am very moved and grateful that I could take part in this conference in Jerusalem, and the fact that I have been coming here for twenty-five years has greatly bound me to the city. I would like also to say, as it is not well known here, that when I received the Peace Prize of German Booksellers and Publishers in 1986, and the ceremony was transmitted and received by 20 million homes in Germany, Austria, and Switzerland, I said I was pround of the fact that I was receiving the Prize a year after Teddy Kollek, who was awarded it as the Mayor of Jerusalem, a city which should be close to people of good will in the world. That is what I think and I am very grateful.
[*Applause*]

Józef Gierowski: Judging by the agreement between Professor Gutman and Professor Bartoszewski, we are surely on a good path and that is the most important result of our discussion today. I would like to thank everyone very much who has taken part by asking questions on our remarks, and with this I close our meeting.

NOTES ON CONTRIBUTORS

Władysław Bartoszewski: (b.1922, Warsaw), is Professor of Modern History, and taught at the Universities of Lublin, Munich and Augsburg and is the author of over twenty books. He was co-founder of the Council for Aid to Jews (*Żegota*) and recipient of the title 'Righteous among Nations', Yad Vashem, Jerusalem, 1963. He has also been awarded the Herder Prize (1983) and the German Booksellers' Peace Prize (1986). He is a vice-president of the Institute for Polish-Jewish Studies, Oxford.

Ewa Berberyusz is a leading Polish journalist. She was born in Warsaw in 1929, the daughter of a high-ranking army officer, who was forced to conceal his identity during the Nazi Occupation, and who was killed in the Nazi uprising of 1944. She was educated in a convent school and studied philology at Warsaw University. She has worked in various publishing houses and since 1980, has been associated with *Tygodnik Powszechny*. Several volumes of her *reportages* have been published in book form.

Jan Błoński is Professor of the History of Polish Literature at the Jagiellonian University in Kraków. His many publications include *Poeci i inni* (Poets and others) (1965), *Zmiana warty* (The Changing of the Guard) (1961) and *Odmarsz* (Departure).

Andrzej Bryk is lecturer at the Legal-Historical Institute of the Jagiellonian University. His fields of research include Modern Political History and the history of Polish-Jewish relations. He has written about Jewish Autonomy in the Polish–Lithuanian Commonwealth in the sixteenth and seventeenth centuries and Polish–Jewish relations in the twentieth century.

Kazimierz Dziewanowski was born in Warsaw in 1930. He is a journalist and author and has written 15 books. He is closely connected with the Catholic press in Poland, with Solidarity and with the opposition. He is a member of the Citizens' Committee formed by Lech Wałęsa.

Viktor Erlich was born in Russia in 1914 and has lived in the USA since 1942. He is Bensinger Emeritus Professor of Russian Literature at Yale University and author of *The Russian Formalists* (1955), *The Double Image* (1964) and *Gogol* (1969).

Józef Gierowski was born in 1922 and participated in the Home Army (AK) during the war. He has held the post of Professor of History, first at the University of Wrocław and now at the Jagiellonian University. He is director of the Department of Modern Universal History and of the Research Center of Jewish History and Culture in Poland. He has written widely on the history of the seventeenth and eighteenth centuries.

Jan T. Gross emigrated from Warsaw, Poland, in 1969. He is currently Professor of Sociology at Emory University, in the United States. He is the author of *Polish Society Under German Occupation, Generalgouvernement, 1939–1944* (Princeton University Press, 1979), and *Revolution from Abroad. The Soviet Conquest of Poland's Western Ukraine and Western Belorussia* (Princeton University Press, 1988).

Yisrael Gutman is Max and Rita Haber Professor of Holocaust Studies at the Institute of Contemporary Jewry at the Hebrew University and Director of the Center of Holocaust Studies at Yad Vashem. A member of the Jewish Fighting Organization, he took part in the Warsaw ghetto uprising. His books include *Anashim ve' afar* (Men and ashes, Jerusalem, 1956), *Mered hanotsrim: Mordekhay Aneliewicz ve' milkhamot getto Varsha* (The Revolt of the besieged: Mordekhay Aneliewicz, and the Revolt of the Warsaw ghetto) (Jerusalem, 1963) and the *Jews of Warsaw 1939–1943: Ghetto, Underground, Revolt* (Brighton 1982). Together with Shmuel Krakowski, he wrote *Unequal Victims: Poles and Jews during World War II* (New York, 1986).

Jerzy Jastrzębowski was born in 1937 and is an essayist and broadcast journalist. In 1981, he was a member of the National Committee of Solidarity. He worked for Polish State Radio until the introduction of martial law in December 1981 and was subsequently a broadcaster on Radio Solidarity. More recently, he has worked for the Canadian Broadcasting Company. He is a freelance writer for *Tygodnik Powszechny, Kultura* (Paris), and *Związkowiec* (Toronto). He divides his work and home between Warsaw and Toronto.

Jan Karski was born in Poland and subsequently entered the Polish Diplomatic Service. He was taken prisoner by the Red Army in August 1939, escaped several months later and returned to German occupied Poland where he jointed the anti-Nazi underground organization. As a courier between the government-in-exile and the underground authorities in Poland, he made several secret trips between France, Great Britain and Poland during the war. In August 1943, he personally reported to President Roosevelt. After the war, he received his doctorate at the University of Georgetown where he teaches Eastern European Affairs, Comparative Government and International Affairs. Among his books are *The Great Powers in Poland 1919–1945*, and *The Story of the Secret State*.

Maciej Kozłowski was born in 1943 and graduated in history from the Jagiellonian University. After studying journalism at the University of Warsaw, he worked as a journalist. He was dismissed from his position in 1968 and spent two and a half years in jail. On release he worked as a freelance journalist and writer until 1982, when he started work for *Tygodnik Powszechny*. He has published a series of historical essays in book form and his book on the Polish–Ukrainian war of 1918–19 will shortly appear in English.

Stanisław Krajewski was born in Warsaw in 1950 into a totally assimilated Jewish family. In the last ten years he has actively developed his Jewish interests and religious identity, giving it expression, among other activities, in his articles and lectures for Polish and foreign audiences. He is active in the Jewish–Christian dialogue, in the Citizens' Committee for the Protection of Jewish Cemeteries and Cultural Monuments in Poland, and recently in the Society for Polish–Israeli Friendship. He is a mathematics scholar.

Kazimierz Kąkol is Professor in the Faculty of Journalism and Political Science at the University of Warsaw. Between 1957 and 1974 he was chief editor of the weekly journal *Prawo i Życie*. From 1974 to 1980 he was Minister of Religious Affairs. Since 1985, he has been Director of the Main Commission for the investigation of Nazi Crimes in Poland and the Institute of National Memory.

Antony Polonsky is Reader in International History at the London School of Economics. Among his books are *Politics in Independent Poland* (Oxford, 1972), *The Little Dictators* (London 1975) and, with Boleslaw Drukiér, *The Beginnings of Communist Rule in Poland* (London 1981). He is President of the Institute for Polish–Jewish studies and editor of *POLIN: A Journal of Polish–Jewish Studies*

Teresa Prekerowa is a historian. She has worked for many years in various publishing houses. She is the author of *Konspiracyjna Rada Pomocy Żydom w Warsawie 1942–1945* (The Underground Council for Aid to Jews in Warsaw 1942–1945, Warsaw 1982) and many studies on Polish–Jewish themes. She is a recipient of the title 'Righteous among Nations', Yad Vashem, Jerusalem, 1985.

Witold Rymanowski is a journalist writing for *Życie Literackie*, Kraków.

Stanisław Salmonowicz is a Professor at the Historical–Legal Institute of the University of Toruń and at the Polish Academy of Sciences in Warsaw.

Rafael F. Scharf, born in 1914 in Kraków, where he attended the Hebrew High School and graduated in Law at the Jagiellonian University. He has lived in England since 1938 and served in the British Army (Intelligence) and after the war in the War Crimes Investigation. He is a Member of the editorial board of *The Jewish Quarterly*, a member of the Governing Council of the Institute of Polish–Jewish Studies, and vice-chairman of the International Janusz Korczak Society.

Władysław Siła-Nowicki was active in the underground resistance 1941–5 and fought in the Warsaw Uprising in 1944. A member of the illegal armed resistance against the Communist dictatorship (Freedom and Independence) between 1945 and 1947, he was arrested in 1947; his death sentence was commuted to life imprisonment and he was released in 1956. An attorney and adviser to Solidarity, he has been defence counsel in several trials of democratic opposition activists. In 1968, he was barred for a period from practising law after defending students who had demonstrated in March of that year.

Jerzy Turowicz was born in Kraków in 1912. A journalist and writer, he was co-founder and editor-in-chief since 1945 of the

Catholic weekly *Tygodnik Powszechny*. He is Chairman of the *Znak* Publishing Institute and Member of the Polish Bishops' Conference Committee for dialogue with Judaism. He is vice-president of the Society for Polish–Israeli Friendship.

Janina Walewska was born in Warsaw in 1931. She worked for 23 years as a librarian in the Institute for the History of Material Culture at the Polish Academy of Sciences in Warsaw. She is retired.

Ryszard Żelichowski was born in Western Poland in 1946 and studied history at the University of Warsaw where he was awarded the degrees M.A. and Ph.D. He is the head of the historical section of the illustrated weekly *Stolica*.

INDEX

aid to Jews 72–80, 139, 142–3, 145, 148
AK *see* Home Army
Allied countries: and guilt 23–4, 114,
154; and Holocaust 23–4, 146,
152–4, 159; Kozielewski's (Karski)
visit to 87–9; passivity of 152–3
Andrzejewski, J. 3, 168
Anolik, B. 144
anti-semitism 4, 54; and anti-German
views of Poles 106; and church 15;
debate over 37–9; dissemination of
155–60; and genocide 104; and guilt
18; Holocaust and 140–1; legacy of
171, 173–4; among Poles 37–9,
99–100, 102, 123–33, 136–8, 140–2;
and Polish indifference 17–18; pre-
war rise of 164–5, 173–4, 200; and
stereotypes 57
assistance, Jews' payment for 74

Baczyński, K. K. 145
Baron, S. 6
Bartoszewski, W. 5, 129, 131, 139,
207–13, 223–8, 231–2
Bauman, Z. 2–3, 25–7
Bełżec concentration camp 89–90
Berberyusz, E. 10, 16, 29, 113, 116,
123, 131, 201; on guilt by neglect
69–71; and Jewish identity in Poland
98–109; on Poland's loss 7; reaction
of Poles 16, 199
Berman, J. 83, 115
Białystok uprising 77, 79
blackmail of Jews 75, 126–7, 129–30,
167
Błoński, J. 1, 8–12; and anti-semitism
123–33; comment by Gutman 28–30;
comment by Scharf 27–8; comments

by Turowicz 20, 134–43, 215–20;
criticized by Rymanowski 155–60;
criticized by Siła-Nowicki 21–2, 23,
24–5, 59–68; defended by
Bartoszewski 207–13; defended by
Dziewanowski 110–17; defended by
Jastrzębowski 118–22; in discussion
185–9; and guilt by neglect 69–71;
home as analogy 12–13, 44–5; in
Jerusalem 24, 31; Oxford
Conference (1984) 9, 45; 'Poor Poles
Look at the Ghetto' 34–52; reactions
to article 14–15, 27–9, 215–16; on
responsibility for murder 11
Bortkowska, A. 204
Borwicz, M. 3
Bryk, A. 8, 14; on the Hidden
Complex of the Polish Mind 161–83

Chciuk, A. 56
church 106–7, 141, 163–4; and anti-
semitism 15
Ciechanowski, J. 87
communist governments and Jews
4–5
concentration camps 67–8, 79, 223–4;
Bełżec 89–90; Kozielewski's (Karski)
visit 89–90; in Poland 222–3; Poles
dying in 135–6
Cranbourne, Lord 91
Cukierman, A. 148
Czerniakow, A. 101

Dalton, H. 91
Datner, S. 79
Davies, N. 54
death camps *see* concentration camps
Disraeli, B. 158

239

Dmowski, R. 113
Dobroszycki, L. 4
Dziewanowski, K. 16, 23, 140;
  criticism of Siła-Nowicki 116–17

Edelman, M. 128
Eastermann, A. L. 92
Eden, Sir A. 91, 151
The 'Eighty-First Blow' 144–9
Elias, N. 1
Erlich, V. 28–9, 199–201, 221
extermination policy 159

Fackenheim, E. 175
Fajner, L. 83
Feigin, A. 115
Fein, H. 15, 162
Ficowski, J. 32–3
forgiveness 125–6
Frankenfurter, Justice F. 87
Freytag, G. 57

genocide 46, 153; anti-semitism and
  104; German intentions of 147
Germany see Nazi Germany
Gerstein, K. 90
ghettos 65–7, 79, 147; see also Warsaw
  Ghetto
Gierowski, J. 15, 184–5, 189–223
  passim, 228–30, 231–2 passim
Gilbert, M. 91, 92
Gomułka, W. 5
Greenwood, A. 91
Gross, J. T. 32, 213–15
Grot-Rowecki, Gen. S. 86, 88, 200
Grynberg, H. 168
guilt: of Allied nations 23–4, 114, 154;
  and anti-semitism 18; by neglect
  69–71; Jews' sharing of 138–9; in
  Miłosz's poetry 145; and passivity
  131–2; in Poland 187
Gutman, Y. 20, 28–30, 201–7, 222–3

Herbst, S. 91
Hering, SS Capt. G. 89
Hesse, F. 153
Hirszfeld, L. 78
Holocaust: Allied governments and
  23–4, 146, 159; and anti-semitism
  140–1; background to 184; impact on
  Poles 2–3; lessons from 194–8;
  military success of Nazi Germany
  146–7; and Nazi Germany 102, 139,

158–9; Polish attitudes to 115, 173,
  175; Polish participation in 20–2;
  Polish silence over 176; 'rationality
  of evil' 25–6; rescue of Jews from 30;
  uniqueness of 210; viewed by Jews
  31
Home Army (AK) 5, 85–6, 162, 174;
  attitude towards Jews 168–70; and
  German occupation of Poland 167;
  Kozielewski (Karski) in 82; Żegota
  167, 174, 204

indifference of Poles to Jews 17–18
'insufficient resistance' thesis 145–6

Jakobovits, Lord 31
Jaspers, K. 141
Jastrzębowski, J. 15–16, 135;
  criticism of Siła-Nowicki 118–22
Jerusalem Conference 184–232
Jews: aid to 73–5, 139, 142–3, 145, 148,
  208–9; appeal to Allies 151–2;
  blackmail of 126–7, 129–30, 167; and
  Błoński's analogy 12–13, 44–5; and
  communist governments 4–5;
  contributions to Polish history 6–7,
  65; extermination of in Eastern
  Europe 159–60; and guilt 138–9; and
  Home Army 168–70; identity
  98–109; and loneliness 209; meaning
  of Poland to 99–101; and mission to
  London 81–97; passive behaviour of
  66–7, 77–8; payment for assistance
  74; in post-partition era 156–8; in
  post-war Poland 54–5; in pre-war
  Poland 155–6; as privileged group in
  Poland 24–5, 157–8; saved by Poles
  30, 72–80, 139, 142–3, 145, 192–3;
  separateness from Poles 63–4, 164;
  stereotypes 56–7; survival, chances
  of 152–3

Kainer, A. 173
Kąkol, K. 22–3; on 'the eighty-first
  blow' 144–9
Karski see Kozielewski
Kawalkowski, A. 91
Kielce pogrom 3–4, 127, 205–6
Kirchenbaum, M. 83
Kisielewski, S. (Kisiel) 58
Klein, D. 30
Koestler, A. 92
Kominek, Cardinal 120

Korboński, S. 87
Korczak, J. 148
Kossak-Szczucka, Z. 104, 166–7
Kot, S. 91, 92
Kovner, A. 204
Kozielewski, J. (Karski) 14, 151;
  assessment of mission 94–7;
  assignment 82–5; mission to West
  90–4, 151–2; visit to concentration
  camp 89–90; visit to Warsaw Ghetto
  87–9
Kozłowski, M. on the Mission that
  Failed 81–97
Krajewski, S. 7, 10, 14; on Jewish
  identity in Poland 98–109

Lanzman, C. 9–10, 30, 107, 125, 146–7
Laqueur, W. 83
Law, R. 92
Levi, A. 67
Levi, H. 67
Lewin, Z. 129
Lickiewicz, A. 102, 133, 158
Loewe (Stroński), S. 159

Machajek, C. 14
Makowiecki, J. 85
Mann, T. 93
Mikołajczyk, S. 84, 91, 94
Miłosz, C. 10–11, 24, 34–6, 40, 112,
  145; comments on by Siła-Nowicki
  59–61; poetry of 49–52
'Mission that Failed', The 81–97
Moczar, Gen. M. 6
moral responsibility, concept 211
moral sensitivity 173, 174
Morgenthau, H. 153

Nazi Germany: extermination of
  Eastern European Jews 159–60; and
  genocide 104, 147; hatred of 126;
  hatred of Christians 141; and
  Holocaust 102, 158–9; military
  success and the Holocaust 146–7;
  proclamation of death penalty 149;
  responsibility of 140
Neuwerth (Nowaczyński), A. 158
Norwid, C. 196

Ossowski, S. 3, 205
Oxford Conference 9

passivity 66–7, 77–8; of Allied

countries 152–3; and guilt 131–2; and
  survival 147–8
Pehle, J. 94
Poles: aid to Jews 72–80, 139, 142–3,
  145, 148, 208–9; and anti-semitism
  37–9, 99–100, 102, 123–33, 136–8,
  140–2; attitude towards Jews 76–7,
  105–7, 191–2, 202; in concentration
  camps 135–6; death of intelligentsia
  136; defended by Siła-Nowicki 61–3,
  67–8; and the 'eighty-first blow'
  144–9; guilt 187; and guilt by neglect
  69–71; and history 161–2; and
  Holocaust 2–3, 20–3, 30–1, 115,
  175–6; indifference to Jews 17–18,
  188; killed by Germans 135–6; and
  Kozielewski's (Karski) mission
  81–94; nationalism 8; in post-war
  period 54–5; responsibility for Nazi
  policy 222; saving of Jews 30, 73–5,
  139, 142–3, 145, 149, 192–3;
  Solidarity years 7–8; stereotypes 55,
  57; views of Jews 191–2
Polish economy, inter-war 164–5
Polish mind, hidden complex of
  161–83; and anti-semitism 164–5,
  173–4, 175; and church 163–4; and
  Holocaust 173; moral sensitivity of
  173, 174; see also Polish–Jewish
  relations
Polish–Jewish relations: decline in
  163–4; divergence of communities
  169; end of 177; and German
  occupation 165; and Holocaust
  167–8; in inter-war years 162–3; in
  post-partition era 156–8; post-war
  173; and separation of societies 165;
  as vicious circle 201
Polonsky, A. 1–33
'Poor Poles Look at the Ghetto' 34–52;
  background to 185; effect of 197;
  Miłosz's poetry and 36, 40–2, 49–52;
  reaction to 1–2
post-partition era in Poland 156–8
Prekerowa, T. 20–1, 23, 134, 139, 143;
  aid to Jews 72–80
Pruszyński, K. 178

Raczkiewicz, W. 84
Ratajski, C. 82
'rationality of evil' 25–6
Ringelblum, E. 30, 74, 205, 209

Roosevelt, President F. D. 91, 93, 94, 151
Rowecki, Col. T. 88
Rymanowski, W. 14–15, 25; criticism of Błoński 155–60
Rożański, M. 115
Rzepecki, Col. J. 86

Salij, Fr. J. 125
Salmonowicz, S. 134; on stereotypes 53–8
Scharf, R. 27–8, 30–1, 220–1; in discussion 189–99; on effect of Błoński's article 197–8; Poles' views of Jews 191–2
segregation of Poles and Jews 165, 167
Selborne, Lord 91, 92
Shoah (film) 9–10, 30, 81, 107–8, 145; discussion on 125; Kozielewski (Karski) in 94–7
Sikorski, Gen. W. 84–5, 87, 91
Siła-Nowicki, W. 14, 16, 26; comment by Walewska 123–33; criticized by Dziewanowski 23–4, 110–17; criticized by Jastrzębowski 118–22; criticized by Prekerowa 72–80; criticism of Błoński 21–2, 23, 24–5, 59–68
Siudak, P. 91
Słonimski, A. 92
stereotypes: of Jews 56–7; Polish 55, 57
survival: chances, of Jews 152–3; and passivity 147–8; of Polish nation 146
Szwarcbart, I. 84, 87, 152

Tolstoy, A. 93

Treitschke, H. von 57
Turowicz, J. 8, 10, 13–14, 17–20, 22, 125, 128, 201; on Błoński's article 134–43

underground see Home Army
'universe of obligation' 162
Urban, J. 10

Vincenz, S. 168

Walewska, J. 14; on anti-semitism 123–33
war criminals 154
Warsaw Ghetto 79, 148; burning of 70; and Czerniakow's suicide 150–1; demand for weapons 85–6; Kozielewski's (Karski) visit to 87–9; and Polish defence of 170–1; uprising 67, 77, 131, 135–6, 148, 153, 215
Wells, H. G. 92
Widerszal, L. 91
Wilkinson, E. 91
Wise, Rabbi S. 94
Woliński, H. 91
Wroński, S. 152
Wyszyński, Cardinal 125, 127

Żegota 5, 167, 174, 204
Żelichowski, R. 23; on allied reaction to the Holocaust 152–4
Zuroki, E. 154
Zwolakowa, M. 152
Zygielbojm, S. 67, 84, 87, 92, 146, 152, 153